Diagnosing Dissent

Diagnosing Dissent

Hysterics, Deserters, and Conscientious Objectors in Germany during World War One

Rebecca Ayako Bennette

Cornell University Press
Ithaca and London

First published 2020 by Cornell University Press

Library of Congress Cataloging-in-Publication Data

Names: Bennette, Rebecca Ayako, 1973– author.
Title: Diagnosing dissent : hysterics, deserters, and conscientious objectors in Germany during World War One / Rebecca Ayako Bennette.
Description: Ithaca [New York] : Cornell University Press, 2020. | Includes bibliographical references and index.
Identifiers: LCCN 2020006258 (print) | LCCN 2020006259 (ebook) | ISBN 9781501751202 (hardcover) | ISBN 9781501751226 (pdf) | ISBN 9781501751219 (epub)
Subjects: LCSH: Military psychiatry—Germany—History—20th century. | World War, 1914–1918—Psychological aspects. | Soldiers—Germany—Psychology. | War neuroses—Germany—History—20th century. | World War, 1914–1918—Desertions—Germany—Psychological aspects. | World War, 1914–1918—Conscientious objectors—Germany—Psychology.
Classification: LCC UH629.5.G3 B46 2020 (print) | LCC UH629.5.G3 (ebook) | DDC 940.3/161—dc23
LC record available at https://lccn.loc.gov/2020006258
LC ebook record available at https://lccn.loc.gov/2020006259

For Ella

Contents

Acknowledgments

I owe my appreciation to many people and institutions that helped make the completion of this book possible. First, I would like to thank the staff at the several archives I visited to undertake my research. They not only helped me find sources vital to my research but also made going to the archives an enjoyable experience. The knowledge and kindness of so many people at the archives I visited have contributed greatly to this book.

I received funding for my research both from the Gerda Henkel Stiftung and from Middlebury College. The generous support of these institutions allowed me to make multiple research trips for this book and devote significant time to its writing.

I also owe gratitude to several individuals who helped me think about the ideas I wanted this book to express, offered advice, found archival sources, attended conference talks, and read drafts. Their suggestions made this book better; their encouragement helped me to keep going. In particular, I would like to thank Paul Lerner, Gundula Gahlen, Joachim Radkau, Bernd Ulrich, Philipp Rauh, Björn Hofmeister, Wolfgang Schaffer, Maike Rotzoll, Regina

Keyler, Erhard Knauer, Susan Burch, Paul Monod, Febe Armanios, Susan Ferber, Jonathan Sperber, David Blackbourn, Helmut Walser Smith, Michael Gross, Martina Cucchiara, Maria Mitchell, Michael O'Sullivan, Mark Ruff, Aeleah Soine, and Lisa Zwicker. I am also grateful to the anonymous readers who shared their time and expertise.

Emily Andrew has been a tremendous editor whose guidance has helped shepherd this project smoothly through the publication process. I have enjoyed working with her and with Cornell University Press.

Finally, I would like to express gratitude to my family. Momo, Lena, and Siggi—my four-legged companions—sat up with me even when I worked late into the night. My husband (and best friend) James Fitzsimmons heard more about this project than anyone else. He has likely memorized certain passages after reading so many drafts. My daughter Ella was a good sport, even as a toddler, despite this book seriously eating into playtime. I will never forget how she reacted one day when my husband and I told her something great had happened. She responded by asking if I had finished my book. (Actually, she had won a local coloring contest for four-year-olds!) I could not have written this book without my family's support and patience. I owe them the deepest gratitude.

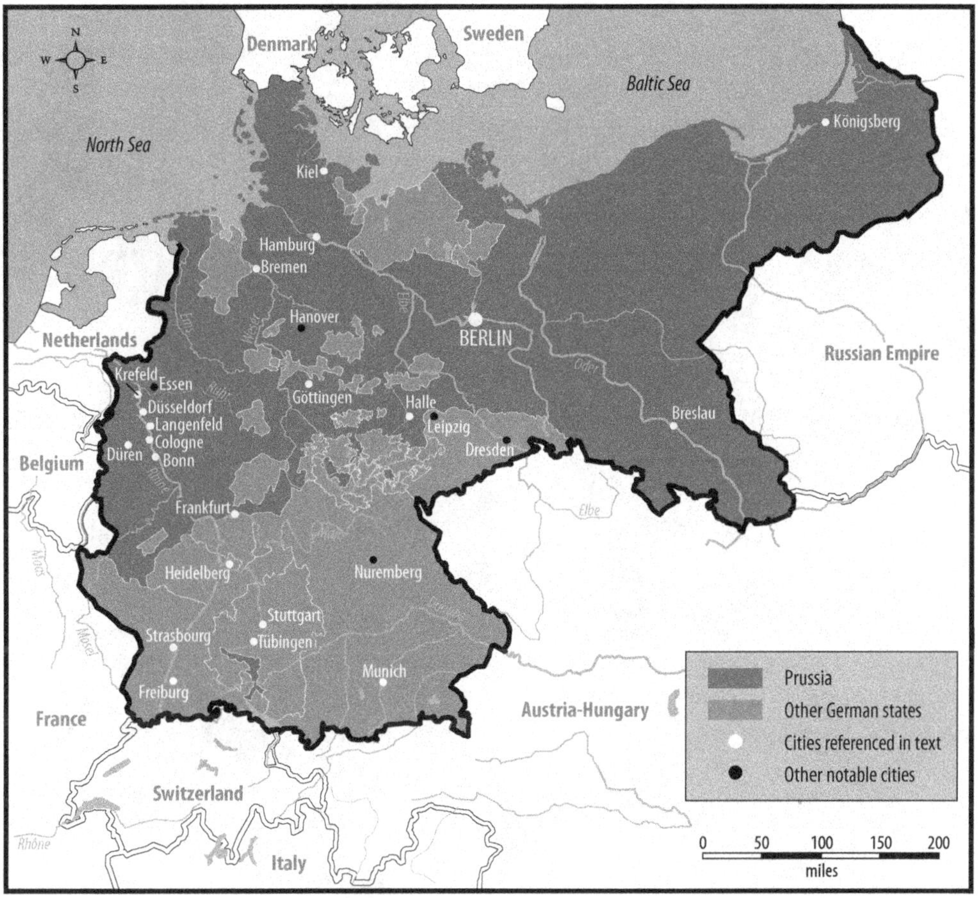

Map of Germany, 1918, by Mike Bechthold

Introduction

On July 14, 1917, a twenty-four-year-old soldier named Wilhelm W. arrived in Düren at the psychiatric hospital for observation of his mental state. Writing home to his sister just days before his hospitalization, Wilhelm W. lamented, "You cannot believe how I have suffered in this war. I have come close to insanity. This time has made an indelible mark on me." No doubt he had been through a lot by this point. World War I had been raging for the past three years across Europe, and Wilhelm W. had been a soldier for much of that time, serving first on the eastern front in Russia and then in the west in France. The stress and dangers of combat likely struck him as quite alien to his life before the war; he was a painter of figures by occupation. Indeed, responding to the intake questions about events leading up to his transfer under military order to the hospital, Wilhelm W. again acknowledged the strain he had been under: "I felt that I was going crazy."[1]

Multitudes of German soldiers likely uttered similar words in military and civilian hospitals across the battlefields and at home. Indeed, the stresses of cataclysmic, long-standing war had created hundreds of thousands of psychiatric cases for the military to deal with by 1917. All told, the official statistics record was over six hundred thousand cases by the time the fighting ended.[2] Some of these cases would likely be categorized completely separately now, like the neurologic disorders of epilepsy or progressive paralysis resulting from late-stage syphilis, an infection for which effective treatment only came later with the introduction of penicillin in the 1940s.[3] Yet, many of the individuals treated during the war suffered from what would become the quintessential wartime psychiatric malady: shell shock, or as the Germans colloquially termed the afflicted soldiers, *Kriegszitterer* (war tremblers), for the telltale symptom of uncontrollable shaking these traumatized men commonly exhibited. Another sizable number experienced episodes of disorders seen commonly in peacetime as well, such as manic depression or schizophrenia. In many cases the episodes were recurrences, but in others the first signs of such maladies that doctors believed were quickened—if not necessarily caused—by the pressures of service appeared only in the field. A first glance at Wilhelm W.'s file would warrant inclusion in the last group, as doctors in Düren diagnosed him with *dementia paranoides*, a term ultimately regarded by Emil Kraepelin as one version of an illness that became unified under the diagnosis schizophrenia.[4]

One can see from the file the details that led the hospital staff to diagnose *dementia paranoides*. By all accounts Wilhelm W. was withdrawn and insisted he wanted nothing further to do with other people. He even answered a question about whether he had any enemies with a resounding "Oh, yes! People to whom one is disagreeable. But I don't have anything to do with that anymore; the names of all souls that were in my company have escaped my mind." That he claimed to no longer recall the names of any of his former troop members could not have been a reassuring sign of health to the hospital staff either. No doubt the diagnosis also took into account Wilhelm W.'s behavior even before he arrived for observation. After all, it was seemingly peculiar behavior that had triggered the psychological evaluation to begin with. Insofar as the hospital staff was informed, this included having to repeatedly be brought back to his post, refusing to follow orders, and believing that a recently arrived corporal was trying to manipulate and control him. The aforementioned letter the soldier wrote to his sister—a copy of which was included in the file for doctors to consult—served as further evidence of mental illness: Wilhelm repeatedly referenced the need for secrecy, noting that he could not reveal the real reasons for his actions to anyone there. He did not even dare write them in the letter.

Certainly, all these details from before and after his arrival at the hospital, both reported by others and declared by the patient himself, indicate a man in the midst of a crisis. Yet, a closer look at Wilhelm W.'s file suggests the young soldier may have been in the midst of a far different internal struggle than one involving an unfolding episode of schizophrenia. When confronted with leaving his post on two separate occasions in June, Wilhelm W. did discuss the treatment he received from the corporal who thought "he could do whatever with me that he wanted to." At the same time, however, he also pointed out that his reason for leaving and refusing to follow orders was that he was "fed up with the war." Indeed, the second time he left was no random moment but right after he was told to join other units in positioning mines, an order that was issued three times but did not change Wilhelm W.'s refusal. Furthermore, the event that appears to have been the final straw in the commander's patience with his intransigence—in other words, the act that precipitated Wilhelm W.'s arrest and transfer to Düren for an evaluation of his mental state—was yet another refusal, this time to position artillery shells for use.

Even Wilhelm W.'s claims of persecution by the corporal and the existence of enemies among his company members can be understood in quite a different light than signs of paranoia when other evidence from the patient file is weighed. Complaints about poor treatment from superior officers and fellow soldiers hardly stood out in accounts of soldiers and were difficult to assess for their validity. Yet, that the relationship between Wilhelm W. and these other members of his company was bad is quite believable when one considers his multiple refusals to follow orders and share in the workload. As both physicians and patients in many other cases attested, soldiers considered shirkers were often harshly treated by other troops, who felt they had to make up the work.[5] The repeated questioning of orders did not likely endear Wilhelm W. to the corporal either, a point confirmed by their last reported interaction. According to testimony by the patient after his arrest, the final incident began with the corporal asking (not ordering) Wilhelm W. if he wanted to help position shells. Upon Wilhelm W.'s answer in the negative—indeed, he went further by adding that he "would rather be shot dead before he went to position them"—the corporal then issued the formal order for him to do so.

Perhaps the best insight into the real struggle raging within Wilhelm W. comes from the letter sent to his sister. Despite his unwillingness to expand on the reasons for his behavior, he provided plenty of clues to his mind-set. Again Wilhelm W. noted the anguish that he experienced while serving, drawing on savage imagery in describing his deeds: "[I] have had to howl with the wolves for so long. The disgust drove me away." Indeed, it was because he felt his fellow soldiers, the "wolves," had no real concern or qualms about the actions they were committing that he no longer wanted to associate with others, let alone confide his true feelings to them. Moreover, he reasoned, no one had any desire to know what he was really thinking. He would not tell the enlisted men around him; he did not tell the military authorities when he was arrested. Nor would he reveal anything to the court if it came to a full trial on the grounds of going AWOL (absent without leave) and refusing to follow orders. Besides, Wilhelm W. concluded, such trials were perfunctory and not concerned with "human, emotional reactions." Even the possibility that he might spend years in jail would not deter him, and Wilhelm W. attempted to calm his sister's worries on this point. Referencing a recent conversation they had while he was on leave, he acknowledged that she counseled him not to make trouble for himself. But, Wilhelm W. wrote, even though he was initially unsure of what to do, he decided to "see it through to the end" and "now [the time] has come." Wilhelm W.'s unwillingness to follow orders linked to placing artillery was no spur-of-the-moment decision, no simple impulse without thought. Despite the many vagaries of his letter, which he knew was being read by the authorities, Wilhelm W. had little doubt that his sister knew exactly what he meant and why he did what he did.

In this reading of the case file, Wilhelm W. was no shirker as his troop members and superior officers thought. Nor was he mentally deluded, as the psychiatrist who observed him concluded. Instead, he was a soldier who had seen and done horrific deeds over the course of years and had finally had enough. While he may have waivered on complete refusal to serve, by the summer of 1917 Wilhelm W. had clearly drawn a line at positioning weapons intended to kill. He had become a conscientious objector.[6]

Certainly, this understanding of Wilhelm W.'s case fits the general context of conscientious objectors in Germany during World War I. Though it may seem strange to identify a soldier who had already participated in innumerable battles as a principled opponent of war, this migration from willing fighter to conscientious objector was not an uncommon one among those refusing to serve. Known for his prewar publications on Africa and his postwar pieces on pacifism, Hans Paasche, for example, not only served in colonial campaigns in present-day Tanzania but also willingly reentered the Imperial Navy for the first two years of the war. As his refusal to fully engage in the duties of his office increasingly caused difficulties, Paasche was eventually given a quiet discharge from the military, a gentle treatment afforded to him no doubt because he also happened to be the son of well-known liberal politician and vice president of the Reichstag Hermann Paasche. Indeed, when Paasche the younger would not desist in spreading his ideas of conscientious objection, a treason trial ensued in which scandal (and a potential death sentence for the defendant if convicted) was avoided largely by a brokered deal that landed him in a psychiatric institution.[7] Though Paasche's path there was more drawn out and tortuous due to his connections, the same fate of hospitalization awaited others who dared make known their opposition to serving in the war effort. Much like Wilhelm W., men increasingly did this in 1917. If one considers other patients explicitly identified either by themselves or by the hospital staff as conscientious objectors (though this did not, of course, preclude a simultaneous determination in the positive of being mentally ill with another affliction), then the label of *dementia paranoides* arises as a common diagnosis seen in connection with those cases. Finally, even the language used by Wilhelm W. to speak of his internal struggle and ultimate acceptance of any potential punishment has a familiar ring to it when compared with the expressions of identified conscientious objectors.[8] While we can never know for certain what crisis befell him leading up to his hospitalization in July 1917, a lot about Wilhelm W.'s case suggests it was not schizophrenia.

Of course, there are many problems involved with attempting to (re)diagnose individual patients from World War I, not the least of which is that reading files can never replace firsthand examination, no matter how complete they may be in cases. Moreover, as has been noted repeatedly in the literature dealing with the history of medicine and the use of patient files, whatever the circumstances of the individual's illness were, the files created to document them already reflect a processing and interpretation of the facts by those attempting treatment, most notably the physician in charge.[9] To attempt definitive diagnosis based on old records would certainly be questionable at best.

What can be done, however, is to examine an array of files within the context of the time to understand how and why physicians made certain diagnoses and proposed particular treatments. While such an effort may ultimately be unable to definitively pin down much about individual patients like Wilhelm W., it can yield multitudes about the practices and perceptions that were prominent in the system of military psychiatry during World War I. As the title suggests, one of this book's goals is to consider how these practices and perceptions played out in a process of diagnosing dissent, an endeavor in which German physicians at times focused more on the medical part of this spectrum and at others on the moral end.

The topic of German wartime psychiatry during World War I has received a lot of attention in the past twenty years. Most of it has focused on the diagnosis and treatment of the *Kriegszitterer* (war tremblers), often referred to in English as shell-shocked soldiers. This topic, if anything, is generously covered in the literature, which generally asserts the following bleak narrative. Especially after a highly publicized wartime medical conference in September 1916 definitively put the nail in the coffin on any real dissention of opinion and practically ushered in a party line among psychiatrists, German soldiers who presented with a notorious mixture of symptoms that could include headaches, body pains, stupor, general weakness, sleep problems, speechlessness, crying, difficulties in moving limbs, and most notably shaking were labeled "hysterics." These men were more or less blamed for their own (feminine) weakness in the face of the ravages of war and denied any pension for what was considered a "sickness" of their own making. It was a sickness of their own making because a fundamental cause of hysteria was seen to be not so much the trauma and strain of the situation but the "desires" dwelling in the own hysteric's heart: desires to leave the battlefield and return home or desires for a pension so one would no longer have to serve or work at all. In other words, the afflicted men themselves, and not anything having to do with what they experienced in war, were the problem, because they did not have the constitution, they did not have the will, they did not have the nerve that they were supposed to have. If not seen as active dissent—though a variety of opinions existed on exactly how aware hysterics were of their underlying motivations—suffering from shell shock was seen at bare minimum as the reflection of internal intransigence that made appropriate soldiering impossible. Because of this, pensions for war injury were denied these men. Instead, they were not to be coddled but given rough, quick treatment (ideally lasting only hours or days, often with electric shock) and sent back to work. This is the view of German wartime psychiatry—as brutalizing, repressive, and focused on the nation, not the patient—that dominates our understanding of the period.[10]

At the same time, despite our increased attention to the case of *Kriegszitterer*, the most blatant form of dissent that played out in the realm of military psychiatry—conscientious objection—is largely missing in the literature. If one wants to learn much of anything about it, the best source to date is Peter Brock's decades-old article "Confinement of Conscientious Objectors as Psychiatric Patients in World War I Germany," which briefly sketches out what is known in less than twenty pages.[11] Slightly more can be garnered in secondary sources mainly devoted to other topics, such as works on religious communities that at times produced conscientious objectors.[12] Yet the larger absence of the subject likely stems from a few reasons. First, the long-standing characterization of the wartime treatment of men by the medical field as repressive, not to speak of the more generalized understanding of the *Kaiserreich* as a highly militaristic society, has led to the underestimation of the potential for dissent to exist within this system. If practices of the time meted out such a dire fate to soldiers suffering from real trauma who were too ill to serve, so the reasoning goes, how could those men who openly and actively refused to do their duty have survived in this system at all? Unlike in Britain, where work has been done on the "conchies" of World War I, for example, nothing similar exists for the German case. In part, of course, this is also due to there being no program that allowed German soldiers to formally object and plead for release from service in the military as there was in Britain. Not just a matter of laws but also of sources, this meant there was no centralized record kept of men who applied for release from service, a clear problem for historians looking for paper trails.[13]

Indeed, even contemporaries who were attempting to substantiate facts surrounding conscientious objection ran up against a brick wall when it came to Germany. An effort by the Quaker mathematician and activist John William Graham to provide a record of conscientious objection during World War I in—not surprisingly—Britain and internationally as well included a short section on Germany in the 1922 book *Conscription and Conscience*.[14] Beyond noting the dearth of information and that even inquiries produced little information, Graham summed up the general fate of conscientious objectors in the *Kaiserreich*: "A common plan was to offer the objector non-combatant service, and if he refused, to get rid of him by declaring him insane." The section concluded, however, by adding, "Apparently the objectors were so few that the question was not prominent."[15]

That the dissent was primarily medicalized—versus criminalized as in most other countries that did not allow for releases—has also meant that what records do exist are often in the form of patient files, not legal proceedings, the former being a type of record that historians are often even less inclined to comb through.[16] Moreover, the very fact that there was no official process through which to apply for release from service as a conscientious objector meant the number of those willing to openly declare their views undoubtedly shrunk. Even if one were to look through all the psychiatric files still extant for German soldiers during World War I, the number of individuals explicitly labeled as conscientious objectors would certainly be limited.[17] In short, scholars have produced little work on conscientious objection in Germany for this period out of both interpretive and practical considerations. There is not much in the secondary literature because little remains in primary sources about a group of men who largely did not exist and were not very significant. Perhaps not all silences are without good reason.

Yet, what if some of the underlying assumptions that have led to this silence were not completely right? While certainly those expressing dissent in and to the military frequently found themselves institutionalized, what if the system was not nearly as repressive and dismissive in dealing with military patients as the literature has asserted? And, what if the ability of patients to express personal agency and negotiate life in such settings was greater than previously thought? And what if this meant that—though unlikely ever hitting the levels that conscientious objection did in a country like Britain—German soldiers expressed more dissent, including full-blown refusals to serve in the military, than historians have recognized possible? Might there then be a far more expansive history of military dissent up to and including conscientious objection in Germany during World War I waiting to be written if only one were willing to dig through "haystacks" of psychiatric files to find these men? This book answers the last question with a resounding yes.

Certainly, this is not to suggest that the extensive work to date on military psychiatry has simply been wrong. But it has told only one part of the story: that of the poor treatment, both medically and in terms of basic human compassion, that many soldiers suffering from very real psychological trauma received at the hands of doctors during World War I. This important and painful episode has been fleshed out frequently in the literature on military psychiatry. Early work on the topic by Ester Fischer-Homberger, for example, detailed the increasing reliance on "hysteria" as a diagnosis not only before the war but also during it as a means of dealing with the increasing numbers of claims for disability pensions brought forth by both civilians and veterans in the last decades of the *Kaiserreich*.[18] Especially considering the needs of not merely their individual patients but also the larger society, physicians stopped viewing hysteria as an actual sickness that required compensation.[19] Touching on the hallmark moment of the 1916 conference, Fischer-Homberger continued on to note that increasingly physicians viewed these traumatized individuals with "contempt" and gravitated to treatments involving "strong-arm methods" that were both painful and potentially deadly.[20] Thereafter, soldiers were to be sent back to the front, another allegedly appropriate regimen to stave off further episodes of hysteria.[21]

Peter Riedesser and Axel Verderber were even more critical of the treatment military physicians provided to traumatized soldiers. Indeed, they discussed the efforts by the military authorities to have physicians limit pension claims, a request that was more than complied with by the treating psychiatrists. They complied, because most physicians were not only ardent war supporters but also "conscious accomplices of a military leadership that demanded the smooth functioning and quick recovery in case of need of soldiers' fitness for action."[22] This meant the proliferation of hysteria diagnoses, the employment of therapies of a "brutal nature," and putting soldiers in harm's way at the front to prevent them from relapsing.[23] Though Riedesser and Verderber did not examine conscientious objectors during World War I, they did explicitly address the ways in which doctors viewed illness and how soldiers, with no other options left to them, fell back on sickness as a form of dissent. Indeed, the view that hysteria was nothing more than weak nerves at best and active resistance or simple cowardice at worst justified that such patients were "silenced for the time being with brutal therapeutic methods."[24] They concluded that one can only view such episodes as "shocking" and "shameful."[25]

This overall picture of military psychiatry in World War I has changed little in much of the subsequent literature on the topic. The preeminent historian of medicine Wolfgang Eckart offers up a standard summary of the wartime events, focusing on the devaluation of soldiers' mental trauma by quick, brutal treatment.[26] Whatever suffering befell soldiers during wartime not only came from the experiences of the front but "also doctors had contributed to it."[27] Some scholars have been careful to note that not all doctors saw the issue in such black-and-white terms. Julia Barbara Köhne, for example, explains the messiness surrounding the hysteria diagnosis, which meant different doctors might use the term to mean quite different things.[28] Livia Prüll prefaces her discussion of the connections between World War I and World War II medicine by specifying that her focus is "on the group of publishing physicians" and "leaders of their field."[29] The finely nuanced research by Hans-Georg Hofer focuses on these issues in the Hapsburg Empire, but he includes important points of comparison with Germany suggesting the latter pulled back from the use of treatments like electric shock sooner than did the Austro-Hungarians.[30] Nonetheless, their ultimate recounting of World War I military psychiatry and the treatment of hysterics largely confirms earlier accounts that focus on the dismissive attitude and brutal treatment.

The emphasis on the repressive and brutal nature of World War I military psychiatry likewise inflects interpretations of the larger trajectory of medicine in Germany. Connections are made among the diagnosing of traumatized soldiers as intrinsically defective (since the hysteria stemmed from their own weakness, not the war events), the brutal treatment meted out to them, and other events like the limiting of food rationed out to those in mental hospitals more generally during World War I.[31] Not surprisingly, the dismissal of individuals' suffering in the face of the needs of the military and national community has been posited as a watershed moment in the descent into the horrific medical policies that reached their depths under the Nazi regime during World War II.[32] While some scholars are more explicit than others, this interpretation is advanced in almost all the works already mentioned.

Certainly, this analysis has not gone unchallenged.[33] Indeed, Paul Lerner's interpretation in the award-winning *Hysterical Men*, likely the best-known English-language work on the topic of shell shock among German soldiers, argues that the impetus behind the shift to hysteria and quick, rough treatment came from modernization and the extension of medicine's purview during the war.[34] It was far more a continuation of rationalization impulses and the emphasis on the economic utility of traumatized soldiers that influenced military psychiatry during World War I than a decisive turn toward the ultimately deadly policies of the Nazi regime. Lerner sees prime evidence for this coming from his research that indicates—contrary to other accounts—

soldiers were not usually returned to the front lines but funneled into jobs in industry and other vital sectors after being diagnosed with hysteria.[35] Of course, as has been pointed out, economics and the basest of racial policy can go and often have gone hand in hand, as an attempt by one scholar to combine both arguments while still highlighting continuity suggests.[36] Yet, Lerner's evaluation of German military physicians as not being substantively different from counterparts in other European countries and his suggestion that traumatized soldiers were treated "with even greater brusqueness" elsewhere undercuts the notion of Germany moving along a different path that from 1914 to 1918 veered fundamentally closer to the policies of the Third Reich.[37] Indeed, Lerner's account nuances the largely monolithic portrayal of medical brutality in a number of instances. For example, he stresses that the efforts to root out malingerers (*Simulanten*) and send them for punishment was not very common.[38] He notes that among the options for more "active therapy" preferred in treating hysterics after 1916, physicians used not only strong electrical current but also a host of other less painful, if still deceptive, methods.[39] He also indicates that some doctors protested the use of certain therapies seen as too aggressive.[40] Most importantly, he explicitly states the "often overlooked" point that "the interests of doctors frequently coincided with those of their patients. Increased psychiatric power and control saved thousands of men—including those suspected of malingering—from both severe military punishment and the dangers of the front, a fact that is obscured by the excessive emphasis on medical brutality and state complicity."[41] Lerner provides a much-needed corrective.

At the same time, *Hysterical Men* offers a far more detailed analysis of the subject that confirms much of the earlier scholarship on the topic. Again pointing to a radical shift occurring after the 1916 conference, Lerner examines how the triumph of hysteria as a diagnosis belittled traumatized soldiers' suffering and freed the harrowing effects of war from blame: "Most German psychiatrists and neurologists concluded that the 'war neuroses' had little to do with war."[42] Such diagnoses fell disproportionately on those of the lower classes, enlisted men who doubly suffered because a diagnosis of hysteria was not seen as meriting the granting of a pension.[43] And while the treatment given to the soldiers certainly gained nuance in *Hysterical Men*, the focus remains on the "often shockingly brutal" procedures used to make men fit for work again within a few weeks.[44] Even after the interventions of Lerner's book, the larger narrative of wartime psychiatry still focuses on the harshness of the system and a seemingly inescapable web of physicians in hospitals and clinics waiting to diagnose hysterics, quickly treat them, and ship them off into the wartime economy. As Philipp Rauh rightly concludes, "The (medical) historical picture of psychiatry in the First World War has to date been strongly shaped by the draconian treatment methods developed and used in these years."[45]

In part, the overwhelming emphasis on brutality stems from an almost exclusive reliance on either administrative papers from military medical authorities or the contemporary journal literature in the field of psychiatry and neurology. The use of patient files as sources and an examination of actual treatment cases have been almost absent from this entire discussion. Bearing out the above point on the reluctance to use patient files as historical sources, only a couple of projects concerning World War I military psychiatry have published research drawn extensively from this type of source. In 2011, Petra Peckl, who consulted the psychiatric records remaining in the military archives in Freiburg for soldiers in various *Lazarette* (military hospitals) during World War I (as a member of the larger project "Krieg und medikale Kultur: Patientenschicksale im Zeitalter der Weltkriege 1914–1945"), published some of her initial findings concerning the actual treatment of these men.[46] Unlike the standard narrative that scholars had generally agreed on, Peckl's research provides a major intervention. Based on treatment records, Peckl argues that the harsh therapy often highlighted in earlier accounts was less commonly used in reality. Instead, the quite traditionally based methods of restoration from rest and good nutrition were often employed, lasting for weeks or months, not hours or days.[47] Beyond this striking finding, Peckl suggests that class did not play a large role in determining how patients were diagnosed or which treatments they received.[48] Furthermore, she complicates the picture of where recovered patients were sent, suggesting a good mixture among those who were sent back to the garrison, to the front as soldiers, or into factories at home as industrial workers.[49]

In her 2012 study, Maria Hermes presents the data from her examination of the medical files of psychiatric patients treated in one city hospital in Bremen, the St. Jürgen-Asyl.[50] Attempting to contextualize the treatment soldiers received, she includes data not only from military men but also from civilians of both sexes who were treated in the hospital between 1914 and 1918. In her analysis of the data, Hermes confirms some of the earlier points about treatment but likewise interjects important new findings. For example, she confirms from the records that malingering, as Lerner has suggested, was not a larger concern in actual patient treatment.[51] She also argues along with Peckl that the reality of treatment for traumatized soldiers was seldom the harsh, quick therapy of electric shock and the like. Furthermore, distinctions of class and rank rarely had a significant impact either, according to her analysis.[52] At the same time, Hermes's attention to the patient files still confirms the assessment in the literature more generally that contemporary physicians posited little connection to the conditions of modern warfare, instead choosing to focus on the inherent constitutional deficiencies of these men. Indeed, Hermes's findings even suggest that this rejection of the war as a cause of trauma was present from the beginning; 1916 was not a watershed moment in terms of how actual soldiers were treated for wartime trauma, at least not at the St. Jürgen-Asyl. Contrary to the prior scholarship, Hermes argues that little changed over the course of the war.[53] Furthermore, the treating physicians there had little concern for the larger debates that may have been swirling in the elite circles of the profession and rarely relied on consistent distinctions between the labels of "hysteria" and "traumatic neuroses," opening up to question how much studies that focus only on differences of diagnoses can ultimately reveal about military psychiatry.[54]

Clearly these studies have shown the importance of moving beyond merely administrative and journal literature for understanding wartime psychiatry. Even from only these two initial studies a picture of far greater variety emerges than that which has been portrayed more monolithically from above. Yet, this research into new sources has not fundamentally moved the topic beyond those questions essentially confirming or rejecting the terms and answers already set out by the research that has focused on more traditional documents. Both Peckl and Hermes largely ignore the actual patients as anything more than objects in these files, the latter not even attempting a reading of ego documents.[55] Neither scholar gives us much of any sense that patients had any room for expression or agency in these interactions. Certainly, the unequal power relationship between the hospital staff and the patients that informed everything—including the production and very survival of ego documents—must be recognized. As important as the worldview of treating physicians is to the story of military psychiatry during World War I, however, it is not the only relevant question. An article by Köhne focusing on medical cinematography in Britain, France, and Germany does raise the possibility that soldiers could derail carefully scripted presentations of their illnesses and is an important step in the direction of examining patient expression. At the same time, her own recognition that such actions may have resulted as much from the inability to perform certain physical actions as from refusal to do so limits the extent of her findings for understanding military patients' agency. Köhne's article reveals a lot about the limits to physicians' control, but it gives little sense of how soldiers may have negotiated medical situations to their own ends.[56]

This neglect in the literature is all the more surprising because the recent works by Peckl and Hermes do highlight findings indicating harsh treatment was not as common as previously thought, which further points to the possibility—introduced into the conversation by Lerner—that physicians and psychiatric care might provide protection to patients in certain instances, like when they were facing military charges for malfeasance. A diagnosis of mental incompetence, for example, would mitigate punishment or avoid completely any conviction for wrongdoing. Yet this possibility is still largely treated as a side issue, one only examined as evidence of less repressive treatment regimens. The protection offered to patients and the role they themselves may have played in negotiating the medical system and using it to further their own ends remain neglected.[57] Perhaps because patients still remain mere objects even in these more recent accounts, the attention overall continues to focus on the limits of this medical system. While Hermes clearly indicates harsh therapies were less common, for example, harsh judgments were not. Indeed, her analysis confirms the consensus in the earlier literature that doctors largely disregarded the horrors of war as a cause of trauma. Instead, drawing on the explanatory power of social Darwinism and ideas of inheritance, they pointed to the inborn deficiencies of the individual soldiers. In short, Hermes still argues that doctors believed patients' suffering stemmed from inherent weakness. Not surprising given this emphasis, even these accounts informed by patient files pose World War I as a fundamental step along the way to the policies of the Third Reich in this understanding.[58]

Patients as Actors

Yet attention to the soldiers' medical files—especially when reading ego documents as well—reveals that patients were not only passive objects but also actors. Admittedly, they were actors with less power and fewer options than others, like doctors and staff within the hospitals. The literature is rife with examples of patients being subjugated, from acts of complete brutality to acts of symbolic degradation, which were just as common and just as important. Similarly, the patient files themselves also reveal plenty of these incidents that cannot simply be chalked up to oversensitive reactions or the ramblings of those overtaken by delusions, no matter how much the involved physicians tended to portray them that way.[59] The aim of this book is in no way to argue that the treatment of soldiers with an array of psychiatric conditions during World War I was good. Here, the extant literature has substantiated something quite true.

At the same time, however, it was not merely dismissive, brutal, and one-sided. Patients not infrequently engaged physicians about their treatment. Sometimes they were rebuffed; sometimes they were not. Soldiers in particular appeared to be in a more advantageous position when it came to asserting themselves, as their role in the war—at least as a member of the military—accorded a basic level of respect during the conflict. This was a card soldiers in the hospital could and did play. Furthermore, the cast of actors involved never only included the hospital staff and physicians versus the ill. It also commonly grew to encompass many others, such as family members, employers, fellow soldiers both in and outside the hospital, military superiors, and personal physicians, many of whom often entered the conversation to lobby for the patients.[60] And, again, these additional voices also realized the potential weight of portraying their requests in the light of just treatment for veterans. Though the retreat from reliance on electric shock ordered by the Bavarian ministry near the end of the war is mentioned in the literature as an indication of the brutality of World War I treatments, for example, it also reveals the limits of physicians' power when dealing with military patients, as the policy change resulted from public pressure.[61] Furthermore, as the recent research involving actual patient files suggests, an overarching reconsideration of how cognizant and sympathetic some doctors may have been to the plight of their patients is warranted.[62] This study will show that soldiers could and did negotiate the system of psychiatric care during World War I to their own ends, often creating spaces for dissent that otherwise would have been impossible. Such medicalization of dissent was not without its costs, of course, as those within the psychiatric system often found their views delegitimized and partially silenced. This is likely a reason why so little has been written of them. Yet, medicalization did provide an array of options that could be protective of dissenters and even allow those on the most extreme end of the spectrum—conscientious objectors—to attain their aims.

Such a view of psychiatric treatment and dissent during World War I is in keeping with important developments in the historiography. Viewing the system as not merely top down but being shaped by influences from below as well is in keeping with the scholarly interventions illuminating how medicalization as a social phenomenon of the early modern and modern era was a two-way street. While certainly the state took a leading role in building up and professionalizing the medical system—a point emphasized especially in accounts of medicalization in Germany—all impetus did not come from above. The needs of common people responding to crises like epidemics or financial hardship could also propel them to invite the "imposition" of a state-regulated medical system because of its perceived advantages.[63] Particularly in the realm of the military, for example, access to comprehensive care was a benefit that came to be expected by soldiers in return for serving.[64] Another larger trend in the historical scholarship has been the emphasis on history from below, a point Roy Porter made specifically for the history of medicine by asserting the need for the "patient's view," as the title of his famous article stated it.[65] The fruits of this history from below have been seen in many fields. Scholars of the history of medicine have given this area less attention, however, though Porter's much-cited call came over three decades ago. This dearth likely stems in part from the impact of thinkers like Michel Foucault or Erving Goffman on the field of medical history. Both specifically addressed psychiatric institutions and emphasized the high degree of control exercised over patients. If the types of sources historians commonly select have been partly to blame for the neglect of patients' voices, so has the influence of these and other thinkers involved with the antipsychiatry movement from the 1960s onward been significant.[66] Military patients have doubly been left behind in efforts to present history from below, as they have also traditionally been seen as the objects of orders, not the actors responding to them.[67] At the heart of this lacuna is the reluctance to see patients as having agency, instead seeing them as dominated and constructed by physicians and discourses beyond their control. As referenced above, this influence on the dominant understanding of German military psychiatry during World War I is clear. Yet, as has been pointed out in the literature, real "patients have by no means been so passive" as many theoretical constructions have suggested, nor have real soldiers been so obedient as military hierarchy would indicate.[68] This is a conclusion borne out by the medical files of World War I soldiers as well.

The focus on patients' voices and agency is also a central concern in the burgeoning field of disability studies.[69] While the field recognizes that individuals labeled as disabled—including those with a "psychiatric disability"—are hardly negotiating an even playing field when dealing with the medical establishment and its institutions in society, affiliated scholars nonetheless emphasize the importance of uncovering patients' "counter-stories" that can also "reveal forms of resistance."[70] Particularly for scholars concentrating on historical disability studies, the endeavor relies heavily on reading documents against the grain and searching for sources beyond those penned by elites in an effort to reintegrate individuals silenced and made invisible in traditional accounts.[71]

Mental Illness and Dissent

Recognizing patient agency is also central to expanding the way in which mental illness and dissent have been linked in the literature. Earlier scholarship has addressed aspects of this connection, long recognizing the relationship by viewing how dissent—or indeed potentially almost any behavior that deviates from the contemporary norms—becomes conceptualized as mental illness in a process meant to delegitimize and silence opposition.[72] This linkage is abundant in the history of World War I, as the focus has been on how many physicians of the era saw war hysterics as, ultimately, expressing their "war reluctance" and even "refusing service."[73] Indeed, even contemporary civilians recognized the power of psychiatry to diagnose dissent in this manner, one of the reasons for increased public scrutiny of medical institutions.[74] The practice of considering conscientious objectors as mentally ill that forms part of this study fits easily into this practice as well. Though less frequent, scholars have posited the flip side of this process, considering mental illness as an expression of dissent by individuals. Elaine Showalter has extended her analysis of hysteria for Victorian-era women to shell-shocked British soldiers during World War I, making a point also posited by scholars such as Eric Leed and Riedesser and Verderber: often "hysterical symptoms [were] the only remaining possibility to express their politically (still) not articulated or no longer capable of being articulated protest."[75] While this view recognizes that illness could be linked to a generalized sense of dissent, however, it does ironically echo the standard explanations of hysteria as "flights into sickness" to escape the war and, again, de-emphasizes the role of significant trauma—regardless of the affected soldier's standpoint on war service—in precipitating the illness.[76] Indeed, the other connection made in the literature between the psychological disorders of World War I soldiers and dissent also reflects another wartime concern of certain psychiatrists: some soldiers simply faked nervous symptoms to escape the battlefield. Tellingly, this is the connection made between mental illness and opposition by Benjamin Ziemann in his overview of dissent outlets available in World War I.[77] That illness can bring "benefits" more generally has been studied in the history of medicine, but again the focus has been on individuals who fake illness to get such advantages.[78]

Undoubtedly, some instances of mental breakdown stemmed from an inchoate rejection of the war, and other cases were merely feigned, though caution should be exercised in any attempt to gauge how common such occurrences were.[79] While this book attempts to offer an overarching examination of the larger spectrum of connections between dissent and mental illness for World War I military psychiatry that the literature has already touched on more generally, such as diagnosing dissent as abnormal to silence it or simulating illness to escape service, it also seeks to highlight what has largely been missing: that individuals truly traumatized—and they were legion—by the effects of a horrific war became ill but nonetheless found ways to negotiate the medical system to achieve aims that included receiving treatment but did not end there. In particular, these ill patients could recognize that their sickness, for all its disadvantages, might also be able to offer some advantages, particularly in the realm of dissent. In this sense, the book hopes to draw on and extend the growing concerns over agency that have influenced both the history of medicine and the real-world treatment of the sick by recognizing that patients are not merely their illnesses but individuals who continue to have agency and goals beyond their malady.[80] In other words, shell-shocked soldiers did not choose their illness, but they often could and did continue to make choices about a number of other things after being diagnosed, some of which reflected certain views about serving and the war effort itself.

Sources

A note on sources is in order. This book is based on a number of different types of sources, including government decrees, military reports, court records, physicians' personal letters, newspapers, and contemporary medical journals. The bulk of the research, however, stems from consulting approximately 2,200 medical files of soldiers treated during World War I. While certainly this is a very small number of the over 600,000 instances of psychiatric treatment undertaken at the time, this examination of patient files likely constitutes the largest of its type for understanding military psychiatry in World War I. Not merely using a larger quantity of files, this study also addresses some of the limitations of patient-file sets used in earlier studies. The sources used by Peckl and her research colleagues, for example, came from 500 cases housed in the Military Archive in Freiburg. While they provide a good overview of military treatment for psychiatric maladies in various settings and also form part of this present study's source material, they are often more basic in their content, an unsurprising quality given that a sizable proportion of the materials stem from doctors often triaging soldiers in various sick bays. This fact also underlies the relative paucity of ego documents in these files. Furthermore, given that the collection is made up of files from many different clinics, the ability to understand the context of any one hospital or *Lazarett* or a given physician is impossible. Those used in the other notable study based on patient files by Hermes all stem from one civilian hospital converted to aiding the war effort by treating soldiers as well. The total files number approximately 1,750, though only a portion of them concern soldiers, as both civilian and military patients were analyzed. This collection's greatest strength is being drawn from one setting that allows context to be studied over time. Given the setting, it is likely that the opportunity to consider ego documents would have been greater as well, if Hermes had chosen to.

While not taking away from either of these fruitful research projects, the present study draws from a larger set of files as well as examines cases in a variety of settings, which were intentionally chosen to reflect a diversity of institutional venues. The sources include the records remaining in the military archives (Bundesarchiv Freiburg), but also those from the civilian hospitals of Düren, Grafenberg (in Düsseldorf), and Galkhausen (in Langenfeld), which treated soldiers as well during the war. The files from the latter three institutions allow for more insight into both physicians and patients, as the completeness of the records from these settings enables one to follow the diagnostic tendencies of individual doctors who worked there. They include surprisingly large amounts of ego documents as well. Also included in this study are files from the first facility set up to house forensic patients in the Rhineland, later known as Haus 5 (in Düren). These documents allow for particular insight into how psychiatrists made delineations between mental competence and incompetence in cases involving legal infringements. Finally, using the patient files from the military *Reserve-Lazarette* of the university psychiatric clinics in Freiburg, Heidelberg, and Tübingen allows for an examination of how elite doctors—those often publishing in journals, contributing to official policy formation, and running "model" institutions—approached patient care in reality. As the inclusion of Tübingen suggests, this examination goes so far as to compare the rhetoric of Robert Gaupp, the notable proponent of the hysteria diagnosis often discussed in the literature, with the very different reality of treatment in the clinic he supervised. Overall, this sizable number of files from multiple locations offers the ability to see differences and similarities in a variety of settings.

As the emphasis on patient agency and two-way influences would suggest, this study takes ego documents and the patient's perspective seriously.[81] Granted, these files do not give equal time to doctors and patients. Commonly composed of a few dozen handwritten pages, though shorter and longer cases are hardly rare, they contain far more from those employed in the medical establishment than they do from patients.[82] Yet the voices of the latter are there, as are those of others who would intercede on behalf of the patients, such as family members. While one cannot ignore the Foucaultian "medical gaze" or the power dynamics of doctor-patient encounters, one can read the files with attention to multiple viewpoints (and not just between doctors and patients) and dissonances among them. Indeed, given the widely acknowledged letter-censoring practices of contemporary psychiatric institutions, that letters were held back in and of itself indicates that some patients were expressing viewpoints contrary to those of the hospital staff. This may not allow all patient perspectives to be uncovered, but it should certainly allow for some of them to be. As Porter famously suggested, to ignore patient files merely because of the inequality inherent in their creation would be to relegate all sorts of fruitful historical records to telling only the story of history's powerful.[83] Considered in another way, it would be a double silencing of those already least listened to. Thankfully, historical scholarship in many fields, including that of patient perspectives drawn from patient files, has already begun to show what would be lost if that were the case.[84]

This book uses these patient files to examine soldiers' dissent during World War I that played out in the medicalized setting of German military psychiatry. Some of the dissent was more perceived than real, the result more so of certain psychiatrists' perceptions than of the soldiers' intentions (though the extent to which all members of the profession viewed it this way has been overdrawn). That is likely true of shell-shocked soldiers generally, though there are important exceptions in which rejection of the war factored into how the case played out. Other instances of dissent were intended as that by the soldiers, but may have stemmed from more general, nonideological concerns. Many deserters snuck away for reasons that had nothing to do with qualms about the war itself. At the same time, without a formal way to refuse serving in the military, many who did have ideological reservations chose this option, a point revealed in the case histories of individual deserters. Finally, at the extreme end of the spectrum was conscientious objection that soldiers clearly grounded in ethical concerns about the killing and dying involved in war, dissent commonly—though not always—recognized by psychiatrists even as they rejected its validity. Examining how psychiatry treated all forms of dissent—both perceived and real, general and more ethically motivated—is important for understanding the possibilities for agency in the military and medical system. Of course, at the heart of this study is uncovering dissent that had ideological underpinnings, a subject the literature has largely neglected.

Outline of the Book

The evidence and arguments of the book are laid out in four chapters and an epilogue. Chapter 1 gives a broad overview of developments within the main areas of psychiatry, the military, and pacifism. Largely based on secondary sources and synthetic, it is nonetheless important for providing the necessary background to understand the conditions prevailing in Germany leading up to 1914. Highlighted are the rising fortunes and expanding purview of psychiatry in the decades before World War I, though the limits of describing these trends as medicalization will also be referenced.

Also explored is the general prestige of the military and the relatively modest role of pacifism in imperial German society.

Chapter 2 begins by providing the standard narrative concerning wartime psychiatry in Germany found throughout the literature of the past few decades. Drawing on a nuanced reexamination of the medical literature of the period as well as the actual treatment files of soldiers seen by psychiatrists during the war, however, this chapter argues that while historians are correct to see 1916 as a pivotal moment in the success of the hysteria diagnosis over others like traumatic neurosis, no such consensus emerged at this time about most other questions surrounding how to understand or treat shell-shocked soldiers. Instead, many psychiatrists still believed "real" wartime horrors were to blame, not merely the weak wills and pension desires of reluctant soldiers. More importantly, regardless of the official debates, the majority of soldiers—even those seen by elite physicians—were not subjected to the harsh and brutal treatment regimens that the standard narrative on wartime psychiatry has presented. In light of this reassessment of wartime psychiatry that presents it as far less repressive than hitherto thought, the chapter ends by revealing the significant space for agency that even traumatized soldiers had. Though placed in hospitals or other mental institutions for treatment during this time, these men could still find ways to negotiate their situation and to express dissent.

Chapter 3 continues the focus on the reality of agency and space for dissent that medicalization offered to soldiers during World War I by illuminating how the tendency to refer deserters for psychiatric observation and treatment (far more commonly than soldiers who committed other acts of delinquency) frequently served to shield these men—even as they committed overt acts of disobedience—from the full brunt of military discipline. Examining the contemporary understanding of the boundary between mental illness "in the actual sense"—as psychiatrists distinguished it, on the one hand—and those who were not truly sick even if they did not allegedly exhibit complete mental fitness, on the other, the chapter reveals the flexibility shown by wartime psychiatrists in determining issues of mental competence for transgressions of discipline related to desertion and the similar charge of going AWOL. Practically this allowed many soldiers to express dissent and avoid significant unwanted involvement in the war, such as direct fighting in combat or other types of service related to engaging the enemy, without legal consequence. Instead, examining psychiatrists frequently interpreted such actions as signs of psychological disorder that warranted leniency. Unlike in other countries where deserters were likelier to be summarily dealt with by the military police and courts, the German system of medicalizing such men meant at times even notable signs that a soldier's absence was precipitated by opposition to the war were considered only secondary details when expert testimony from a physician suggested some level of mental incompetence had played a role.

Chapter 4 rounds out the analysis of the interconnections between psychiatric medicalization and the dissent of German soldiers during World War I by focusing squarely on the largely ignored topic of men who took an explicit and decisive stand against the war by refusing to serve. Almost always sent for psychiatric observation to determine what illness lay at the heart of their allegedly incomprehensible—and according to some, reprehensible—refusal to defend Germany, conscientious objectors during World War I faced examination by doctors who sometimes dismissed them as mentally ill and, hence, incompetent. Yet, on the whole, psychiatrists involved in such determinations frequently expressed far more cognizance of the limits of their own diagnostic abilities and purview in such cases than the standard view of the wartime medical community would lead one to believe. Moreover, as even the standard observation without a determination of mental illness "in the actual sense" frequently marked the conscientious objector as illegitimate in contemporaries' eyes, military and state authorities often felt no need to pursue such men further, even after their release from the hospital. Hence, conscientious objectors, whether they were determined to be mentally ill or not, often found both outcomes left them with significant room to remain out of the war and express dissent. Indeed, the medicalization of conscientious objection as the most overt form of dissent was not only a method promoted by authorities to their advantage in dealing with such men but also a tactic that appealed to many of the objectors themselves because of the greater room for maneuver it offered versus criminalization (the standard procedure for dealing with such individuals in other countries). Furthermore, a close examination of the patient files of the period and the medicalized treatment of such men suggests the number of conscientious objectors was more significant than previous research has revealed.

The final section of the book is presented as an epilogue, as it includes both an extension of the narrative of dissent and medicalization during World War I into the post-1918 era and a summary of some of the larger conclusions that can be taken from the reexamination of wartime psychiatry. While prewar pacifism never embraced conscientious objection as a stance before the war—and indeed most pacifists did not do so during the fighting between 1914 and 1918 either—those who did refuse to serve during the conflict became both inspirations for and, in some cases, even the leaders of the growing movement of more radical pacifism during Weimar Germany that did reject military service. One cannot understand the subsequent development of this more radical pacifism of Weimar without recognizing its roots in the dissent that was far more evident in the medicalized system dealing with everything ranging from psychologically traumatized soldiers to committed conscientious objectors than scholars have previously noted. After completing this narrative arc of dissent into the postwar era, the book ends by drawing together how such a reevaluation of wartime psychiatry fundamentally informs larger historical questions concerning modern German history. Far from being a scholarly curiosity or minor historical aside, the medicalization of dissent and the ability of soldiers to gain agency and expression even within the walls of psychiatric institutions during World War I provide insights into the fundamental questions concerning Germany's path to modernity.

Chapter 1

Antecedents

Psychiatry, the Military, and Pacifism in Late Imperial Germany

"Our psychiatric map of today no longer shows the many dark stretches of space and blurry borders as it used to," the psychiatrist August Fauser confidently claimed at a 1903 conference held in Stuttgart.[1] Certainly, as the director of the local hospital acknowledged, much remained to be learned, and doctors could not always definitively determine the exact affliction a patient was suffering from. Yet, Fauser touted "the recent developments" in his field that meant practitioners now had a far better understanding of psychiatric disorders.[2] Indeed, recent advances "guarantee[d]" not only the ability to make specific diagnoses but also a fuller understanding of the causation and prognosis of a variety of afflictions, according to the director.[3] Nonetheless, Fauser realized many members of the audience came to the field from a far more traditional background in asylum work focusing on providing a proper environment for patients that often had little in common with the cutting-edge research being carried out in the hospitals and clinics increasingly associated with academic medical faculties.[4] Because of this, he acknowledged the service such traditional practitioners had rendered to the care of the mentally ill. Yet, the director's embrace of and emphasis on all the information the latest work in the field had made available—research into etiology, better classificatory systems based on symptoms, and pathological-anatomical findings—made his identification with "the newer psychiatric direction" centered around the universities clear.[5] This was where the future contributions of psychiatry to society would be found.

Fauser's confidence stands in stark contrast to the estimation of the noted historian of medicine Erwin Ackerknecht concerning the field at the start of the twentieth century: "The position of the psychiatrist around 1900 was not a particularly happy one. . . . His patients were prisoners and in a way he himself was a prisoner caught up in the difficulties of the field in which he had chosen to work."[6] Ackerknecht lamented the limits of psychiatric knowledge, especially the rudimentary treatment options available to help those gravely suffering. Certainly, one might suggest that Ackerknecht's interpretation reflected a more general pessimism regarding psychiatry; his low estimation of the field's progress even decades later found reflection in an aside about his own experiences with the system as a trained physician.[7] A similar argument could be made about Fauser's optimism. After all, it was Fauser's research that made headlines in publications like the *New York Times* after he confidently claimed at the 1913 conference of the German Psychiatric Association that he had discovered a blood test to determine *dementia praecox*, an earlier diagnosis largely supplanted by the modern-day term "schizophrenia." It was a claim that merely a few years later would be completely disproved.[8]

While Fauser's and Ackerknecht's estimations of psychiatry around 1900 inhabited opposite ends of the opinion spectrum, it is notable that the scholarly literature on the subject has tended to reflect more of the latter's pessimism concerning the field at the turn of the century. Worsening work conditions in a field already marked by serious problems and the poor standing of psychiatrists within the medical community as well as in society more generally added to the more specific concerns about scientific knowledge and treatment efficacy to produce a situation described as one of multiple "crises."[9] Indeed, drawing on the same quote from Ackerknecht, Paul Lerner characterizes the field and its practitioners as "plagued" by a variety of problems.[10] At the same time, one cannot simply dismiss the optimism of Fauser. To an extent, both the pessimism and the optimism reflected different sides of the reality of the situation, akin to seeing the glass half empty or half full. Even though scholars have tended to emphasize the limits of psychiatry around 1900, these very shortcomings were made all the more glaring in light of real improvements and advances over the previous century. As Eric J. Engstrom and Volker Roelcke have noted, finding weaknesses and strengths in the standing of psychiatry at the end of the nineteenth century might not reflect finding one "despite" the other but more a case of being able to see both of them "maybe even because of" the contrast.[11]

Certainly, Fauser's optimism would have been understandable when looking at the improvements made in psychiatry—or what passed for it—over the previous century. Part of the more general conceptual shift initiated by the Enlightenment that highlighted reason and progress, a new outlook in the care of those deemed "insane" emerged by the beginning of the nineteenth century that recognized some of those suffering individuals might be treatable. Far from ascribing mental illness to religious or supernatural causes, practitioners—some more quickly than others, of course—increasingly came to view those under their care as afflicted by ailments best addressed by the medical sciences. Instead of merely warehousing the ill alongside other "undesirables" like the poor and women of ill repute, with nary a person with any medical training in sight, institutions began to focus on healing.[12] A prime example was the establishment of the institution in Siegburg (near Cologne, Germany) in 1825. The intake guidelines for Siegburg indicated that only those deemed curable be admitted, an outcome that should be achieved in two years or less. Failure or a change in the prognosis of any individual was supposed to lead to the patient's immediate discharge or transfer to another facility. Nonetheless, the optimism embodied in Siegburg certainly contributed to its "distinguished reputation" both in Prussia and beyond.[13] While one would be right to note that not much had changed, especially in the early decades of the nineteenth century in the actual therapies available to cure sick individuals in Siegburg or elsewhere, it would be anachronistic to underestimate the importance of simply recognizing the goal—and a potentially attainable one at that—of curing the "insane."

Institutions opened up in many places beyond Siegburg as part of a European-wide phenomenon in which newer institutions grew in size and more beds for patients became available. While religious asylums for the mentally ill continued to exist, often properties secularized right before the end of the Holy Roman Empire in 1806 came to serve new purpose as public hospitals for the mentally ill. In Germany specifically, it was the last third of the nineteenth century that saw exponential increases: around 1900 approximately twice as many public institutions for the mentally ill existed as had merely a few decades ago around the founding of the nation in 1871. Indeed, dozens more would be built leading up to the eve of World War I. The numbers of patients tell a similar story of expansion in care. They rose from 33,023 (in 1877) to 111,951 (in 1904) to 239,583 (in 1913). While most of these institutions did not have the sole focus on treatable cases as Siegburg did, and many individuals seen as incurable continued to be housed in these newer institutions as well, efforts to rehabilitate patients continued, a process with some success given the marked difference between patients seen and number of beds available in 1913, which was 164,708. A sizable portion of those who were treated must have required stays of less than a year.[14]

Psychiatry not only became less limited by growing its institutional capacity and moving away from the endless confinement of individuals, but also its patients—and by extension the field as a whole—became less liminal over the century. While attitudes toward the "insane" had previously lumped them in with the larger category of the poor, the clientele of institutions became less indigent over the nineteenth century. Of the four levels of care a patient could be placed under in an institution, the least expensive fourth class always made up the bulk of the patients. But the very existence of more well-appointed classes of care indicates the increased presence of those from beyond merely the bottom of the social ladder. (This is not to speak of the wealthy who had long found places in expensive private sanatoria, of course.) It is not surprising in light of the changing social profile of patients that more attention was paid to regulatory oversight and reform. Not only did care come in a variety of classes of comfort, for example, but also it increasingly came without some of the most obvious forms of physical repression. Chains and other restraints began to disappear over the century. However much one—either doctor or patient—may have felt a prisoner in one of these asylums around 1900, the real "prison section[s]" of many a former institution were long gone by then, as Ackerknecht himself noted. Beyond merely the socioeconomic profile of patients in residential institutions shifting, psychiatrists over the century increasingly found better-off individuals turning to them for help with issues related to "nervousness," which became a highly "fashionable" disorder especially en vogue among the bourgeoisie in Germany and elsewhere.[15]

The rising fortunes of psychiatry over the nineteenth century could also be seen in a number of further developments that generally fit into the professionalization of the field, especially in the latter half of the period. Though caution is advised in attempting to pigeonhole all groups into a similar, predetermined path regarding their development into modern professions, the common hallmarks of the process are all visible in the case of German psychiatry (as well as for the medical field more generally). Well into the century, practitioners who ministered to those suffering from mental illness tended to have little specialized training. What knowledge they did gather—something completely devoid of any regulation—often occurred haphazardly and once on the job itself. As already noted, some asylum administrators had no medical background but were instead appointed based on other factors like religious learning. With such a mix of individuals involved in tending to the insane, it is no surprise that little sense of group identity, much less exclusivity, existed.[16]

Though unlikely clear at the time, the creation of a psychiatry chair at the University of Berlin in 1864 formed a watershed moment in the rise of professional psychiatry in Germany. The first of its kind, the position was taken up by Wilhelm Griesinger, who also oversaw the establishment of a new clinic at the affiliated Charité hospital. Beginning slowly with only one more such position created at the University of Göttingen that decade, the stream of establishing new chairs flowed by 1900, with sixteen of them and many new clinics linked to universities as well.[17] The research taking place in the universities by a "new generation of psychiatrists," who firmly associated themselves with these academic institutions as Fauser did, now dwarfed what little investigation those employed in the old-fashioned asylums were conducting.[18] No doubt the shift received a fillip not only from psychiatry's anchoring in academia but also from Griesinger's successful efforts to meld neurology—often considered part of internal medicine at the time—to psychiatry. His emphasis on the physical, brain-based origins of disorders allowed psychiatry to enjoy in the second half of the century the prestige not only of university inclusion but also of a connection to the much-esteemed hard sciences of the period.[19]

By 1900 "university psychiatry" had clearly won out over "institutional psychiatry."[20] Whatever concern this likely caused for old-style asylum practitioners, it meant a notable rise in the status of psychiatry. By that point, a common identity could be found among psychiatrists that drew on increasingly common training in universities, membership in common professional organizations, and readership of certain field-specific journals. Not only gaining clear demarcation from those outside the profession, psychiatrists became internally distinguished from general practitioners as part of a process that saw specialization among a variety of subfields. The reform of the medical curriculum in 1901 would include psychiatry among the specialties required. By that point, psychiatrists not only enjoyed increased status at home but also formed the forefront of the field internationally.[21]

Psychiatrists not only gained professional "jurisdiction" over the care and treatment of the "insane"; they increasingly expanded their realms of influence beyond this core constituency. In addition to treating patients suffering from "nervousness" and colonizing neurology, psychiatrists began enlarging their area of concern to claim additional individuals who were less gravely ill as potential patients within their purview. Such "borderline" cases involved a variety of perceived abnormalities that often found a home in broad diagnoses like psychopathic inferiority (*psychopathische Minderwertigkeit*) and claims of degeneracy.[22] Indeed, interest in the "grey zone" between insanity and complete mental health only rose as psychiatrists further expanded their purview to another horizon by increasingly considering the health of not merely individuals but entire populations. Concerns for public welfare and social hygiene by psychiatrists increasingly meant a far larger domain of expertise than merely a few decades earlier. It also dovetailed with the function of physicians more generally growing beyond merely being doctors concerned with their individual patients' welfare to instead increasingly being incorporated into the workings of the social welfare state. There they not only offered treatment but also functioned as gatekeepers to benefits like pension payouts.[23]

Psychiatry's Expanding Influence beyond Medicine

The expansion of psychiatry's province of expertise occurred not only within the field of medicine itself but also into others as well. One of the most important realms that psychiatrists increasingly played a role in was that of the law. Already dating back to the sixteenth century, judgments in the Holy Roman Empire generally followed a stipulation in the *Constitutio Criminalis Carolina* recognizing those of unsound mind who committed a crime should not be penalized for their actions. In earlier centuries, the determination normally proceeded without any medical input. By the second half of the nineteenth century, however, courts commonly called on physicians to provide expert testimony on the question of a defendant's mental state, even though the decision ultimately rested with the judge. Indeed, under German imperial law the field of psychiatry specifically received a boost in the recognition of its competence to make such determinations, as an 1879 law allowed for the accused to be remanded to an asylum for a period of observation. Increasingly, the courts sent defendants for the six-week observation period, and the number of such cases expanded rapidly up to the eve of World War I, far outstripping a rather modest rise in crime during the same period.[24]

Of course, one should not overestimate this unmistakable expansion of psychiatry's purview into the courts as an unmitigated triumph. Engstrom is right to caution against overlooking the real limits of psychiatry in the legal realm. Many causes promoted by doctors never came to pass, such as the desire for an official, intermediary category of diminished responsibility (*geminderte Zurechnungsfähigkeit*) to bridge the hard separation between mental competence and incompetence that psychiatrists often found insufficient to account for many borderline cases.[25] Moreover, it bears repeating that judges—not medical authorities—were the ultimate arbiters of mental competence, and they could and did go against expert testimony. Furthermore, as Ann Goldberg has pointed out, medicalization was one option for understanding deviancy, but it was not the only one. Focusing on accused Jews in her research, she emphasizes that many of them were not pathologized but reduced to their racial qualities associating Jewishness with a host of negatives, including criminality.[26] Yet, more generally, it is hard to overlook the degree to which psychiatrists did assert themselves in court cases and legal determinations of mental competence. Although judges retained the ultimate right to decide whether a defendant would be considered mentally sound, the very proliferation of requests for expert medical testimony highlights the notable degree to which doctors had expanded into the field of law with forensic psychiatry, as Richard Wetzell concludes.[27] Furthermore, while recognizing the multiplicity of debates and discourses contesting their authority and suggesting other nonmedical actors were more qualified to judge such issues, the reality of the case files nonetheless confirms that medical opinions generally held in final court rulings.[28] Certainly, medicalization is a complex term that should not be applied monolithically in light of its many facets, levels, and limits. Yet, keeping in mind that it was not a zero-sum process but more "a lasting co-operation" between members of the medical and legal fields in many instances, the expansion of psychiatry into the courts was a major boost to its place in imperial Germany.[29]

Indeed, the turn-of-the-century antipsychiatry movement, one of the most noted limits to psychiatric expansion, in part grew out of the very success of this field in gaining currency in the courtrooms. Most notably represented in Germany by the organization Bund für Irrenrecht und Irrenfürsorge (Association for the Rights and Care of the Insane), the movement included many individuals who had firsthand experience of one kind or another with the psychiatric profession. Some members had been former asylum patients themselves, and their suffering became popular knowledge in a series of memoirs and other tell-all books published as part of an entire body of literature that came to center on revealing psychiatric abuses. Yet, not surprisingly, many other members of the antipsychiatry movement came from the areas increasingly having to cede territory to psychiatric experts altogether or, at the very least, share the field with them. Religious officials were among the former; jurists—increasingly having to expect the presence of doctors in courtrooms—were among the latter. Indeed, even the concern for psychiatric abuses expressed in the public realm more generally can also be seen as a response to the very real successes of the field over the nineteenth century. After all, such fears of unwarranted incarceration in a mental asylum came on the heels of decades of institutional buildup, greatly increased access to medical (including psychiatric) care, an expansion of the field into less severe mental afflictions, and an acceptance of psychiatry's role in ensuring public welfare. What could be used for good in helping and healing, of course, was also at times used arbitrarily, repressively, and even maliciously against those deemed in some way unfit. The public scrutiny of psychiatry's expansion—a crucial safeguard, as practitioners had indeed amassed considerable opportunity to curtail the rights of individuals diagnosed as ill—that made its way into parliamentary discussions and efforts to ensure the existence of sufficient legal checks came exactly because of the field's power and increased prestige by the turn of the century.[30]

Another area into which psychiatry had made vast inroads was the military. Part of the link stemmed from the same use of expert medical testimony in military courts as in the imperial legal system more generally. Just as psychiatrists became the accepted source for recommendations on the mental status of defendants in civil criminal cases, so too did military judges frequently order soldiers to undergo medical observation when issues of competence came into question. Indeed, far from merely calling on outside medical opinion when a certain defendant appeared mentally unsound or the details of a particular case stood out as bizarre, military authorities tied fundamental concerns of discipline and dissent to the application of psychiatric knowledge and expertise. Behavior anywhere from laziness and absenteeism to outright desertion came increasingly to be viewed as a potential medical issue in a process Ulrich Bröckling calls "the pathologizing of military disobedience."[31] It was a medicalization of dissent that appears not to have been as pronounced in other countries at the time, which mainly continued charging such transgressions as military criminal infractions without considering any potentially mitigating circumstances, medical or otherwise.[32]

Of course, psychiatry was also established in the military for its primary function as a specialized field of medicine important in caring for the minds and bodies of soldiers more generally. Indeed, the value modern psychiatry could bring to treating patients was arguably recognized by those within the military realm even sooner than in general society. After all, the 1901 reform of the medical curriculum made the study of psychiatry a requirement for all doctors in training, but similar stipulations had existed since the 1870s for those being educated at the Friedrich-Wilhelm-Institut. Renamed the Kaiser-Wilhelm-Akademie in 1895, the institute had been founded to ensure medical officers would be trained in sufficient numbers and quality for the Prussian military. Much has been written about the advances in medicine more generally and their correlation with times of war; certainly the rising interest in military psychiatry and its introduction into the curriculum at the institute owed much to the wars of unification and their importance. In particular, the Franco-Prussian War, a war that presaged many of the "modern" aspects of warfare that would fully erupt after 1914, gave a fillip to interest in military psychiatry.[33] By the turn of the century, it was a "popular and fashionable sub-discipline of German psychiatry."[34] Not limited to those serving in the military, the subdiscipline also held the attention of and received input from many of the leading psychiatrists at the height of their academic careers.[35]

Beyond playing a role in determining mental competence in martial courts and in the providing of medical care for German soldiers, psychiatry had a third, important function connected to the military: the regulation of recruitment. While the specifics of the military structure and size are beyond the limits of this discussion, an important factor to keep in mind when considering the law of universal conscription in the imperial German army is its complete unattainability in reality. Universality was true in the requirement that all males report for potential conscription into the military; yet, only a portion of those would ever actually serve. The budget constraints and corresponding size requirements of the military meant a far greater supply of recruits existed than the demand called for. So, in a process of whittling down the number, various medical authorities would examine the potential recruits, considering both physical and psychiatric fitness. To ensure those with alleged mental shortcomings did not slip through the commonly rushed exams, a variety of psychiatric institutions and special schools providing education to developmentally disabled children (a field also widely populated by psychiatrists) were required by the War Ministry from 1906 onward to report any males who could be potential recruits. Furthermore, intelligence testing, still in its infancy, was also introduced around this time by a number of psychiatrists working not only with schools but also with soldiers to manage recruitment levels and discharge enlistees later found to be "feebleminded." Such disqualifications on medical grounds—both physical and psychiatric—could account for significant deductions in the recruit pool, with fully clean bills of health often given to only about half the men presenting for conscription. Those tagged for psychiatric problems could amount to a couple percent of the entire group, or approximately one-third of those deemed completely unfit for service, which made military psychiatry an important brake on recruitment numbers. By such means, contemporary military authorities believed they were ensuring that only the best men served. Even in the last years before World War I, and after a notable expansion in the size of the German army from four hundred thousand to six hundred thousand, only about half of all young men had actually served.[36]

As this multiple-pronged role played by psychiatry in military affairs was quite extensive by the turn of the century, it is no surprise that both these specialists and physicians more generally had been steadily integrated into the military. Again highlighting the potential connection among wars, medical advances, and increased planning for the care of sick and wounded soldiers that became standard procedure in modern warfare, the regulation of the status of a group of soldiers specifically identified as medical officers (*San-*

itätsoffiziere) appears in military protocol beginning in 1873, shortly after the seminal Franco-Prussian War. According to enacted regulations, medical officers were to be uniformed and due the same honors and deference as their regular, nonmedical counterparts in the officer corps. While medical officers may never have fully reached the same level of status as hardened regular officers who had proved themselves in battle, by World War I military doctors were quite comfortably positioned in society. The importance of (and professional status of) physicians had been recognized as central to a modern military, and this further reflected on the prestige of doctors within imperial Germany generally. And psychiatrists—now highly integrated into multiple areas beyond merely the treatment of the "insane" in asylums—shared in this prestige by association with the military. Certainly, they themselves recognized the importance of psychiatry's link to the military for their standing in society. Indeed, it was not a luster merely limited to those actively in the military. Demands for psychiatric facilities and care commonly required reliance on civilian doctors and institutions as well, both before and during World War I. Yet, even psychiatrists contracted as civilians by the military still gained the right to a rank and the corresponding deference.[37]

Military Cachet

Psychiatry arguably benefited from its cooperation with the military more than any of its other associations.[38] For whatever can be said about the problems facing psychiatry around 1900, no such doubts could be cast on the widespread esteem and importance in which the military was held. Even though conscription limits meant the military as the "school of the nation" did not match reality in a direct sense, martial values and prestige resonated throughout imperial society. Always dressed in uniform for public engagements, Wilhelm I and Wilhelm II presented themselves as military men above all else. Not only important to the crown and nobles, the military and the prestige gained from association with it meant many sons of the bourgeoisie likewise aspired to service in the armed forces. Approximately two-thirds of officers came from nonnoble backgrounds by 1914, though their proportions remained lower in some more exclusive regiments like cavalry. Yet, the prestige of the military did not only serve to reinforce the status quo or bolster the position of the nobles and the wealthy bourgeoisie. Even enlisted men from lower social backgrounds could employ their attained status as an argument for receiving better treatment, and sometimes claiming ownership of martial values meant less privileged groups could get their voices heard alongside the traditional bastions of power. At the same time, persons lacking in honor, such as convicts, often lost the right to serve, an exclusion intended to mark them off and prevent tarnishing the prestige of the military.[39] Indeed, the historian Isabel V. Hull describes how "both real and symbolic power were so heavily militarized" because of the central importance and esteem given to the military in light of its formative role in national unification after 1871.[40] Even martial habits and methods spread out beyond military institutions proper, evidenced by the proliferation of "harsh, order-giving tones of military routine" that "seeped into civilian life."[41]

Of course, one should neither overstate the level of glorification of the military in the *Kaiserreich* nor overemphasize its importance in Germany vis-à-vis the same sentiments in other countries at the time. Some men did not report for conscription; others were undoubtedly relieved to find out they had not passed muster for recruitment. No doubt this in part stemmed from the notoriously grueling rigors of barracks life that enthusiastic recruits often conceived of as a rite of passage steeling both body and mind but likely left more reluctant participants feeling broken. Indeed, heightened suicide rates among conscripts meant they were fourteen times likelier to kill themselves than members of the general populace. There was regional variation in the attractiveness of service as well; the middle class in southern states was more skeptical of the military, for example. While the middle classes more generally sought the social status becoming a military officer could confer, their increasing presence also brought bourgeois values to bear on life in the military. Certainly, the desire to serve did not fill as many hearts at the lower end of the social hierarchy as at the top, and the growing socialist movement in Germany often worked to expose problems within the military. While overconfident soldiers sometimes treated civilians impertinently, the latter rarely accepted such behavior without complaint and contestation. As much as military service was associated with manliness, it was never the only route to becoming a man. Moreover, while the military played a central role in imperial society, so too did the civilian institutions of the legal courts and the bureaucracy as a whole. Highlighting the prestige of the military in the *Kaiserreich* need not equal subscribing to a view that Germany was particularly beholden to militarism.[42]

Pacifism on the Margins

Yet, recognizing the prestige and importance of the military, as well as how psychiatry benefited from association with it, also highlights another important aspect of imperial society that fundamentally affected how dissenting views concerning martial affairs and, ultimately, World War I played out in the *Kaiserreich*: pacifism was an ideology on the margins. Indeed, Germany did not have a pacifist organization "of any significance or durability" until the founding of the Frankfurt Peace Association (Frankfurter Friedensverein) in 1886.[43] A national peace organization did not appear until six years later with the founding of the German Peace Society (Deutsche Friedensgesellschaft). There had been smaller peace groups before, though they did not last. The first such ephemeral organization formed in 1850 in Königsberg only to be outlawed a year later. Even after the founding of the German Peace Society, the movement grew only modestly. Helene Stöcker, the leading advocate for women's rights who increasingly became involved with pacifism during World War I, quipped that the first handbook for the German pacifist movement, published in 1911, appeared long before there was any movement to speak of. By 1914, the movement had approximately one hundred local organizations, though they were concentrated in the southwest of Germany. Perhaps the membership totaled ten thousand people, though those individuals truly committed to the movement likely numbered merely in the hundreds. (For comparison, even small areas like the Palatinate had 540 veterans' associations with around thirty-five thousand members.) The profile of the membership did not lend itself to bolstering greater acceptance in society either, as the individuals involved were disproportionately elderly or female compared with the general population. This created an image of pacifism as unmanly and soft. Another limit on the growth of the peace movement in Germany was the distance socialism kept from it until shortly before the war. For the most part, members came from the middle class and identified with left-leaning liberalism.[44]

Of course, there was more to speak of concerning the intellectual roots of pacifism in Germany in the early nineteenth century, as Roger Chickering has noted.[45] Foremost among thinkers laying the foundation for pacifist ideology was Immanuel Kant. In "Perpetual Peace" ("Zum ewigen Frieden") Kant laid out a series of guidelines that would allow nations to avoid war, including the elimination of standing armies. Indeed, Kant suggested that man's reason would triumph and ultimately lead to the adoption of an international system alleviating the need for war. Given Kant's subsequent influence on the movement, it is unsurprising that the first noted German peace organization arose in Königsberg. After all, it was the site of the eminent philosopher's birth a century earlier. Yet, these strong intellectual currents did not translate into a more significant organizational presence in Germany until the end of the nineteenth century. Elsewhere, in countries such as Britain, France, and the United States, pacifists had successfully organized decades earlier, often in response to the horrors of the Napoleonic Wars and the War of 1812, which was proportionally more lethal for American soldiers than most other conflicts, including World War I. Even when notable peace societies were founded in the 1880s and 1890s, non-Germans played leading roles. The Frankfurt Peace Association grew out of the efforts of local democrat Franz Wirth as well as Frederik Bajer, a Danish activist. Two Austrians played a central role in establishing the German Peace Society in Berlin. Bertha von Suttner, author of the widely read pacifist novel *Die Waffen nieder!* (*Lay Down Your Arms!*) and the best-known woman on the continent according to a Berlin newspaper poll around the turn of the century, as well as the journalist Alfred Fried took the initiative in the society early on, though organizational efforts soon passed to German natives.[46]

Perhaps unsurprising given its largely bourgeois and liberal membership, the German peace movement promoted a rather moderate program, especially in comparison with the direction many pacifists in Germany and elsewhere subsequently went in during and after World War I. While disputes remained over the extent to which the larger public should be involved or more specific efforts should be pursued by lobby groups, the focus remained on creating a system of international agreements and agencies that could provide an arena for arbitration of disputes among sovereign nations. Hopefully made unnecessary, war was to be avoided. Nonetheless, these early peace advocates generally accepted the validity of war in certain cases, above all any wars of self-defense, something their counterparts in many other European countries acknowledged as well. Consequently, the idea of refusing service to one's country—in peace or wartime—was a nonissue among members of the German peace movement. Indeed, Fried went so far as to call such actions tantamount to treason. Though he adamantly championed the use of the word "pacifism"—only coined in French in the early twentieth century—for the German movement during the *Kaiserreich*, the ideals of pre–World War I peace activists were quite different from what is commonly understood by the term today. The shifting meaning of the term has foreseeably often led to confusion.[47]

For the background of pacifism in the sense of a refusal to serve or conscientious objection, one must also look to a different thread within German history: privileges granted by royal authority to religious minorities in the early modern period. While various places in German-speaking Europe granted different privileges at different times, such exemptions commonly applied first to Mennonite communities. In 1623, for example, Duke Friedrich III of Holstein-Gottorp granted Mennonite settlers to the new city of Friedrichstadt the ability to refuse service as a combatant on religious grounds. In Prussia, both King Friedrich I and his son Friedrich Wilhelm I offered various allowances to the kingdom's Mennonites, though it was finally in 1780 under Friedrich II, also known as "the Great," that the situation was more closely regulated by an agreement allowing freedom from service in exchange for a yearly payment from the community. Soon Quakers were also allowed to use the exemption. At times some of the actual cases of exemption could be drawn out and require appeals and intercession from more well-known individuals to higher authorities, but generally members of these religious minorities did not have to serve. Though the law under the North German Confederation initially did not provide for such exemptions, a royal decree in 1868 guaranteed that certain religious minorities would not have to undertake armed service but could instead act as members of the medical corps or other auxiliary troops. The instruction continued to be followed in many cases after 1871 as well.[48]

While there was some growth in the peace movement in the years leading up to 1914, both from shifts to a more "scientifically" focused system and from some initial instances of cooperation with socialists, no sizable attention ever arose regarding a more general application of conscientious objection, either as a right or as a tactic to prevent military conflict. Alongside the general acknowledgment of defensive wars as just, it hardly surprises that the peace activists in Germany—as well as in cases elsewhere—threw their support behind their national governments in 1914 when the fighting broke out in the middle of summer. After all, the war in Germany was pitched as a defensive war, a move that also ensured the votes for war credits from all political parties, especially the initially tentative Social Democrats. While peace advocates may not have joined in the initial enthusiasm—noticeable in some cases, though the widespread nature of this outburst has often been overestimated—or the aggressive propaganda that became common, they nonetheless backed the war effort alongside other Germans. Just weeks after the outbreak of hostilities, the German Peace Society put out a flyer proclaiming, "Concerning the duties that have now arisen during the war for us friends of peace, there can be no doubt. . . . Every German friend of peace has to fulfill his duties to the Fatherland exactly like every other German," a statement that left little unclear about the organization's stance. Thus began what was a period of political truce (*Burgfrieden*) that would mark the early stages of the war. The German Peace Society proved so acquiescent to the war effort that only months later more critical activists would create a new organization called the New Fatherland League (Bund Neues Vaterland) to fill the void of concerted work against the raging conflict, especially in opposing jingoistic calls for territorial annexation during the war. Both organizations and others like them had to contend with wartime censorship measures and similar repressive acts from the government and military authorities attempting to stifle any public debate over the war, which soon saw the New Fatherland League silenced. Some members of the peace movement then formed another organization, the Zentralstelle Völkerrecht, in 1916, but again, it had to contend with a variety of repressive measures. By 1917, the most notable, organized criticism of the war came not from pacifist groups specifically but from the newly created Independent Social Democratic Party of Germany (USPD), which had formed in April after a split from the Social Democratic Party (SPD).[49] Nonetheless—as moderate and muted as they may have been in opposition to the war during the conflict itself—these pacifist beliefs, socialist ideology, and religious convictions all formed elements that the individuals examined in this book who would express dissent between 1914 and 1918 could and did draw on in their decisions to avoid service. Of course, the cases highlighted in the following pages also make clear that often the reasons for refusing to serve came less from any organized movements and more from the very experiences of war and its horrors, especially as they were extended and heightened by the duration of the conflict fought with modern weaponry.

While the importance of military culture and the moderation of prewar pacifism help explain why the outbreak of hostilities was generally met with acceptance of the service—military and otherwise—that would be required and willingly given by the German populace, the established presence of psychiatry as a discipline in German medicine as well as in the functioning of the military meant it was hardly surprising that the pronouncements regarding the war turned around issues of "nerve" without much need to explain such metaphors to the public. It also meant, as the military increasingly had to deal with issues of dissent—whether from soldiers actually intending opposition or from the rising numbers of psychologically traumatized troops no longer able to fight, who were nonetheless conceived of by some in the military leadership as semi-intentional failures of willpower—that the reliance on psychiatry to deal with disciplinary issues of all kinds arising during the war was a foreseeable continuation of a process with roots dating back several decades. Indeed, even the efforts to handle more explicit instances of dissent and outright refusal to serve in military courts were largely medicalized with the psychiatric assessment of such objectors being the first—and frequently the last—word on such cases. Of course, it formed part of an effort to dismiss such ideas as nothing more than the irrational rantings of unstable and even mentally ill individuals, a process that delegitimized dissent. At the same time, however, a close examination of wartime psychiatry and the actual treatment of soldiers in a variety of institutions reveals that such medicalization also allowed for the greater expression of a variety of dissent and refusal to serve than has been recognized.[50]

Chapter 2

Hysterics and Other Patients

Diagnosis, Treatment, and Negotiation

As is often recounted in the literature on military psychiatry between 1914 and 1918, the fate of countless German soldiers who would be seen for nervous disorders by the end of World War I was finally decided in September 1916 by a small group of neurologists and psychiatrists at a special wartime meeting of their professional association in Munich. Drawing on long-standing discussions about the underlying causes of illness linked with trauma that originally focused on industrial accidents and phenomena like "railway spine" in the late nineteenth century, the debate reached a fever pitch in the midst of the war. Numerous doctors contributed to the conversation on how to effectively understand and treat the masses of soldiers pouring into military hospitals and exhibiting the signs of mental and physical disturbance that would become known in English as shell shock. The German term focused more on the outwardly visible shaking, earning the affected men the label "war tremblers." Lack of clarity over the causes of war neurosis—another term associated with the complex of symptoms—and the inability to effectively treat afflicted soldiers not only created an economic problem for the imperial government similar to the earlier concerns over the pensions paid out to victims of accidents under the Bismarckian social insurance system but also created manpower shortages by taking men out of the military ranks in the midst of a world war.[1]

The problems the war tremblers created for the government did not end there, either. In addition to the practical concerns of money and manpower, war tremblers undermined the morale of Germany as it fought a war that the scholarly literature has amply shown was conceptualized around "nerves."[2] Germany would allegedly win because its army had long "cultivated the power of the will over the body, over [both] muscles and nerves."[3] That a flurry of advertisements touting a variety of medicinal supplements designed to foster "healthy nerves" often ran alongside such statements only underscored their importance.[4] Given the significance of presenting a unified front void of any troubling issues that might undermine the war effort, which the widespread censoring of reportage was meant to ensure, no irony was intended in the acknowledgment of a market for such aids that also implied German nerves may have been flagging.[5] Instead, much was made of problems with the nerves of the enemies' troops, with propaganda often playing into the long-term use of France as a foil to positively portray German attributes. At the same time, the overall health of Germany's own troops was proclaimed.[6] Indeed, as martial masculinity reached a high point during the war, an intensified emphasis on the value of composure and self-control as well created an ideal, emotional, and psychological profile for soldiers that revealed how ingrained the importance of "nerves" had become to military success in World War I.[7]

Yet, by the middle of a war that had lasted far longer than initially expected, the countless soldiers being pensioned off from military service for unresolved nervous disorders could not be ignored. Drawing on a constellation of influences, including the long-term sway of etiologic explanations that favored inherent disposition and "inferiority," the efforts to augment professional standing, and the recognition of the dicey situation the rising numbers of war tremblers was presenting for the military command's pursuit of victory, top neurologists and psychiatrists in Germany gathered in the fall of 1916 to reach a solution.[8] In contrast to the vagaries of causation and treatment that existed up until then, those present rallied around the approach represented most pointedly by professors Max Nonne of Hamburg and Robert Gaupp of Tübingen. From among the multiplicity of diagnoses that were associated with war tremblers—including terms like *Granatschock*, *Nervenschock*, and traumatic neurosis—rose one in particular that was championed by Nonne and Gaupp: hysteria. More than just a terminological clarification, the conference also represented a decisive shift away from the position held most notably by Herman Oppenheim. Oppenheim originated the traumatic neurosis diagnosis, which asserted a degree of underlying physical damage to the brain as part of the explanation for the disorder, instead of the completely psychologically based causality championed by Nonne and Gaupp.[9] In particular, the psychological explanation posited the uncontrollable shaking, emotional suffering, and all imaginable varieties of physical dysfunction, from limb paralysis to mutism to blindness, that plagued war tremblers as effects of the afflicted men's intense desire to be free of the hardships of military service, which caused them to wish themselves sick, literally. The September 1916 conference signaled that "the great majority of German psychiatrists reached a consensus that these conditions—like the accident cases of the 1890s—were best labeled hysteria. 'War hysteria,' a direct parallel to 'pension hysteria,' became the diagnosis of choice."[10] At the heart of war neurosis was the individual patient's desire: desire for release from the rigors of military life, desire for the comforts of home, desire for a handsome pension. Moreover, such a "flight into sickness" arose in those with a "deficient will," linked to an inferior "constitution" often inherited as a "hereditary burden," meaning the experts "ruled out a connection between lasting psychological suffering and concrete war experiences."[11] "In short," as Paul Lerner has resolved, "most German psychiatrists and neurologists concluded that the 'war neuroses' had little to do with war."[12] Hysterical men, then, were those who lacked a healthy constitution that could both withstand the hardships of wartime service and accept the sacrifices that it entailed. Given the increased emphasis on self-control and composure as characteristic of good soldiers, the diagnosis called into question the very masculinity of such men. More specifically, the term "hysteria" brought in direct associations not only with female anatomy but also with the long-standing medical images of women's bodies as out of control.[13] Far from rewarding these soldiers for their shortcomings with rest, visits home, and pensions, the appropriate treatment regimen for hysteria was to be short, brusque, and focused on getting men back into the war effort, though more as workers than as soldiers, as Lerner has importantly demonstrated.[14] Underlying this heavy-handed approach, of course, was the medical view that cast these war tremblers as disciplinary problems in addition to being patients in need of treatment. Dissent—as much as sickness—was often the lens through which these men's conditions were viewed.[15]

Likely the conference of 1916 and the decisive shift in conceptualizing war tremblers has particular resonance as it also involved the professional (and ultimately personal) downfall of Oppenheim, who had been a leading figure of prewar neurology. Author of the widely acclaimed textbook *Lehrbuch der Nervenkrankheiten*, which enjoyed multiple editions and translations, Oppenheim—a Jew—likely never received a university position because of the anti-Semitism of the period. Especially in accounts that posit a fundamental shift beginning in World War I toward the later policies of the Third Reich, the abandonment of Oppenheim and his potentially more sympathetic view of war tremblers (as suffering from "real," physical injuries instead of simply being weaklings who had lost their nerve) in 1916 fits well in such a trajectory, particularly as both Nonne and Gaupp later had involvement in intellectually justifying or even enacting the racial hygiene policies of the Nazis. Noted as well is that the devastating blow to Oppenheim—who found his position unsupported by any other members present at the conference—may even have contributed to his early death a few years later.[16]

With the diagnosis of hysteria triumphant and treatment regimens promising quick and almost universal success decided on after September 1916, traumatized men were branded as constitutional weaklings at best and unpatriotic dodgers at worst. Henceforth, both medical and military authorities worked to root them out by setting up a vast system of special treatment clinics that employed a variety of treatments ranging from merely deceptive to physically excruciating and even deadly.[17] Often remarked on as quintessentially typical of such methods, the Kaufmann cure was defended by the neurologist who developed it, Fritz Kaufmann, at—unsurprisingly—the Munich conference as well. Involving strong, painful electric shocks to the body and repeated exhortations to the patient that healing would be successful, the treatment could last hours and also involve exhausting exercises performed under the strict disciplinary watch of the attending physician. Though it initially met with some hesitation—often over how treating physicians would deal with the rigors of such therapy and not over what the effect on patients would be—the Kaufmann cure became the preferred method of dealing with war hysterics: "It became the cornerstone of active treatment and quickly revolutionized the organization of wartime psychiatric services."[18]

Not surprisingly, Gaupp came out firmly in support of Kaufmann's methods.[19] Even though subsequent fatalities from the use of electrical shock in treating war hysterics did precipitate investigations into treatment both during the war and after, patients who had been subjected to such brutal therapies did not even have the satisfaction that their French counterparts likely got from the suspended sentence handed down to Baptiste Deschamps, the soldier convicted for coming to blows with a physician attempting to treat his bent body with electricity. German investigations into similar issues of physicians' misconduct led to no such definitive outcomes undermining military psychiatrists. All this was seen as necessary to quell dissent among the troops and restore the military discipline required to wage a "war of nerves."[20]

At least, these are the issues surrounding the treatment of war neurosis that have been emphasized in the literature. The settling of the etiologic issue in favor of psychogenic causes, the ensuing consensus (at the bare minimum among elite doctors who set the standards), the emphasis on the inherent, personal shortcomings of the soldiers afflicted corresponding to a larger denial of modern warfare's impact, and the link to refusing hysterical soldiers pensions that served the interests of the nation and not the individual have all dominated how the issues of war neurosis and military psychiatry have been presented for the period.[21] And, there is certainly truth in this portrayal. But there is also a lot that is either overlooked or, just as important, underemphasized to the point of distortion, and this has consequences not only for the more direct understanding of how trauma was treated in World War I Germany but also for understanding the way in which dissent could and did exist even within this medicalized and at times repressive setting.

This chapter attempts to rebalance the baseline view of wartime psychiatry by presenting a reconsideration of three areas. First, the etiology of war neurosis was not nearly as settled an issue after 1916 as the literature has presented it to be. Certainly, traumatic neurosis and organic causation had largely been abandoned, but what exactly psychogenic causation meant and, importantly, what this suggested about the impact of modern warfare and the alleged inherent inferiority of afflicted individuals was far from agreed upon, even among elite doctors. In particular, there was a great diversity of opinion about whether hysteria stemmed from psychogenic effects, like shock and terror from war, or from those causes also labeled more specifically ideogenic in nature. The latter referred to thoughts—wishes often considered by contemporary experts as quite separate from the feelings of horror at war experiences—that aimed more specifically at certain outcomes, such as discharge and pension awards. Not surprisingly, it was the latter, ideogenic cause that most closely aligned with the view that war played little role in causing neurosis. The extant scholarship of war neurosis has largely conflated this important distinction.[22] Only the meticulous research by Gundula Gahlen has begun to challenge the existing view of consensus, though her focus has been on reconsidering officer-enlisted dichotomies in the literature.[23] The narrative of consensus among leading doctors on hysteria more generally has largely gone unquestioned.

Indeed, even the more recent contributions that have focused on patient files and actual treatments have done little to question the rhetorical unity among contemporary doctors publishing on the topic. The reality of a far less uniform treatment in daily life on the front lines and in hospitals throughout the Reich has been understood as the limits of the elite discourse—still considered uniform—permeating down to the daily level.[24] Hence, second, this chapter not only questions the extent to which there was rhetorical consensus but also draws on the case files of a variety of hospitals to argue that the reality of treatment on all fronts, including those in leading hospitals run by elite doctors, was likewise a far from reliable reflection of what the standard, scholarly narrative has described.[25] Indeed, the patient files of the reserve military hospital at the psychiatric clinic in Tübingen, led by none other than Robert Gaupp himself, reveal treatment that was far less uniform and, importantly, less brutal than the literature indicates, a point that also calls into question previous explanations for such variability.

Third, this chapter focuses more closely on the reality of daily life for many of these men being treated in hospitals for a variety of forms of trauma linked to war neurosis. Building on the reconsideration of both the rhetoric and the reality surrounding the treatment of war neurosis as well as drawing attention to some of the important conditions in which patients received care during the war, the many ways in which soldiers could express both agency and dissent in this medical system are highlighted. Far from being a system of total repression that brutalized soldiers and left little space for anything else, the system allowed for men to express themselves in many ways on the spectrum of dissent.

In February 1917, Private Gustav B. reported to the military reserve hospital in Krefeld for reexamination to see if his condition had improved enough for him to be reenlisted into the active military. Presenting with complaints of seizures that occurred approximately every two weeks as well as a stumbling gait, the private remained there largely without incident save an episode of spasms that followed a misunderstanding over the soldier's request to go out for the afternoon. Nonetheless, Gustav B. was not reassigned to active military duty but released from the hospital as fit for work at home. The treating physician—Dr. Voss, a specialist in nervous disorders—concluded that Gustav B.'s episodes both in the hospital and prior to that were "undoubtedly of hysterical origin."[26] Indeed, such a determination agreed fully with the diagnosis of the earlier examination performed in June 1916 that had also been undertaken in Krefeld, but under the direction of a different physician. Dr. X, as that physician was anonymously referred to by Voss, had diagnosed the private as suffering from "hysterical seizures."[27] Dr. X explained in the diagnosis that "such a hysteria always has a psychogenic cause," emphasizing that "hysteria never develops" from the kind of military service performed by Gustav B., who had manned a watch post in Belgium.[28] Instead, the seizures were nothing more than "escaping into hysteria" induced by "wish complexes."[29] Not surprisingly, Dr. X rejected the episodes as a service-related injury to preempt any "pension desires."[30]

At first glance, this case fits perfectly with much of what research on war neurosis has suggested, especially as both the first and second examinations fell right before and after the time of the 1916 Munich conference. Certainly, hysteria as a diagnosis was ascendant; few people beyond Oppenheim still considered an organic cause as underlying this familiar complex of symptoms. Voss's purpose in publishing on the examinations of Gustav B., however, was not to highlight the consensus concerning war neurosis that had set in but to draw attention to the continued "differences of opinion."[31] While he in no way contested Dr. X's findings of hysteria or the psychological (i.e., not organic) origins, he made a huge distinction between how they each saw "the essence of hysteria and of psychogenic symptoms in general."[32] Stressing not only the theoretical importance but also the real impact such determinations had on soldiers, he rhetorically asked, "Now what is the situation in the present case in reality?"[33]

That "hysteria never develops" from such service was an argument Dr. Voss believed made no sense if one gave any basic thought to the stress that Gustav B. served under, concluding, "People who are not (inherently) nervous can also become upset when the rebellious population takes shots at the watch post at night." Not only did Voss rule out a constitutional predisposition for the private's hysteria, but he also fully dismissed any idea that Gustav B.'s sickness had its origins in "wish complexes." Hysteria was psychogenic, he reiterated, but that meant such cases "are caused, here, as always, through affective events." Not content only to reject both a constitutional underpinning and a "wish complex" causation, Voss laid the origins of hysteria squarely at the feet of the emotional trauma elicited by events. In this case, it was the trauma of the war that Gustav B. experienced in Belgium. Not only wrong, the ascription of hysteria to "wish complexes" was "dangerous": "It is not freedom from service and pension visions that allow a relatively large number of our often especially hardworking and brave soldiers to become hysterical." Instead, Voss concluded, "the cause is to be found in the tremendous demands of the present war placed on psychological strength at the front, on the base and sometimes also at home."[34]

Such a strong defense of traumatized war tremblers as "hardworking and brave" and the clear ascription of causality for their sickness to the traumas of the situation and not to their individual shortcomings might lead one to think that Voss was an extreme outlier in these diagnostic debates that had been waged over wartime trauma. He was not. While this article certainly was one of the strongest singular statements rejecting a dismissive approach to war hysterics, contemporary medical journals contain far more recognition of the ideas Voss was arguing for than has previously been acknowledged. Voss was neither an outlier nor an outsider. While he may not have had the scholarly credentials of the top men involved like Gaupp or Nonne, for example, Voss was not without academic achievement. He had published on a variety of issues in several contemporary psychiatric journals, edited volumes, and monographs, as well as taught at the university in Düsseldorf. Indeed, his work—on the very issue of hysteria and its causes—featured in the *Deutsche Militärärztliche Zeitschrift* as well as other leading journals perused by many physicians involved in treating shell-shocked soldiers.[35]

All of these main points—the significant effects of war trauma, the ability of healthy men to also be affected, and the rejection of the etiologic role of desires in hysteria—found support and reflection in the wider literature both before and after the Munich conference in 1916. Just as Oppenheim and his ideas had suffered their defeat, Karl Birnbaum—tasked with periodically presenting a comprehensive overview of the latest state of research on war and mental illness for the community in the leading journal *Zeitschrift für die gesamte Neurologie und Psychiatrie*—explained that while traumatic neurosis might now be folded into the term "hysteria," the diagnosis was still problematic because too much remained undetermined about its types and causes. To emphasize this point, he continued to list a number of leading scholars who had superficially reached conclusions about a variety of disorders that might all be classified as hysteria but in reality suggested quite different things, repeatedly adding the words "in the sense of" to each case to highlight that a closer look would reveal more difference than similarity of opinion in what the term meant.[36] Indeed, on issues like the role of wish complexes, Birnbaum's overview emphasized that not much had changed recently to alter the split between those who considered their presence essential to understanding hysteria and those who did not.[37] Birnbaum even noted when summarizing the work of another scholar that the latter's sense of how much weight the field ascribed to the function of wish complexes in hysteria was off, as German doctors had "kept clear of an overestimation" of desire's role.[38]

Little had changed by the time the next report came out, with Birnbaum explicitly referencing the Munich conference and Oppenheim's downfall.[39] On the important issue of what hysteria itself meant, Birnbaum merely concluded that the same questions remained, as "no fundamentally new viewpoints or experiences have been advanced." In other words, the victory of Nonne and Gaupp over Oppenheim had done little to settle this. While certainly the debate over whether the war tremblers were suffering from a disorder with an organic or a psychogenic cause was settled, as the wider scholarly literature of German military psychiatry indicates, this had done little to further clarify remaining, fundamentally important debates concerning whether these psychological influences were more affective or ideogenic (i.e., wish complexes). Of course, Oppenheim had rejected wish complexes, but so did many other scholars who did not support an organic etiology.[40] This open question remained until the end of the war, as Birnbaum would continue to report commentary on both sides of the desire debate in the subsequent reviews. He merely ended his series with no definitive consensus on this issue, as even by the last year of the war there had been "hardly much new presented" to settle things.[41]

If not caused by desires specifically, hysteria could still be seen as a defect in the afflicted soldiers themselves if a so-called inferior constitution was involved. Even here, though, the diversity of opinion continued. Indeed, the best example that underlines the extent to which September 1916 settled only one specific debate but left open many questions that significantly affected how leading doctors discussed war tremblers in the scholarly literature is the disagreement on this issue between the two "victors" of Munich: Gaupp and Nonne. While Gaupp emphasized the importance of a soldier's "psychopathic disposition" in the etiology of hysteria, Nonne continued to reject its greater significance, instead opining "resolutely" that "every campaign participant" can be afflicted.[42] In other words, even the healthy could fall victim to hysteria, a position Birnbaum noted Nonne shared with "many others" including—mentioning him by name—Oppenheim.[43]

If not caused by wish complexes or constitution, then, the etiology was still psychogenic but lay in the strong emotions that welled up within afflicted soldiers. Certainly, that could be slanted in a dismissive manner inclined to lay blame at the feet of the men themselves. The affective reaction of overwhelming fear, for example, could be portrayed as fundamental cowardice, which was really only at most one step removed from a constitutional argument centered on issues like inferior or psychopathic constitutions. At the same time, however, psychogenic explanations focusing on affective issues—as Voss did and modern-day research on trauma disorders does as well—could also not only recognize the complete horror experienced by individuals during their service but also by extension acknowledge the effects of the war itself on the psychological health of soldiers.[44]

Indeed, Birnbaum could summarize early on that there was generally consensus concerning etiology and the effects of war insofar as the "harmful influences" of the campaign were concerned: "Tribulations, over exertions, and privations on the one hand and mental trauma, feelings, emotional strain, and strong sensory impressions on the other hand are all recognized as operative pathogenic factors."[45] The degree to which each was weighted differed greatly among opinions, but this basic recognition that the events and experiences of war could be harmful to combatants' mental health was widespread, a fact Birnbaum saw as having less to do with "accident neuroses" and more to do with the research done on "psychotraumatic" factors and "the consequences of catastrophes."[46] Moreover, even after September 1916 and the shifting tide against organic causes, many continued to place heavy emphasis on these external factors. Recounting the research of Semi Meyer on hysteria, for example, Birnbaum went beyond merely summarizing and offered confirmation of the doctor's viewpoint: "Certainly Meyer is right with this emphasis on the affective moment in its pathogenic meaning for the psychotraumatic disorder."[47] Max Levy-Suhl suggested that most soldiers from the front were negatively affected in some way, and for those men who specifically developed hysteria it had more to do with the "sickening psychological stimuli" of "today's battles" than anything else, recognizing the particular nature of modern warfare that Voss also alluded to. Reporting on another study that cited the "consequences of tumult resulting from the chronic emotions of life during war" as a central cause of mental disorders, Birnbaum did suggest that the larger body of opinion and evidence supported the contrary view of a constitutional underpinning for war neurosis; yet, he cautioned, the other possibility linked to war's "harmful influences" had "not insignificant" support.[48]

Indeed, even some physicians who placed more emphasis on men's dispositions still recognized the unprecedented nature of combat in World War I.[49] Consider, for example, Gustav Liebermeister, who was investigated for excessive brutality in treating war hysterics. He noted that the "external causes, which in the war have grown to enormous forces," could certainly make constitutionally sound men sick.[50] Even neuroses like hysteria could affect the healthy, though he added that these men would likely not have been in possession of much "mental discipline."[51] Similarly, C. von Hösslin (a collaborator on other research with Alois Alzheimer) also considered constitution more important but nonetheless recognized that "none of our earlier wars has interfered in the same way as the current one in the fate of individual families and threatened and actually exterminated so many existences."[52] While there is no doubt that many lauded the invigorating effects of the war on soldiers, there was not uncommonly a recognition among others—including elite physicians—that modern combat could and did have negative effects.

A further consideration also increasingly brings into question the oft-noted obliviousness of contemporary military doctors to the sickening effects of war, including for cases of hysteria. Among doctors who argued for the importance of constitution in the etiology of hysteria—a position historians have associated with rejecting the influence of war—a further disagreement existed over whether this disposition was inherent or could also be acquired. Some scholars firmly espoused the idea of inherent or hereditary predisposition, yet others recognized that external events might also play a role in forming an individual's constitution. While there were many ways this disposition could be acquired, one of the most common ways that doctors who espoused this view pointed to was through wartime experiences, such as "chronic exhaustion and acute emotional impacts."[53] Indeed, Birnbaum indicated that this issue of where the disposition to sickness came from was "pursued on several occasions," and he judged the substantiation of "the particularly large impact of an acquired disposition" on mental health to be one of the significant advances of the war, a position that was not rejected at any point later.[54] In other words, even among the physicians who linked hysteria to dispositional causes, some of them considered the external effects of the war to be contributory to an acquired disposition that meant it took very little for these men to finally break down. Not a direct recognition of the effects of wartime trauma, it clearly acknowledged its role in creating war hysterics and was central to how service injury and pensions would be determined.

Beyond Hysteria: Neurasthenia and Other Diagnoses

Another important point in considering the extent to which the prevailing opinion did not simply dismiss men suffering from wartime trauma and blame them for their own sickness is the continued focus in the wartime scholarly literature on neurasthenia. This continued to be the diagnosis given to many soldiers presenting with the telltale symptoms in question.[55] While the expression of hysteria and neurasthenia may often have been extremely difficult, if not impossible, to distinguish (a point made repeatedly in the contemporary medical literature), the etiology was different. Though one should not overlook the diversity of opinion among experts on the underlying causes of neurasthenia any more than on hysteria, the scholarly literature on military psychiatry is right in recognizing that the former diagnosis represented fewer potential downsides for the patient in question. Unlike hysteria, which could be attributed to wish complexes and the desire to be free of one's duty, for example, neurasthenia was conceptualized more commonly in terms of a nervous system that had simply been worn down and depleted by the very real tribulations and privations of war in this case. Further emphasizing the different valences of these two diagnoses was the gendering of each, with a clear feminine association attached to hysteria, though likely not to the same extent as in other countries.[56] Indeed, this negative connotation of hysteria helps explain why the earlier scholarship so often posited that officers were less frequently given this stigmatizing diagnosis than enlisted men. It seemed to correlate to a higher opinion of these officers to begin with as well as a quite different understanding of the types of treatment suitable for them, as neurasthenia was thought to be best treated by replenishing efforts like rest and good diet.[57]

Of course, all of the most recent research that has examined the reality of patient treatment in the files indicates that the officer-enlisted distinction had far less impact on diagnosis than previously believed, with hysteria and neurasthenia being used extensively for both groups.[58] Yet, this important recognition that the rank-and-file soldiers also frequently received the diagnosis of neurasthenia and that this continued long after the 1916 conference has largely not been remarked on in itself (and regardless of how men diagnosed with hysteria were considered) for its larger implications for understanding the extent to which contemporary psychiatrists and neurologists at all levels recognized the deleterious effects of the war on soldiers' mental health. The characterization of the hysteria diagnosis as triumphant after the Munich conference, which it indisputably was in terms of defeating Oppenheim's traumatic neurosis concept, is often too easily conflated with overlooking the frequency with which soldiers presenting with the same group of symptoms (as those ultimately diagnosed with hysteria) continued to be categorized in both the medical journals and the actual patient files as suffering from other ailments as well. In short, neglecting the continued prevalence of such non-stigmatizing diagnoses like neurasthenia leads to an underestimation of the extent to which military psychiatrists recognized the impact of the war even on healthy men, through no fault of their own.

Take, for example, the case of common soldier Josef A., who was seen in the forensic department of the Heil- und Pflegeanstalt in Düren in July and August 1917.[59] Under observation for leaving his post, the soldier could easily have been classified among the hysterical given his general presentation of symptoms. He had been experiencing various episodes of dizziness, headaches, and unexplained "whirring and pressures in his head." Even more notable, the physician reported that the reason Josef A. abandoned his post was the "yearning to see his family again," something quite similar to the desires seen by many as constitutive of hysteria. The patient's limited "willpower" did not allow him to resist such impulses either. Instead of focusing on Josef A.'s constitution or hereditary disposition, however, the case file made extensive reference to the many big battles he had fought in as well as his earlier experience of being buried in earth and other debris after a grenade explosion, an event linked specifically to the dizzy spells.[60] Josef A. received the diagnosis not of hysteria but of "nervous exhaustion (neurasthenia)" or, more specifically, of being in a "neurasthenic twilight state," a condition that he was seen to have no responsibility for and also made him unpunishable for the offense of going AWOL. In short, the trying experiences of war had simply exhausted his nerves and made him unable to function or resist the desire to go home, a summary that could just as easily have been made of many a soldier diagnosed with hysteria. But, like so many others, Josef A. did not have to deal with any consequences that this potentially more negative diagnosis brought with it.

Indeed, even the use of diagnoses that are frequently considered to be close relatives of or even synonyms for hysteria could in some cases be an indication that the treating physicians had reservations about either the theoretical or practical implications involved with that particular term for war neurosis.[61] Georg D. received an initial diagnosis at an onsite, battlefield hospital in 1917 of "nerve shock after burial."[62] As he needed further care, Georg D. was transferred to a reserve military hospital for treatment in November and December of that year, where he was diagnosed with "hysterical episodes," a common-enough determination given his repeated references to headaches, dizziness, and shaking. It was also more in line with the diagnostic trend toward hysteria. Interestingly, though, the diagnosis line again specifically made reference to more than just the soldier's condition, including explicit notation of Georg D.'s experience of being buried, likely also by debris from a battle explosion and collapsing trench walls.[63] Certainly one might explain this change in diagnosis from nerve shock to hysterical episodes as an example of the reduced receptivity to war's traumatic effects by physicians treating patients far from the actual fighting versus those doctors on the front line.[64] Indeed, some physicians shied away from terms like "nerve shock" as they too easily were taken to mean that the injury had a "real" component to it.[65] The diagnostic change might also be reflective of the distinction that existed at the time between transitory traumatic shocks and hysteria, which some physicians attached only to soldiers whose symptoms did not resolve within a short time.[66] It also likely reflected the different diagnostic approaches of individual doctors.[67] What is also important, however, is that not only was hysteria not the first, go-to diagnosis in this case, but even when it was used, the diagnosis was made with explicit reference to a wartime event. This addition to the diagnosis line—a common practice found in countless other patients' files as well—suggests a continued recognition of wartime trauma's role in precipitating Georg D.'s illness despite the terminological change to hysteria.

Perhaps even more striking is the diagnosis for another soldier named Georg who was treated at the same reserve hospital earlier that year: "nervous complaints after gas poisoning."[68] Presenting with the symptoms of headaches, pains, difficulty sleeping, and shaking, Georg W.'s condition had deteriorated to the extent that he insisted on walking with a cane when outside his quarters, although the file recorded that "there is no detectable cause for that; otherwise can walk well in [his] room without a cane." Indeed, Georg W. had been in such a poor state for so long that his file included multiple references and documents from earlier treatments in three other battlefield and reserve hospitals over the past four months, during which time none of the documents include much attention to his earlier years or family history to determine his constitution or hereditary disposition. After months of rest and medicines to both aid sleep and ease physical pain, Georg W. was released back to his garrison for service. In the case of this Georg, hysteria never arose as a diagnosis, despite the doctors involved in his final course of treatment being far removed from actual fighting as well as his condition lasting a long time. Even more striking, the reserve military hospital in question was none other than the one for psychiatric disorders in Tübingen headed by Robert Gaupp, the major proponent of the hysteria diagnosis. While Georg W. appears to have been treated by one of the doctors under Gaupp, the patient files more generally indicate frequent consultations between these other physicians and the director himself. Hence, the choice of diagnosis and explicit reference to a causal event from battle suggest a far more varied and nuanced view of how war tremblers were conceptualized and treated than even the latest research on patient files indicates.

Indeed, the sources consulted for this study from the many different types of civilian and military hospitals suggest that to understand how contemporary physicians viewed war tremblers it is vital to look at the multiplicity of diagnostic terms that continued to be prevalent as well as to go beyond merely labels by examining the nuances of what the files actually emphasized in describing the etiology of a patient's illness. Studies that tally the statistical appearances of various diagnoses such as hysteria or neurasthenia are useful, but they also have their limits, especially given shifting and often murky delineations among terms. A diagnosis of "fright neurosis"

(*Schreckneurose*) might reflect the view that the sickness was only short-lived and had not yet progressed to the pathological state of hysteria. Or, it might mean basically the same thing as a hysteria diagnosis complete with wish complexes and alleged constitutional deficiencies. Or, it might mean something quite different, as it likely did to the diagnosing doctor in the Heil- und Pflegeanstalt Grafenberg when he applied it to the partial, psychogenic mutism of Wilhelm N. Even though he remained for treatment in April and May 1917, little more is known of this patient than the point emphasized in his file that he had been in the field for over two years serving both in Russia and in France by the time he was transferred to a military hospital.[69]

Even the general distinction between neurasthenia and hysteria—one that fundamentally structured how wartime psychiatric disorders were categorized and discussed—held little weight in certain instances. This appears to be the case for patients treated at the military reserve psychiatric station set up at the University of Heidelberg. From a close reading of several hundred cases there, the etiologic descriptions, diagnostic terminology, and treatments ordered indicate that the local usage of the two terms was often interchangeable.[70] This may explain the rather peculiar diagnosis given to Friedrich K. in December 1917, when he presented with headaches, difficulty sleeping, and shaking.[71] Despite the physician involved emphasizing the lack of an organic reason for the patient's disorder and the "subjective nature" of the issues, as well as calling earlier episodes "undoubtedly hysterical in nature" (while at the same time ruling out any constitutional hereditary issues), the final diagnosis was "light traumatic neurosis." Not only had this diagnosis largely been discarded by this point, but the very description of the patient militated against its use. Yet, the largely interchangeable nature of neurasthenia and hysteria in that particular hospital suggests that the physician referenced traumatic neurosis to substantiate the external etiology he saw at work, a point explicitly noted in the longer file: "The neurosis extant for [Friedrich] K. is undoubtedly the consequence of the long-term wartime service. Thus, wartime military service injury is present." This effort to sidestep the direct use of the diagnosis of hysteria does indicate its prominence and the many negative associations often swirling around it, as the scholarship on this topic suggests. Yet, what these cases and the numerous other examples throughout the patient file archives also indicate—as this chapter has argued—is the skepticism plenty of physicians continued to have regarding the alleged consensus on hysteria, a counterposition that was far more widespread among all levels of doctors (including elites) than has been assumed in the scholarship.

Beyond the Rhetoric: Treatment Realities

While recent research has largely left untouched the idea of rhetorical consensus on war hysteria among the tone-setting, elite doctors and not probed the extent to which diagnostic labels in actual cases failed to line up with the typical understandings often repeated in the historical scholarship, a few innovative and notable studies have examined the degree to which the reality of treatment for hysteria matched the harsh rhetoric, as noted in the introduction.[72] Interestingly, however, the overall assessment of these studies finds that the more varied and less harsh treatment actually received by hysterical soldiers could be understood as resulting from the gap between elite and common doctors. The latter doctors were more sympathetic for a number of potential reasons, such as greater proximity to the actual fighting or less concern with regulating national standards.[73]

This chapter has already stressed that the elite opinion was not nearly as uniform in dismissing the suffering of war tremblers as the literature has suggested; it also argues that the reality of the patient treatment even in elite institutions did not necessarily match the alleged rhetoric, a point that looking at the fate of soldiers who were sent to the Reserve Lazarett II Tübingen at the university psychiatric hospital headed by Robert Gaupp can substantiate. Certainly, no argument can be made that Gaupp did not publicly promote a hardline concerning the treatment of war tremblers, championing as he did one of the dominant interpretations of hysteria to emerge from the Munich conference in 1916. Harsh and dismissive commentary on hysterics from Gaupp is ubiquitous, including his description of those in his clinic as including "quite a few criminals, degenerates, and mentally and morally defective men, . . . crafty fellows who want to create life-long pensions out of a short military stint."[74] How could such individuals not warrant decisive treatment, even when painful? Yet did this rhetorical severity match the treatment prescribed for those soldiers cared for in Tübingen? Based on several hundred case files from the Tübingen Reserve Lazarett and a closer statistical analysis of a randomly selected subset of 150 files from the year 1917, the answer is clearly no.

Despite all of Gaupp's well-known pronouncements in both medical journals and consultations to set military policy, soldiers treated in Tübingen by doctors under Gaupp as well as by the director himself did not generally receive the harsh, quick treatment so often described in both his public pronouncements and the historical scholarship on the period. Of the 150 cases, 53 involved hysteria.[75] Of these 53 soldiers, only 23 are noted as having received any form of the more active treatment proposed in the literature at any point during their sickness, including time spent in hospitals before arriving at Tübingen as well. Furthermore, while many of these 23 men did receive the more terrifying treatments frequently emphasized in the scholarship, like electric shock, simulated choking, or being swaddled to the point of immobility, some of them received nothing more than hypnosis or suggestion therapy, with no references to application of any of the harsher forms of active treatment.[76] Regardless, the other 30 soldiers, or well over half of them at 57 percent, received merely treatments of rest, good diet, and calming tinctures.

Given the frequency with which such hardline treatment was often tied to economics and the hopes of quashing alleged pension hysteria by denying that the injury was linked to service, it is also worth noting that the soldiers treated in Tübingen do not fit the traditional picture in this sense either.[77] While only fifteen received an affirmation that their illness was related to wartime service, the issue was commented on either way in only twenty-eight (not all fifty-three) of the cases. Hence, in 54 percent of the instances where a determination was made, doctors confirmed war-related injury. Indeed, if one evaluates the cases for both of these important markers—wartime injury status and type of treatment—only eighteen of the fifty-three soldiers treated under Gaupp's direction in Tübingen fit the commonly portrayed picture of having received harsh, dismissive treatment. In other words, even in this elite institution where one might expect to find the most conformity to the official rhetoric, perhaps only a third of all soldiers fit the pattern that the scholarship on military psychiatry during World War I has emphasized.

In the other two-thirds of the cases statistically analyzed here, one can find recognition of the damaging effects of war as well as a reliance on mild, restorative treatment. Even the idea of moving men swiftly through treatment centers was not the reality in Tübingen, with over half of the men remaining there for more than one month, a long stay especially when many had already spent time in and would subsequently be transferred to other care facilities in the network set up to treat soldiers.[78] Several soldiers remained in Gaupp's clinic for months, with multiple stays hitting the half-year range. Indeed, far from these being periods of unpleasant isolation and the disciplining of weak-willed men, a few of these soldiers were allowed visits home to their families, an additional indication of how long treatments could last.[79] Not merely a practice of other doctors under Gaupp's supervision at the clinic, these treatment patterns also include files in which the director personally commented and signed off on the prescriptions.[80]

The case of Wilhelm B. is illustrative.[81] In May 1917 the soldier suffered from what the field hospital described as "nerve shock after burial," which ultimately required him to be transferred to the reserve hospital in Tübingen. Arriving in June, Wilhelm B. remained there until September of that year. This occurred in large part because, after Gaupp examined him, the director concluded that the patient suffered from a "psychogenic condition. . . . Prognosis good. For the time being treatment in hospital necessary." The determination of the problem largely mirrored the formal diagnostic label given: "Nervous disposition, psychogenic twilight state." That Gaupp's team was treating him for the more specific psychogenic disorder of hysteria is clear, however, from the references in the notes to Wilhelm B.'s "hysterical twilight state" as well. While much of the daily care likely fell to orderlies and subordinate physicians, by the end of the patient's summer at the hospital, Gaupp signed off on the final prescription: "a restorative vacation of 6–8 weeks," after which Wilhelm B. should try working. While Gaupp remained optimistic about the soldier's long-term recuperation, the director also confirmed a 30 percent disability that qualified as a wartime service injury. Nowhere do the files mention any use of active treatment to cure Wilhelm B., whom Gaupp apparently discharged still partially uncured and eligible for a pension.

While this case is particularly illustrative of how vastly actual treatment could differ from the medical rhetoric, it is not unique among the cases from Tübingen or elsewhere. There are certainly countless examples of the harsh treatment meted out to soldiers in hospitals, including in Gaupp's own.[82] Yet there are also countless examples of quite the opposite. If anything, the general impression from consulting over two thousand patient files from many institutions—both elite and nonelite as well as the specific statistics from Tübingen—suggests more of the latter, mild treatment than the former, with many cases that fall somewhere in between.

How might one explain the dissonance between the harsh rhetoric and the reality? Certainly, though they may have played some role, issues of battlefield proximity or nonelite status do not satisfy as general reasons, as the examples from Tübingen indicate. In part, the vast variety of treatments given to traumatized soldiers fits more with the recognition that the theoretical debates surrounding war tremblers had hardly been resolved for average or elite doctors in a way that the literature has supposed. We might also consider in the case of Gaupp that he—like other doctors—felt less constrained in his actions and opinions when conducting himself "privately" in patient settings versus when writing to determine national policy.[83] Indeed, there are numerous examples of Gaupp making private notations and decisions that reveal more humanity and understanding and less military and financial zealotry, while the latter concerns are clearly exhibited in his public pronouncements. In one case where the organic or hysterical nature of a wound could not be determined for sure, Gaupp erred on the side of the patient and approved a pension.[84] Similarly, his subordinates repeatedly showed such caution in pension cases.[85] While publicly defending Liebermeister's actions when the fellow physician was investigated for heavy-handed treatment practices, Gaupp privately noted his reservations about such methods, commenting that his fellow physician's preference for unpleasant treatments was uncalled for.[86] Though he certainly earned much of his unflattering portrayal in the scholarship, Gaupp undoubtedly was a more complex man than has been shown.[87]

Finally, we might also question the extent to which even leading physicians like Gaupp believed in the use of active treatment to miraculously cure hysterics. Certainly, physicians touted their treatments and results as nothing short of miracles able to solve the potentially disastrous problem of war tremblers and the loss of manpower. For example, the Munich-based psychiatrist Karl Weiler stated that treatment should be continued until "complete success" was achieved, leaving the patients as convinced of recovery as "the visitors to [the pilgrimage site of] Lourdes."[88] Doctors wanted to enhance psychiatry's reputation and prove their own indispensability for the war.[89] Yet, the actual patient files reveal at times a sense among physicians that these new treatment regimens of shock and suggestion could only do so much. On the one hand, such treatments were not necessarily the first, go-to solution in even a "model" hospital. This is substantiated not only by their use in less than half of the cases statistically analyzed but also more generally by the way in which Gaupp and others commented in the files. In the case of hysteric Johahn G., for example, Gaupp and a subordinate suggested all the man needed was to be treated with the "necessary caution" at the military base and he would soon be ready for the front again.[90] Doctors took a similar, wait-and-see approach to hysteric Wilhelm E., who was also sent back to his base.[91] Others, like Georg B., were sent home to work even though they were not healed, with the presumption—noted explicitly in the files—that keeping busy would likely produce more results than treatment.[92] On the other hand, there are cases where hints of doubt regarding the treatment itself appear. Concerning the hysteric Karl B., Gaupp concluded that "hospital treatment at the moment promises no more success. We have oriented B. concerning the healable nature of his illness; likely an improvement of the complaints will happen at home."[93] More explicit is the rejection of further action after failed attempts at the use of active methods. After treatment for two months that included the use of suggestion, a soldier suffering from hysterical deafness was released because "further hospital treatment is pointless."[94] Gaupp judged further efforts concerning a mute soldier similarly useless, as strong electrical current had failed to cure his mutism.[95] After two months in a special clinic designed specifically for application of more active treatments, a soldier suffering from multiple hysterical symptoms was released "because an imminent change of this inhibited state is not to be soon expected" despite everything undertaken up to that point.[96] Certainly some of these instances in which the treatments publicly touted as most effective were either not tried or simply given up on involved hardened psychopaths, a category of patients recognized for its particular resistance to all types of treatment.[97] But most were not. Doctors of all ranks likely just realized that the reality of sickness and healing was far more complicated than the rhetoric surrounding it.

Regardless of the specific reasons, what is most important to note is that the standard narrative of treatment for war tremblers was likely the experience of only a minority of men. When one tallies up all the men diagnosed with other, less fraught disorders like neurasthenia; those who were diagnosed with hysteria by one of the many physicians who conceived of its etiology more as Voss did; and even those who were treated mildly by a standard bearer of the hardline in the profession like Gaupp—whose actual behavior surprises for its moderation in comparison with his rhetoric—the conclusion must be that the lion's share of the hundreds of thousands of cases of nervous disorders treated in World War I experienced treatment that was far less brutal, quick, and dismissive than the literature has emphasized.[98]

Wartime Conditions: Material and Manpower Shortages

While reconsidering the rhetoric surrounding wartime trauma and the reality of the treatment for those deemed to be suffering from hysteria is important, so is keeping sight of the more general conditions that prevailed in field sick bays and hospitals during the war. The number of doctors available to treat the masses of soldiers wounded—both physically and psychologically—quickly came up against limits. The vast majority of physicians in Germany became involved in treating military patients during the war in one way or another. Many were drafted into the military directly and served both in frontline situations and at home. This still did not meet personnel needs, however, so of the doctors remaining in Germany without any military service obligations, countless had to be contracted to treat soldiers as well, often in civilian institutions. Among doctors in the subfield of psychiatry, involvement in wartime care of traumatized soldiers was almost universal. As pressing an issue was the lack of support staff, which became increasingly less qualified over the course of the war, as the need for rapid replacements took precedence over training and testing. Advertisements for positions began explicitly stating that no prior experience was necessary to apply. Hospitals could easily experience turnover of a third of their employees in any given year of the war.[99]

Wartime created not only personnel shortages but also material shortages. Well known are the hundreds of thousands of civilians who starved during the war, not to mention the much larger group that likely succumbed to disease from malnutrition. Less obvious are the tens of thousands of patients in various mental health institutions who starved during the same period. Meals in institutions almost immediately suffered in quality and quantity. Soldiers being treated in both military and civilian hospitals received better rations, but their food also reflected the limited resources. Physical space also came at a premium, with room needed in civilian hospitals for the establishment of departments devoted to soldiers, which of course placed both groups of patients in less than ideal conditions.[100]

Complaints from patients as well as physicians about the conditions during this period are ubiquitous. Examining the caregivers' reports on what the soldiers were saying as well as reading patients' outgoing letters that were never sent reveals repeated comments about the poor state of meals. (Indeed, the inclusion of complaints in the letters was perhaps the very reason the censor did not allow them to be sent.) Soldiers wrote of going hungry and being given nothing more than "stale bread," leading one patient to ask if being in the hospital was actually a "punishment." Beyond the food, the treatment patients were receiving in the hospitals struck many as pointless. One soldier, for example, demanded to leave in part because allegedly no doctor had seen him since his intake interview, which was over two months earlier. Others focused more on the entire process of being placed in a hospital for psychiatric illness, arguing that the treatment was an unworthy "reward" for their military service. Undoubtedly such complaints stemmed from not only the limited supplies and treatments offered to them but also the stigma many attached to being admitted to a psychiatric institution. The entire situation was so grave, some claimed, that even healthy men quickly became sick in such places. Indeed, one soldier who was examined and found not to be ill later lodged a request to be awarded a pension because the hospital stay itself had allegedly driven him mad.[101]

Doctors expressed their frustrations as well. In response to the accusations of poor care more generally, doctors cited rationing and—in civilian institutions—the fact that nonmilitary patients were getting even less. They pushed back against requests from authorities to provide various forms by citing such limited manpower that they could not even accept certain patients, let alone provide detailed reports on them. Indeed, denials of admission due to overcrowding litter the archival files of treatment centers. Though Freud may have blamed his peripheral role in the efforts to deal with traumatized soldiers on the disregard many psychiatrists had for his ideas, the marginalization of a labor-intensive therapy like psychoanalysis had a lot to do with practical limits too. Staff were so overworked in one hospital that they claimed there was not even time to inform family members of the impending death of a loved one. Only death notices could be provided afterward, when a spare moment to write such a letter was found. Even elite, "model" institutions felt the effects, as Gaupp's plea that the authorities refrain from constantly drafting his trained orderlies indicates. Otherwise, the director added, the necessary reduction in intakes would merely further exacerbate the problem of finding soldiers beds in hospitals.[102] Far from necessarily being a reflection of doctors' views of the etiology of various psychological conditions like hysteria or the men who succumbed to them, the inadequate treatment soldiers received during the war was often linked more to the impact of the limited resources, with staff trying to do a lot with a little.[103] Indeed, even a quick look at the patient files of soldiers suffering physical wounds—undoubtedly seen as very real and in need of treatment—reveals how the reality of wartime medicine left a lot to be desired.[104]

Soldiers' Strategies against Institutional Abuses

There are cases where—even considering the lopsided access to leaving a paper trail in the patient files and the efforts of hospital staff to often hush up complaints—the existence of abuse far beyond that explained by limited resources and staff seems quite likely. The case of soldier Kaspar W. is illustrative.[105] Initially admitted to the civilian hospital in Düren in February 1916, he was released almost a year later in January 1917. Far from a successful treatment, however, much of his time was punctuated by documented physical altercations, though various individuals disagreed over how to characterize such incidents. In one instance involving a female orderly, Kaspar W. allegedly received a blow to the head.[106] Afterward, he was moved to another ward for patients considered more difficult, though again viewpoints differed on whether this was done as a necessary precaution or out of spite. In another instance, an orderly took Kaspar W.'s soup away from him after he allegedly misbehaved, which led to four additional orderlies physically subduing the patient and tying him to his bed with wet sheets. It is not entirely clear, but the file suggests he may have been at least partially stripped naked when this was done. Yet another instance involved a blow Kaspar W. received, allegedly for spilling a glass of water. While the director of the hospital confirmed the use of physical force, he characterized it as necessary to control the patient, who was being treated for various outbursts. Of course, all witnesses confirming such an assessment of the altercations were hospital employees. Moreover, while there does appear to have been a longer record of unruly and strange behavior noted in the file concerning previous stays in different hospitals, Kaspar W. was described as otherwise "harmless," a characterization his family also offered. Indeed, even the records from Düren remark on the patient's diligence in helping with tasks around the hospital. Moreover, one thing seems incontestable: Kaspar W. suddenly lost a lot of weight in his last few months in the hospital, dropping from approximately 155 pounds at intake to 135 by December 1916, a quick reduction that cannot be explained by any issues of rationing. For his five-foot-nine-inch frame, it is clear he did not eat enough. While one cannot know for sure exactly what happened or why he was not getting enough to eat, the likelihood of abuse is all the greater when considering the clear exasperation and contempt with which even the director wrote about the patient by the end of his stay. In response to pleas for release from Düren due to mistreatment, the director concluded in a letter to a local authority: "We would be thankful if you could free us from Kaspar." Finally, on January 22 he was released, suddenly "improved." Even though much of the literature has focused on brutal and abusive treatment—and the attempt here is to put that in context as being the minority response—it is important to explicitly recognize that such horrifying behavior was undeniably a part of wartime psychiatry and the treatment of the mentally ill more generally during World War I.[107]

More important for the issue of dissent, perhaps, is that even when the response from doctors and staff was less than desirable, whether from a lack of resources, an attempt to keep military discipline among the soldiers, or cases of intentional denigration and abuse, soldiers were not merely passive objects without agency or advocates to help them. Not only did soldiers complain to hospital staff and family members about treatment they considered unacceptable, but they went further by lodging official complaints and drawing in multiple other individuals to aid them.[108] Often this began with close family members, whose interventions could produce results. The wife of soldier Josef W., for example, successfully brought her husband home from the hospital in Galkhausen (to later have him admitted to Grafenberg) when she thought the staff's efforts to diagnose and treat him were not sufficiently taking into consideration the effects of his wartime service.[109] The father of Karl W. in the Düren hospital made quite clear to the staff that multiple family members were keeping an eye on the patient's treatment, including ensuring that any letters or packages they sent actually reached him.[110] Regardless of whether the orderlies had been messing with Karl W.'s mail, the hospital director personally responded to the accusation, an act no doubt partially motivated by the threat that the family would report the hospital to

Düren's mayor if they were not satisfied.[111] Indeed, the files reveal so much about the likely abuse suffered by Kaspar W. because a number of people outside the hospital—including the mayor of the patient's home town—became involved. They questioned not only the physical altercations and treatment Kaspar received but also the work the patient was required to do in the hospital. Indeed, one complaint lodged with the mayor made specific reference to the constant cleaning assigned to the patient, who several staff members said "clean[ed] better like a woman," a comment the family undoubtedly took double offense at because of its emasculating implications for Kaspar W.[112] Such pressure and inquiry required the hospital director to justify the staff's actions repeatedly and, ultimately, sign off on the release of the patient, which had been the family's goal all along.[113] Some cases involved military authorities investigating and questioning witnesses as to what transpired, with patients being represented by lawyers as well. Other soldiers not only turned to the military authorities but threatened to appeal to the "public" if they did not get a satisfactory response.[114]

Such involvement should hardly come as a surprise, building as it did on several decades of increased public scrutiny of psychiatric practices and the rise of "lunatics' rights" groups, which led to patients having far more ability to accuse abusive doctors.[115] Certainly, wartime likely shifted the focus away from such issues to the more pressing concerns of the war at hand. Yet, any lull in the focus on patients more generally was likely made up for, in the case of soldiers, by the symbolic capital the military men—even those who were sick—had during wartime. Indeed, the patient files are rife with demands from not only soldiers themselves but also their advocates—from family members to public officials—for better treatment and consideration for these mentally traumatized patients exactly because they were veterans.[116] If dismissive physicians cowed some military patients into accepting whatever treatment was meted out to them, others reacted as Leo S. did by clearly demanding more in return for his service and sacrifice when he retorted, "Yes, I am a soldier. I'm proud of that."[117] Similarly, Georg B. also demanded better treatment not only as a person but as a soldier, adding that "my person and my uniform are constantly impugned."[118] Indeed, Kaspar W.'s family in no way accepted his illness as reason for shame and settling for lesser treatment, stating, "Really, there could not be any bigger war disabled [than him]. . . . Here there is no justice and that would be a stain on German honor."[119] While soldier patients certainly did not have equal power with doctors in such cases, they were also not without the ability to change their situation.

Of course, issues of patient opposition to harsh treatment and doctors being forced to reckon with their abuses have been mentioned in the literature. When noted, however, they are almost exclusively linked to the very end stages of the war and the impending (or fulfilled) collapse of the empire from mid to late 1918 to the November Revolution, more of an "aftermath" than an integral part of the treatment of soldiers by military psychiatrists.[120] Yet, while one can certainly consider the resistance and scrutiny to have been far too little and far too late, the stronger impression one gains from reading countless actual patient files is that such patient agency and intervention by others played an important role from the beginning. Investigations not only involved leading physicians like Liebermeister or public discussions like those held in the Reichstag in June 1918, but also could consist of a local public official making inquiries or patients enlisting the help of family members and others in the community.[121] Indeed, far from seeing Gaupp's call for greater protections for physicians after the Liebermeister trial (even though he was not found culpable) as possibly giving them carte blanche to enact whatever treatment they saw fit, one might instead note that doctors were clearly aware of the scrutiny and limitations under which they were treating soldiers. It was a realization Gaupp had already come to when he referred to himself only months after the Munich conference as a "defendant" in April 1917, alluding to having to constantly account for his actions. Indeed, proceedings at the state parliamentary level that year already heard calls challenging the treatment of war neurotics.[122] If anything, this suggests not that scrutiny came very late in the war but that it came not long after the diagnosis of hysteria had won out. This interpretation is further bolstered by Hofer's account of treatment in the Hapsburg Empire, where he argues that skepticism regarding the use of painful electrical treatments took longer to coalesce than in Germany.[123] Especially given the reconsideration of the frequency with which soldiers actually received the brutal treatment emphasized in the literature, such more national as well as more local influences should not be underestimated in their significance for impacting the treatment the majority of traumatized soldiers received. These cases often involved a far larger set of actors, many of whom were allies and weighed in as advocates of the sick soldiers. While German hysterics may not have had the vindication that their French counterparts got from victory in a cause célèbre like the Deschamps case, they did have countless concrete examples from both everyday hospital life and more publicly that psychiatry did not operate without oversight or limits, as it did earlier in the nineteenth century and would most clearly later in the twentieth.[124]

A Space for Dissent by Psychologically Wounded Soldiers

While the expression of agency may seem hard to imagine in settings for the care of mentally ill soldiers as they have commonly been portrayed, it was within this system described above—where harsh assumptions about constitutional inferiority and brutal therapies were far from the automatic outcome of treatment and, even when they did happen, patients could often call on a variety of additional individuals to help ameliorate the situation—that one can see soldiers actually articulating dissent. It could take numerous forms along a spectrum. The more explicit ones like conscientious objection will be discussed in later chapters; here, one should begin with the cases where individuals negotiated hospital stays to multiple ends. In most instances, these individuals not only were ill in the estimation of contemporary physicians but likely would also be recognized legitimately as such today. Their sickness required convalescence. But upon entering the hospital they did not cease to be complex individuals who could both be ill and have very clear opinions about issues like the war or continuing to fight.[125] Though hospital life and treatment were far from perfect circumstances for expressing dissent—any more than they were for curing the variety of psychological illnesses plaguing soldiers—they could and did clearly serve such an end for some men.

Take, for example, the case of Josef W.[126] His time at the hospital in Düren began early in the war in December 1914. The event linked most closely to his admittance was not any battle commotion that befell him directly but the death of his son, who had been serving on the eastern front. The forty-two-year-old father could not stop crying over his loss and refused to talk about it. Indeed, far from initially wanting to be in Düren, the patient called his intake there a "disgrace," no doubt worried that others would find out he was in the "madhouse." Clearly devastated by the loss of his son—the physician's determination of melancholy is understandable—Josef W. nonetheless demanded to be released. Yet, not only did the soldier not leave Düren that year, but he did not leave the next year either. Rather, his discharge from the hospital took place in April 1916, a year and a half later. By that time, far from demanding to be released, Josef W. had gotten into a routine at the hospital. Many reports indicate he worked well in the onsite garden, liked receiving visits from his family, and got along well with other patients. At the same time, however, staff also noted that he often got very upset and excited when speaking about the war itself. He spoke of the "military leadership" having ruined or "disturbed his happy family life." He promised a "settling of accounts" that would take place for this. Though not a specific statement of dissent, such comments make Josef W.'s opposition to the war effort clear. We also know that by the end of his stay in Düren he was keeping his distance from the doctors, apparently to avoid being reevaluated and potentially deemed fit for release. Indeed, he expressed a desire to stay in the asylum "till the end of the war." Not till he got better, not till he rested, not even forever. Simply, he wanted to stay until the war was over. The clear sense that the hospital provided a refuge from returning to fight a war he no longer believed in becomes even more evident from the soldier's parting comments: "If they try to start something with me, I'll just become crazy again! I know where Düren is." Apparently, he felt sure enough that this would allow him to avoid active duty in the future. Certainly, none of this is to suggest Josef W. was not sick. From all accounts he was, and the records indicate he continued to have difficult days well into 1916. Yet the records also give substantial evidence that his illness was not the only thing keeping him in the hospital.

The agency involved in Josef W.'s actions during his hospital stay becomes more obvious when viewed alongside examples of the opposite: cases in which soldiers who were also ill demanded (successfully) to be sent back into service. Ludwig O. also referred to his time in Düren as a "dishonor" and wished to go with his company "to the front." Though that specific stay left him diagnosed with "acute mental confusion"—not uncommonly linked to war neurosis—the files mentioned a long history of problems. Nonetheless, within eight days Ludwig O. got at least part of his wish and was released from the hospital in November 1915, though it is unknown whether he rejoined his original company.[127] Demanding to return to one's comrades was hardly an uncommon plea in the files. Indeed, some soldiers left without even waiting for a doctor to discharge them, as did two patients from the same company who simply returned to their fellow troops, making clear that they wanted to go back to duty.[128] Men like Ludwig O. and men like Josef W. were ill and received treatment, but they also had the agency to make quite different choices about how that played out. In the case of the latter, that was an expression of wartime dissent.

The files of other soldiers reference comments like those of Josef W. that make clear their rejection of the war effort. Not uncommonly it took the form of pointing out how lopsided the privations were spread throughout the German populace, such as Albert F.'s sarcastic quip did: "I can thank the scoundrels that they have brought me so low." Traumatized, worn down, and sitting in the hospital waiting to be treated along with so many other common soldiers just like him had not endeared him to "the scoundrels" responsible, by which he quite likely meant—given his railing against the situation more generally—the nation's leaders that had gotten Germany into the war.[129] He remained in Grafenberg for six months. Similarly, Eugen F. clearly stated that he was done with fighting after entering the hospital in the midst of being transported to the western front. The soldier was diagnosed with a "nervous personality," and his medical reports noted clear signs of trauma, including "manic sleep" filled with nightmares of battles he had been in, like the Somme. While Eugen F. referenced this, he concluded that it was not just his own personal loss of health, but "when one sees how it is going at home in Germany one loses the inclination to be out in the field as a soldier." His hospital stay, though only approximately six weeks long, was enough to stop his transfer; the attending physician recommended he be sent to work or, at most, used in garrison duty.[130]

Nonetheless, as this chapter focuses on the circumstances of military psychiatric treatment and the space created for the exercise of agency by individuals whose acts indicated dissent but never moved to the other end of the spectrum with more concerted efforts of opposition like conscientious objection, for example, the intentions of the soldiers must at times be pieced together from more general, circumstantial evidence. Such is the case of Hermann R.[131] Called into service not long after the outbreak of the war, the soldier entered the hospital in October 1914 with a diagnosis of "state of agitation from a neurasthenic basis," which led to his stay in Düren until the end of June the following year. This did not mean the end of his treatment or his presence in the Düren files, however, as Hermann R. continued to correspond with one of the physicians there, providing updates on his treatments elsewhere. Noting his appreciation for the good treatment he received in Düren multiple times, Hermann R. also apparently had good luck with his subsequent doctors too. Indeed, the only complaints one finds in his letters are about other soldiers and his own company. This was a group from which Hermann R. always positioned himself apart, making it clear that the man had no interest in military service. While Hermann R. was almost certainly ill—there are indications he was receiving treatment that included hospital stays long after the war ended—his symptoms did appear to wax and wane depending on how likely he thought it was that he would have to do heavier service. The letters to Düren often included pleas for the doctor there to intervene on his behalf. Similarly, a clear recognition that his (legitimate) illness could be used to multiple ends comes out in a retort he made to a sergeant who would not cease ordering Hermann R. to undertake duties outside of the barracks: "I will remain here and would like to ask the sergeant to be considerate of me and cut out the bitching. My nerves cannot take it." Immediately after, Hermann R. begged the doctor in Düren to communicate with the company physician so the latter could discharge him from the military altogether. The soldier already had a civilian job lined up in Cologne. Such cases do not even include those in which little contextual evidence is available beyond issues of timing. Johann B., for example, stayed in the Galkhausen hospital for over a year, not surprising given he had been treated multiple times over the previous years for "nervous complaints and alcoholism." Despite several reports indicating he was doing much better—the first such entries begin in July—Johann makes no mention of wishing to leave until the very end, when he presents a flurry of requests not long after the armistice was signed in November.[132]

While the intentions of Johann B. can never be known for sure—and certainly in many cases the dissention was more perceived by some psychiatrists than real—the preponderance of evidence in many such cases like those above suggests that dissent among soldiers and indirect refusals to continue service were not uncommon in psychiatric settings. It was not simply soldiers faking illness, the notorious "simulants" that contemporary medical literature spilled so much ink on.[133] Such cases did occur, though the reality of treatment reveals it was neither a major concern among doctors in actual cases nor apparently attempted much by patients.[134] Neither was the dissent linked to issues of wartime trauma and illness merely inchoate, a kind of last-resort effort to protect one's self in a world gone mad, as some scholars have viewed illnesses like hysteria.[135] Focusing too exclusively on these ideas of dissent does a disservice to those soldiers who were quite ill but also quite aware of their stance on continued fighting and the war, and who availed themselves of one of the few ways in which they could express this. Moreover, the exclusive focus also ironically echoes aspects of the way some elite specialists denigrated traumatized veterans at the time as little more than discipline problems. Nor was the dissent merely a phenomenon that appeared late in the war, though opposition certainly grew louder as the privations increased and disillusionment set in. Yet, this chapter has argued that a reconsideration of contemporary medical opinion, actual treatment regiments, and real hospital conditions reveals that general dissent among soldiers was more possible and more prevalent than has previously been recognized.

Chapter 3

Deserters

Delinquency, Psychological Disorder, and Dissent

In the spring of 1917 a soldier named Jakob S. slipped away from his unit only to find himself right back there just two days later, though it is unclear whether he returned voluntarily or was caught. Upon being placed in military jail to await disciplinary action, Jakob S. destroyed the inside of his cell and managed to break out. Instead of quietly fleeing again, however, he took the time to hurl abuses at his superiors. Unsurprisingly, Jakob S. did not get very far this time either, as the military quickly apprehended him. Shortly thereafter, the court ordered him to undergo a six-week observation to determine his mental competence, which is how he ended up in the Düren psychiatric hospital on May 16 of that year.[1]

Jakob S. did not accept being in the hospital any more than he did being in his unit or in the jail cell. He questioned the staff as to why they were holding him. He explained that he had not had vacation in a while and had gotten in a fight with the sergeant. "It is not such a big deal," he reasoned, as he had been gone for only two days. The soldier did not stop at merely trying to plead with the hospital staff. Within a week he had complained to the court that he did not belong in the hospital because he was not mentally ill. Indeed, Jakob S. wrote multiple letters protesting his stay at Düren to military officials, a lawyer, and his family. Some of the correspondence remained unsent and in his patient file, but other pieces clearly went out, as the military court acknowledged receiving his complaint. It reviewed the matter—even sending a representative to the hospital to speak with Jakob S.—but ultimately denied his request to not undergo the ordered examination.

The next several weeks did little to render being in the hospital more acceptable to the soldier. The soldier's medical file indicates repeated conflicts. According to the staff notes, Jakob S. acted "rowdy and childish." He made complaints of an "outrageous" nature concerning both the doctors and other staff members at the hospital. Even the manner in which the patient addressed the doctors reportedly showed no restraint, as he commonly used an "insolent and unfruitful tone." While the characterization blaming the soldier for these incidents is debatable given the one-sidedness inherent in the composition of the patient record, the ongoing conflicts between Jakob S. and the staff are not, as the soldier continued to write his own complaint letters about the hospital. Given the tense relationship that played out between the soldier and the hospital staff, the end of his extended stay at Düren—which inexplicably lasted twice as long as a normal observation period—must have been greeted with relief by many involved.

The attesting doctor's disdain for Jakob S. came through clearly in the formal expert opinion he wrote. He took ample time to highlight just how bad of a soldier the patient had been, noting that Jakob S. had repeatedly been punished for leaving his unit without permission. The soldier's conduct in civilian life had not been that great either. The physician also spared no space commenting on the multiple complaints the patient had leveled against the hospital staff, all completely unreasonable according to the doctor. Such gripes reflected more about the patient than they did about the hospital, he assured. In the doctor's expert opinion, all of this indicated nothing "sick" about Jakob S. but instead pointed to an "intentional revolt of a willful and undisciplined person of the highest degree." So certain was the doctor in his explanation of the soldier's behavior that he accused Jakob S. of putting on a show just to appear incompetent when the doctors came around to evaluate him. Believing none of what he saw as the patient's histrionics, the attesting physician ended his expert opinion with the clear statement that Jakob S. did not fit the requirements for being declared non compos mentis, or a condition of unsound mind that would have absolved the soldier of responsibility for his actions and made further legal action unnecessary. According to the expert's opinion, Jakob S. was simply a faker who was trying to get out of being punished by simulating illness.

Given the results of the observation, the doctor sent Jakob S. back on August 8, 1917, to await further legal action. Yet, merely six days later, he arrived at the hospital in Düren again. The day before, a court officer had penned a request to the hospital asking if it could keep Jakob S. there. The letter explained that the soldier was very unruly and presented "a danger to the maintenance of military discipline." Given the clear diagnosis by the attesting physician that Jakob S. was not sick but merely a shirker who deserved to be punished, the hospital expressed reluctance to readmit him. After all, the hospital response pointed out, Düren was for the mentally ill, and Jakob S. clearly was not. Only further instruction from the military and a request for "another short testimonial from the responsible doctor" to reconfirm that the soldier in question was not sick and "if simulation can be accepted with certainty" appeared to secure the transfer back to Düren. Jakob S. stayed in the hospital for another several weeks, but the determination by the attending doctor did not change. Further examination found no evidence of sickness, and the doctor concluded that "simulation can be accepted with certainty." Given the soldier's proclivity for running off, five men—including a petty officer with an unholstered weapon just in case Jakob S. tried anything again—came to pick up Jakob S. to face the charges against him, specifically of being AWOL. The authorities did not charge him with the related crime of desertion, because the short duration of the soldier's absence made it hard to prove that more serious allegation.

Much about the case of Jakob S. is instructive in understanding how military psychiatry—or civilian institutions contracted to help with the overflow of cases—dealt with issues of soldiers going AWOL or outright deserting. What is most revealing about his case, however, are two interconnected, atypical aspects of it: the accusation of simulation and the request for the diagnosis to be reconfirmed. While some scholars have noted simulating an illness—either mental or physical—as one of many ways soldiers found not to serve, psychiatrists examining soldiers very rarely leveled the accusation in reality, a point already noted in discussing the treatment of shell-shocked men.[2] Even when doctors knew the consequences could be bad for a soldier who was not found ill, as definitely was the case in court-ordered psychiatric observations, they almost never believed simulation lay at the heart of the problem. Writing in January 1919, by which point he had gained a position as an assistant psychiatrist in Robert Gaupp's clinic in Tübingen, Alfred Storch considered the psychiatric data for soldiers who had been accused of going AWOL or deserting and concluded, "In agreement with most other observers, I have only very seldom seen pure simulation."[3] At most, psychiatrists spoke of individuals occasionally exaggerating or overemphasizing symptoms; but even in these cases doctors accepted the general reality of how the patient was presenting in the hospital.[4]

The physician's charge that Jakob S. was simulating and the certainty with which he stated it as a fact, not merely a suspicion, likely led to the second highly atypical aspect of this case: the call for a second examination of the patient and reconfirmation of the diagnosis. It did rarely happen in legal cases that a second opinion would be requested concerning a soldier's mental competence.[5] Yet, what the military court asked for in this case was something even rarer: it wanted the same doctor to reexamine and reconfirm his conclusion. In part, this may have stemmed from wartime exigencies and the inability to find another hospital that could quickly provide a true second opinion. It also may have been related to the difficulty several people had in dealing with Jakob S., from the officers of his regular unit, to the members of the military court, to the hospital staff. Rightly or wrongly, all parties involved saw Jakob S. as a hassle. (One might even wonder if such feelings of irritation played a role in how the doctor evaluated Jakob S.) Yet what probably played a larger role in the request to reconsider the case of Jakob S. was the very infrequency with which such clear charges of simulation were made. After all, the communications from the court asked specifically about this particular element of the opinion, wanting the doctor again to state how sure he could be that Jakob S. was simulating.

While the request to immediately reexamine Jakob S. was highly unusual—it is the only one like it found in the over 2,200 actual cases and all the contemporary literature consulted for this study—it did stem from the quite typical efforts of both the military courts and the psychiatric experts in general to seriously assess whether mitigating circumstances might apply to soldiers charged with crimes, a process frequently overlooked in the scholarly literature. Each inquiry could require significant time and scarce resources in the midst of a long war, yet expert opinions about a defendant's mental state played a role in cases involving a variety of offenses such as theft, fraud, and assault. Soldiers accused of the crimes of desertion or going AWOL, however, overwhelmingly made up the majority of court-ordered psychiatric observations, highlighting the link between insubordination and supposed mental disorder that grew over the nineteenth century.[6]

It is likewise telling that the court official asked the hospital staff to confirm not only simulation but also that the patient really was not sick. Granted, the questions were related, and an expert opinion declaring the patient fully responsible for his actions was in no way so uncommon in itself as to provoke follow-up questions as the simulation charge did. Yet the request to reconsider the case of Jakob S. not only for simulation but also for his general sanity reflects how commonly such cases of psychiatric observation returned opinions that either pronounced the patient non compos mentis or, at the very least, emphasized mitigating circumstances that supported a lesser punishment of soldiers even of sound mind when they committed their offenses, as this chapter will argue. For in this request to reexamine the patient on both counts, the authorities revealed that health was not necessarily a presumption in such cases. Instead, additional evidence was needed to substantiate it. As more than one doctor at the time noted, military courts showed a notable degree of "accommodation" around issues of mental incompetence, and psychiatrists were frequently quite willing to provide evidence indicating just that for a variety of reasons.[7]

The issue of desertion in World War I has not gotten a lot of attention in the scholarly literature. What has been written on the topic has commonly focused on World War II, often considering desertion as a form of resistance to Nazism and its crimes. Of course, the tumult of the last few months of World War I after the failure of the German Spring Offensive in 1918 is repeatedly mentioned; scholars clearly recognize that many soldiers took themselves out of the fighting. Some intentionally lost their weapons; others allowed themselves to be captured. Still more soldiers simply stole away, no longer fearing desertion charges from a military command in the midst of total chaos that would end in defeat before the year was out. But such accounts rarely look more closely at the men who deserted, nor do they consider desertion as anything more than one of a number of ways the complete breakdown of the German military manifested itself at the end. They are used as examples of soldiers who recognized the reality of the end, not men who rejected service for a variety of reasons.[8]

Especially when compared with the extensive coverage scholars have given to soldiers taken out of commission by psychiatric illness throughout World War I, the literature on soldiers who intentionally left their posts is limited. Granted, the occurrences of each type of event are disproportional. The official government report tallied six hundred thousand cases of psychiatric treatment for soldiers throughout the war.[9] The projection compiled by Christoph Jahr—as detailed records are no longer extant—for numbers of men receiving judgment on the charge of desertion or going AWOL during the same period suggests approximately forty thousand such cases. While certainly a smaller number, it is still a matter of tens of thousands of men, and it reflects only those cases from the field army. It also encompasses only the cases in which an investigation was carried out and a verdict issued, a proportion of all reports that in some cases was as high as two-thirds but could commonly also range as low as less than one-third in a given year and division. Certainly, some of these cases in which the authorities did not pursue a verdict may have been completely spurious. Yet many others were likely dropped for a number of reasons, like insufficient evidence or exigency, and some men received amnesty later in the war.[10] Taking into consideration individuals who would not have been included in Jahr's calculations, like soldiers who were not tried because they successfully fled to neutral countries, Benjamin Ziemann provides an estimate that is more than double: ninety thousand to one hundred thousand. The extent of the difference between the two estimations is even larger than the absolute numbers suggest if one considers that Jahr's numbers include cases of short absences as well as those cases in which the soldier likely intended to leave service permanently, but Ziemann's estimate highlights the latter.[11] Whether or not such a level affected the course of the war and its ultimate end—a subject of historiographic debate beyond the scope of this study—does not change the importance of this phenomenon for understanding dissent among soldiers or how the military attempted to deal with it.[12] As Benjamin Ziemann rightly concludes, regardless of whether one espouses his numbers or even Jahr's lower estimates, "Desertion was the most significant form of disobedience and refusal in the German wartime army."[13]

Indeed, both Ziemann and Jahr—the two scholars who have focused on intricacies of desertion in the German military during World War I—offer many insights into the phenomenon, from how men tended to slip away from their units to where the soldiers went after leaving. Both also deal with the important issue of how authorities investigated and punished soldiers convicted of going AWOL or outright desertion, though here there is more disagreement. Jahr largely concludes that the military legal system was "Janus-faced." Many elements of the process for dealing with deserters adhered to standards similar to those used in civilian cases and fit the ideas of a rule-of-law state. At the same time, other elements meant such protections remained elusive in reality. Minorities within the military, like Alsatians or Poles, especially experienced the limits of the system, according to Jahr. Overall, however, he stresses the relative mildness of military justice in dealing with deserters, noting the tendency not only to hand out light sentences but also often to commute portions of them. Such leniency becomes all the more striking in light of Jahr's comparison with the tougher punishments handed out by the British military.[14]

Though Ziemann's focus on desertion relates mainly to investigating the extent of such actions at the very end of the war, he does address how the crime was handled more generally. Unlike Jahr, however, Ziemann emphasizes that German military action regarding deserters could be decisive and harsh. He sees this as particularly true for those offending soldiers who came from one of the ethnic minorities within the Reich. Relying heavily on the account of a Catholic military chaplain called to offer consolation to an Alsatian soldier about to be executed for desertion, Ziemann argues that such harsh punishment became routine, meaning "far higher numbers of executions than historians have previously assumed" were carried out.[15] While not a direct commentary on the entirety of military justice regarding the acts of going AWOL and deserting, Ziemann does suggest doubt about its general mildness, especially when taken in unison with his point that ethnic minorities were disproportionately represented among those committing such offenses.[16]

What both acknowledge in their accounts is that psychiatry played a considerable role in the military's efforts to deal with desertion. At least in Jahr's case, he is in part emphasizing the effort to weed out those individuals deemed unfit from ever being conscripted, hence heading off the problem of delinquent soldiers before they had a chance to commit any offense. Both scholars also acknowledge that soldiers charged with the offense of going AWOL or deserting often had to undergo psychiatric observation and that such determinations of non compos mentis could affect outcomes. Yet, neither goes into detail on such processes. Instead, both scholars sum up the scant attention given psychiatry's role in settling cases of going AWOL and desertion by referring to the dismissive diagnoses and brutal therapies undertaken by attending doctors to "cure" these allegedly weak-willed soldiers. They emphasize that the treatment "in many ways recalled the practices of 'modernized torture,'" as Jahr specifically asserts, and largely transfer the dominant characterization of how the military dealt with psychologically traumatized soldiers to the cases of deserters as well.[17] If anything, this medicalization appears as a caveat to the leniency shown to deserters that Jahr argues for and a further confirmation of the harsher treatment that Ziemann asserts could befall such men. For more on how psychiatry approached desertion one has to consult the research of Ulrich Bröckling, though he deals mainly with the conceptual approaches psychiatrists took in the shift from disciplining the bodies to disciplining the minds of offending soldiers in the nineteenth century. He recognizes, however, that psychiatric intervention could work to soldiers' advantage in preventing harsh punishment, a factor to which he attributes the low numbers of executions for desertion carried out by the Germany military.[18] Still, one gets only rare glimpses of how actual deserters were treated in the medical files, such as in Hermes's discussion of cases of suspected simulation and desertion.[19]

This chapter provides a more detailed examination of how military psychiatry conceptualized and treated men accused of going AWOL or deserting that reveals—even in the midst of a catastrophic war and in the face of rising numbers of offenses—the notable leniency and flexibility that the concern for determining whether a soldier was of sound mind and should be held responsible for his actions injected into the system. Indeed, far from only recommending that men suffering from grave mental illnesses be absolved from punishment, psychiatrists routinely considered a wide-ranging set of circumstances in determining whether the soldier in question should be held responsible for his actions. Sometimes the determinations pointed to degeneration and deficiencies within the deserters themselves, but not always. Either way, psychiatrists found ample reason to reject the harsh and rigid dichotomies of sick versus healthy and responsible versus not responsible and to introduce far more nuance and consideration into their attestations that frequently argued for moderating any sentences the soldier would have to face. The regular use of psychiatric observation and expert testimony in these cases meant more space for dissent—in the highly blatant forms of leaving one's post and abandoning service altogether—not less. Indeed, that remained the case regardless of whether the dissent was more "straightforward" (i.e., desertion for a basic reason like homesickness) or more potentially "loaded" with ideological motivations, an overlooked and underestimated component in some of these cases.

Rates, Reasons, and Regulations

Leaving one's post and deserting were problems long before the advent of modern warfare. Even under Frederick the Great's oversight of Prussia's rise as a military power during the later 1700s, desertion was a sizable problem. Before the rise of nations and leaders who could call on soldiers' duty to their country as a way of inducing many to stay at their posts even in difficult times, earlier militaries often had to rely on far more practical and physical means of preventing mass desertions. Constant drilling, tight oversight, and harsh punishments lay at the heart of the early modern military's desertion prevention tactics. Deserters could commonly be sentenced to running the gauntlet, a brutal process that often involved the shirtless soldier making multiple passes by a couple hundred men as they beat on him. Despite the name, running was not usually allowed, and another soldier commonly held a weapon on the sentenced man to prevent him from moving through the beating too quickly. A soldier's punishment might be spread out over multiple days if several passes were ordered; in cases requiring the condemned to run many times, the sense prevailed that it was often akin to a death sentence.[20]

Over the nineteenth century, however, other means of stemming desertions that emphasized the mind, not the body, rose to prominence. In part, authorities could increasingly rely on greater ties of duty and allegiance and even intimations of patriotism that arose, especially around the time of the Napoleonic Wars. The high prestige that the military enjoyed in imperial Germany also likely played a role in making desertion less common. The incidence of desertion fell not only because soldiers had more reason to stay but also because the military had become far more mindful of who it let in. As part of its use of psychiatry to ensure the best recruits in a system of universal conscription that never came close to enlisting all young men, the military kept out those it saw as potential problems. Those men not keen on serving in the military undoubtedly used the system to their own ends as well in cases. Even when a soldier did desert, the military no longer relied on the corporal punishments it once had; running the gauntlet, for example, was eliminated in the slate of reforms under Hardenberg and Stein beginning in 1806.[21]

With the beginning of World War I, desertions again became more numerous, and not merely at the very end of the war. Though, as noted above, the exact numbers are difficult to ascertain, desertion rates calculated from the numbers known for particular subdivisions of the army indicate a doubling of cases in field troops from 1914 to 1915. A similar increase occurred again from 1916 to 1917, not to mention even larger amounts after the spring of 1918. By the middle of the war, one is speaking of thousands, indeed, tens of thousands of soldiers per year, especially if including both troops in the field and those on home soil.[22]

These men left for a number of reasons. Some desired to meet up with a lover or check on a wife suspected of being unfaithful, for example. Others left because of a more general homesickness, which was a feeling—often referred to at the time as nostalgia—that many believed could prove to be a potential comfort to lonely soldiers if kept in check but also pose a threat to morale if uncontrolled. Still others left not because they were being pulled in another direction but because something was driving them away. Often noted in connection with the latter is desertions by men who either did not want to face a punishment that awaited them or had simply become fed up with the rough treatment that sergeants meted out to them on a daily basis, not an uncommon complaint among soldiers. Psychiatrists also identified fear for one's life as a reason that drove some men to run away. It was an emotion widely acknowledged by both contemporaries and subsequent scholars, though such a reason was rarely admitted to by the deserters themselves. These were the more basic, "comprehensible" reasons men deserted, as one psychiatrist categorized them, even if they did not make them any more acceptable to contemporaries.[23] Other deserters had more "complex" reasons behind their actions. Some soldiers objected to the social injustice the war heightened, with the masses eating meager rations and dying for the gains of the elite few. Others opposed the senseless carnage of the war, especially as the war dragged on. These ideological motivations behind desertion are even harder to tease out, however. Not only did courts often have neither the time nor the inclination to delve deeply into motivations, but accused soldiers had every reason—practically speaking at least—to hide such opposition to the war more generally.[24]

In large part, this ambiguity had to do with military law defining the crimes of going AWOL and desertion. Both considered failures of "perseverance in service" and handled together in paragraphs 64–80 of the *Militärstrafgesetzbuch* of 1872, the pertinent distinction between the less serious charge of going AWOL and the graver crime of desertion was intent, or whether the soldier intended to remove himself from service permanently.[25] Since the burden remained on the prosecution to prove such intent—a notable protection that the military afforded soldiers despite the dismay expressed from some of the authorities—the default charge lodged against most offending soldiers was for being AWOL. This practice undoubtedly allowed men who did indeed wish to leave for good to go undetected in many cases, obscuring an accurate read of the ratio between going AWOL and deserting. Unless the soldier admitted deserting or gave sufficient evidence of motivations that suggested more than a passing absence was planned, being AWOL was the most that could successfully be argued by the prosecution. This recognition of the difficulty in distinguishing between cases of being AWOL and those of desertion in reality has led many both during the war and subsequently to analyze them as a whole and even to use the term "desertion" as a shorthand for both, a practice used in this study as well.[26]

It is not hard to see why only the most committed and vocal of opponents to the war who wanted to make a stand chose to spell out their reasons upon being caught. Being found guilty of a quick trip home to check on loved ones might be punished with a short term in jail of months, whereas sentencing for the attempt to remove one's self from the war permanently (to avoid service in an unjust war, for example) could be years of incarceration. Though some scholars tend to discuss desertion and conscientious objection together—and there certainly are commonalities and overlap between the two phenomena that defy a hard border between them, especially when considering leaving for ideological reasons—this study addresses the two in separate chapters, categorizing as objectors those who foregrounded the reasons for their actions and usually chose to make their point by remaining but still refusing to serve.[27] More likely, the connection between desertion and ideological opposition to the war became explicit only if the soldier was beyond the reach of the military authorities, either geographically or temporally. One can be certain of the conscientious objection behind the desertion of a common soldier like Adolf Armbrust, who railed against the "futile murdering" and "heavy burdens [placed] on the humbler people," only because he wrote a detailed letter that the authorities received after he was safely "over the Dutch border."[28] For others it is mainly their stature after the war that has allowed an unmistakable understanding of their ideological reasons for desertion. Such is the case with Wilhelm Pieck—first president of the German Democratic Republic—who also fled to the Netherlands to avoid service and further acknowledged his opposition to the war after 1918 and the end of the empire, for example. A similar argument could be made for another East German leader, Walter Ulbricht, who deserted at the end of the war and was sentenced to two months in prison.[29] Yet, this level of clarity is uncommon in the evidence for desertion cases. Sometimes medical records from the court-ordered psychiatric observations can offer more insight into complex motivations, as this chapter will argue, but even here one must usually piece together the purpose behind any given act of desertion.

Medicalization of Desertion

What stands out regardless of the great diversity of situations in which men deserted is that the charge frequently meant the accused would be sent for observation of his mental state. This reflected the increased reliance on psychiatry to solve issues of disobedience.[30] Max Meier, who served as a doctor in a military hospital in Cologne, saw the emphasis not only on the deed but also on the defendant's mind-set as a reflection of how far judicial proceedings had come from the time of simply sentencing people to brutal punishments regardless of their responsibility. Instead, such procedures reflected "humane, modern considerations" to determine justice.[31] The University of Göttingen physician Wilhelm Schmidt concluded that the military called for expert testimony from psychiatrists even more frequently than did civilian courts.[32]

Not merely the first stop for soldiers charged with any type of crime, however, psychiatric observation appears to have been particularly linked to desertion cases, though the results from a larger inquiry made during the war into the numbers of mental competence determinations requested are no longer extant.[33] Yet, the statistics from individual institutions support this.[34] In a report indicating the reasons why the military hospital in Königsberg had to see soldiers to issue mental competence determinations, 80 of the 176 cases dealt with charges of desertion, for example.[35] Schmidt's research based on

107 individuals remanded for observation to the university clinic in Freiburg, where he collected his data, included 50 soldiers charged with desertion.[36] Another study on determining non compos mentis reported 79 instances out of a total of 158 had been attestations for cases involving desertion.[37] Similar numbers appear in a study that analyzed the 73 cases of desertion out of a total of 130 issued attestations.[38] Taken together, the extant evidence suggests that commonly half of all defendants sent for psychiatric observation had been charged with the crime of desertion.[39] Without being able to ascertain the exact numbers of each type of crime committed, it is impossible to be more specific on what percentages of all men charged with desertion were remanded to hospitals compared with those for other types of crimes. Perhaps one way of further contextualizing the tendency to medicalize desertion in particular, however, can be drawn from the observation that approximately half of all attestations concerning mental competence dealt with this particular charge that did not likely make up half of all offenses—such as common thievery, fraud, offending superior officers, brawling, and serious assaults—handled by the courts.[40] In other words, even if some motivations for desertion were considered more "comprehensible" than others, this particular transgression, which constituted "nothing less than the breaking of the oath the soldier swore to his flag" and struck at what was considered to be the fundamental order of the military, made authorities likelier to doubt the mental soundness of men who would dare to commit it.[41]

That attempting to desert was in and of itself seen as something raising the question of mental soundness can be seen in the case of the soldier Willy J.[42] He was sent to the Düren hospital for psychiatric observation after committing two offenses: thievery and attempted flight from his company. The doctor in Düren had to inquire further with the authorities about the attestation they wanted and in relation to which deed it was specifically being written, stealing or fleeing. The physician ultimately crafted his report with more attention to determining responsibility for the property offense (one might assume this was the more pressing crime as it had actually been committed, whereas desertion had only been attempted), but the soldier's intended flight featured prominently. Indeed, the attempted desertion of Willy J. came up multiple times, specifically in connection with his mental state.[43] As the physician related in his notes of their conversations, even the soldier recognized that "one considers him [i.e., Willy J.] mentally disturbed because he slipped away one night." Though the soldier admitted to knowing that he could be punished for stealing when he committed the act, the psychiatrist found him to be unresponsible for his actions, declaring Willy J. covered by the protections of Paragraph 51 in the Reich Penal Code, which allowed for punishment to be avoided in cases where the person charged was found to be of unsound mind at the time of perpetration.[44] The medical file does not give any indication that charges were ever filed for the attempted desertion.

Men charged with desertion not only made up a lot of the cases of psychiatric observation, but psychiatrists frequently found them to be suffering from some pathological disturbance, as the reactions to the flight attempt of Willy J. suggest. One physician concluded that among all the deserters he provided testimony for, "I have found not a one of them among all seventy-three . . . that did not more or less have psychopathological symptoms at the time of the commission of his crime."[45] Another doctor's findings offered a bit more variety: forty-eight of the fifty deserters he examined suffered from some disorder, leaving room for two "normal" men.[46] While other psychiatrists reporting on the incidence of pathological findings among deserters did not always break down their cases so neatly to single out those soldiers who received a completely clean bill of mental health, the general impression drawn from these various forensic studies paints a similar picture.[47]

Not just referred for observation and determined to have some degree of psychological disturbance, soldiers charged with desertion often received recommendations of relief from punishment, either completely or at least partially. This represented an even further step in the medicalization of dissent, as it indicated treatment—not punishment—as a solution. Again, from the extant statistics provided in the various reports made by psychiatrists in contemporary medical journals during the war or just after, declaring men mentally unsound and meeting the standards of Paragraph 51 occurred commonly. Stoll, the director of a psychiatric station for the military, declared 35 percent of the deserters he examined as not responsible for their actions. A further 5 percent were found to partly fit the stipulations laid out in Paragraph 51.[48] Meier pronounced 62 percent of the soldiers in question not responsible, a higher number even more notable when considering that a further 26 percent fell into a middling category that the physician believed warranted leniency. Only 12 percent of the men, or six of the fifty individuals he offered testimony for, should be held fully responsible and receive no special consideration in sentencing.[49] Hösslin found just over half the deserters he examined unquestionably fell under the protection of Paragraph 51, a lower percentage than that of Meier. Yet, Hösslin also added that an additional 23 percent of the cases probably fit the conditions as well, bringing the total proportion of certain and likely cases to 74 percent. Finally, for 26 percent of cases, he declared the men competent but added that they should also receive leniency due to mitigating circumstances related to their mental state. In other words, his expert testimony offered to the military authorities did not find one of the seventy-three men he examined to warrant the full extent of legal punishment allowed.[50]

While other contemporary studies of forensic cases, including those for desertion, do not present the full findings necessary to tabulate the statistical outcomes concerning Paragraph 51 determinations, the information provided generally corresponds to this picture of widespread observation and frequent declarations of non compos mentis. No statistical analysis was undertaken of the countless cases of expert testimony included in the archival holdings for the hospitals in Düren and Grafenberg (two hospitals where the entire span of military cases during the war years was consulted for this study), but the files leave a similar impression, with the former institution being closer to the lower range of non compos mentis declarations and doctors at the latter appearing more inclined to make such determinations at higher rates similar to those reported by Meier. Overall, the extant data points to deserters sent for psychiatric observation being declared not responsible according to the stipulations of the legal code at rates meaning half of all men may have fallen into such a category, though such levels clearly could vary from institution to institution and reflected the practices of the physicians at each. In other words, not only were men charged with desertion not necessarily punished harshly, as research has shown, but also those men sent for psychiatric observation usually received even more consideration and recommendations of milder jail sentences, if their cases were even pursued any further at all.[51]

Diagnoses, Degeneration, and the Damage of War

Doctors associated certain diagnoses with deserters more than others. Epileptics, who were not only known at the time for their seizures but also considered commonly to suffer from attending psychological problems, emotional disturbances, and reasoning difficulties, formed a notable contingent among deserters, according to psychiatrists. Even more prevalent were psychopaths (often a catch-all category that will be discussed in more detail in connection with conscientious objection), who could make up around a third of all cases. Men diagnosed with schizophrenia or considered feebleminded also featured prominently among desertion cases, as did hysterics or neurasthenics in some statistics. Alcoholics did not feature prominently, though doctors also separately noted the influence of alcohol as a common factor in desertion.[52]

What stands out more than the particular diagnoses for deserters, however, is the frequency with which the specific written attestations and the hospital notes are filled with references to issues of degeneracy and inferiority, terms that could be associated with any number of the above conditions. Examining the archived patient files, one finds such labels repeatedly added to diagnoses or used to explain the etiology of conditions in preparing the expert testimony for accused soldiers. Degeneration (*Degeneration*), degenerative constitution (*degenerative Constitution*), and degenerative disposition (*degenerative Veranlagung*)—sometimes shortened to a reference merely to the patient's disposition (*Veranlagung*)—frequently could serve as diagnoses by themselves in such cases. The more proper German version of the word "degeneration" (*Entartung*) appeared as well, though less commonly given the origins of the theory behind the terminology in the works of the French psychiatrist Bénédict-Augustin Morel, author of the 1857 book *Treatise on the Physical, Intellectual, and Moral Degeneracy of the Human Race*.[53] Similarly, descriptions of men sent for observation abound with the use of the term "inferior" (*minderwertig*), which could refer to their intellectual, moral, or general mental capacity depending on the situation.[54] One must also view this in particular connection with the notable presence of the psychopathy diagnoses among deserters, especially given the close associations among all these terms for psychiatrists at the time.[55] While the degree to which psychiatrists located the causes of shell shock in the afflicted soldiers' own inherent shortcomings has been overdrawn, as shown in chapter 2, the link between desertion and some form of individual deficiency or inferiority was strong.

Given the emphasis on degeneracy in the question of criminality and behaviors more generally considered social ills, it is unsurprising that similar associations carried through to diagnosing those charged with offenses in the military.[56] As Robert Gaupp quipped in one expert opinion that he wrote in early 1917 for a deserter named Karl S., who took flight when an anticipated vacation did not materialize, such an "undisciplined" man belonged in the military "like a fist in the eye," or in this case, not at all.[57] Indeed, Gaupp continued, the man "reacted to unpleasant experiences as many degenerates do: with senseless outbursts of rage." The psychiatrist predicted that the soldier would only continue to cause problems for the military and work for the courts, as he would likely offend again and again. With a harshness and decisiveness that has become associated, though not always rightly so, with his treatment of soldiers during the war, Gaupp recommended that Karl S. be sent to the front immediately.

Yet, even in cases where the attesting psychiatrist declared the soldier to be suffering from degeneracy or otherwise allegedly inferior, such harshness as that exhibited by Gaupp toward Karl S. was uncharacteristic. Take, for example, the treatment Otto B. received in Tübingen a few months later. Despite the attending physician (it appears to have been one of the other doctors at Tübingen working under Gaupp) declaring the soldier Otto B. "undoubtedly a *mentally degenerate* personality" who "belongs to the degenerate group of swindlers," the expert testimony recommended a "reprieve" to any sentence the deserter might get.[58] Although Otto B. did not fit the parameters of Paragraph 51, the psychiatrist nonetheless argued that a reprieve would be best in light of the soldier's "mental state." Just a few months later in the fall of 1917, the soldier Julius G. also underwent observation in Tübingen in connection with a desertion charge.[59] Diagnosed with "psychopathic inferiority," being of limited intelligence, and suffering from the side issue of (hysterical) mutism, the man was found to be partly accountable for his actions. While Julius G. was well enough to serve out a sentence, the psychiatrist's report again recommended a "reprieve." If allowed to work instead of being jailed, the report argued, Julius G. might be ready to serve again in the war effort after a few months. Not only would his mutism likely resolve itself, but the doctor thought such a break would "give [the soldier] an opportunity to show his good will." Indeed, the psychiatrist added that Julius G. had been instructed on this point at the hospital.

Such allowances even for soldiers that doctors alleged were clearly degenerate and inferior stemmed from efforts military psychiatry had increasingly been involved with over the past decades: curating conscripts.[60] Under normal circumstances, psychiatrists researching the issue of desertion concluded, such men would likely have been kept out of the military by the increasing reliance on screening and testing. That the war had necessitated mobilizing many men whom doctors considered only marginally fit for service at best was widely commented on in the psychiatric literature of the time, even beyond the issue of dereliction. Likewise, the medical files of soldiers could include explicit reference to previous instances when the man was either declared unfit for conscription or dismissed due to unsuitability for service. The advent of war had made such selectiveness impractical, especially with its long duration requiring new recruits faster than boys were turning into men. "That also those of little suitability would have to be enlisted for military service" was a given, despite the usual "considerations on psychiatrists' part against recruiting such people."[61] At the same time, however, one had to realize that more "unpleasant events" would unfold in connection with such recruits.[62] Far from punishing such men for not being up to the task of military life, their enlistment meant it "appears justified from the start, that the *Militärstrafgesetzbuch* also takes into account these changed circumstances" in the composition of the troops.[63]

The idea that expectations had to be moderated when dealing with soldiers declared unfit appeared in court attestations as well. Writing on behalf of Nikolaus S. in 1917, for example, the attending physician in Düren went to lengths to explain all the problems facing the soldier.[64] Nikolaus S. had a patchy record in the military even before the offense that landed him in the Düren hospital. In August 1916 the soldier had deserted, apparently an act committed while in a state of extended inebriation during which he went home to his family. The file also included the information that the soldier's father was a "drinker," information possibly considered important because of the role alcoholism supposedly played in degeneration.[65] For the offense Nikolaus S. was sentenced to three months' jail time, but then received a reprieve. A month later, he left his position at the front, disappearing into various local Belgian villages and buying food from foreign troops to survive. It is unclear what, if any, punishment the soldier received that time. Yet, he was back at his post shortly thereafter, only to desert again in January 1917. Consequently, the psychiatrist explained, Nikolaus S. did not have "sufficient" ability to understand the impact of his actions and "as a result of this sick disposition" lacked the "strength, profundity, and perseverance" necessary to fulfill his duties. Therefore, the attestation concluded, "that now such an inferior [*minderwertig*] person with those types of sick conditions must fail in regards to military discipline is, from all that has been said, easy to understand." Though the doctor could not certify that the soldier fit the conditions of Paragraph 51, he did find him less responsible for his actions.

While observations of men charged with desertion often revolved around issues of fitness and degeneracy, they hardly formed the only factors considered in explaining why men deserted or why leniency might be called for. While Hösslin believed that it was "almost exclusively the inferior individuals" who were "susceptible" to desertion, he questioned whether this "endogenous" component was more important than the "exogenous" circumstances.[66] Among the latter, he noted exposure to "drumfire," "gas poisoning," and "close-landing grenades," as well as general conditions like "exhaustion."[67] These "severe physical and psychological traumas that were hardly ever in effect in this frequency and strength in an earlier war" could make even the totally healthy become disturbed; "how much likelier might we then expect," he reasoned, that those soldiers already predisposed would be affected by such experiences and cause problems.[68] Meier used the same reasoning to help explain why wartime had seen such an uptick in the commission of military offenses.[69]

Some psychiatrists went so far as to suggest that even those soldiers who began the war psychologically fit could be driven to commit all sorts of crimes, including desertion, if exposed to the strains and stresses of war long enough. Storch, for example, agreed that some deserters had a particular "disposition" that helped explain their behavior.[70] Yet, he distinguished between such soldiers who were predisposed and those who might suffer from a degree of nervousness but not have any of the underlying traits linked to committing offenses. These men committed crimes only after being broken down from exposure to a variety of "emotionally arousing war situations and experiences."[71] Even among these men, Storch noted that some were already "nervous," but others only became so during the war. Again, the cause behind this "acquired" condition was much the same terrifying and stressful war exposure noted by him and others time and again as damaging to soldiers' mental health.[72] Without the war, he continued, some deserters would likely have lived out their lives happily and never had any problems. While many deserters were nothing more than "inferiors," "shirkers," or the "criminally inclined," Storch concluded, the proportion of men committing this offense who would never have come into conflict with the law had it not been for the damages the war inflicted on them was also "not minor."[73] Similarly, in his overview of the literature, Birnbaum emphasized how necessary it was to look at the exceptional conditions of the war—both in the makeup of the army and in the damaging influences exerted on soldiers—to understand fully the connections between psychiatric disturbance and military misconduct, suggesting that healthy individuals might offend as well.[74]

The idea that even healthy men could succumb to deserting after being exposed to so many psychologically trying events found resonance beyond the confines of the medical journals as well. While certainly not mentioned as frequently in understanding the causes of desertion as degenerative or constitutional deficiencies, the damaging influences of war took center stage in some psychiatric attestations. For example, military authorities sent Wilhelm S. to Grafenberg for observation twice, each time after he was caught deserting. In both instances, the psychiatric attestation argued for leniency. Though the soldier did not fit the requirements of relief from responsibility under Paragraph 51, each time his diagnosed "nervousness" that stemmed from "his war experiences" served as a reason for recommending him "to be judged more mildly."[75] That the war had highly damaging effects on men—even those considered upstanding soldiers—found its most wide-ranging acknowledgment in the multiple reductions in minimum sentences for military crimes. Both in 1917 and in 1918 the minister of war Hermann von Stein made presentations to the Reichstag that successfully supported easing sentences, recommendations that came after discussions with the military authorities in the field as well. Each time the justification for the reduction was the far greater "nervous strains on the soldiers compared to previous wars" that could wear down even "respectable soldiers," especially as the conflict had continued on for years by that point.[76] Far from remaining a theoretical position in medical journals or a mercy shown by everyday doctors providing court testimony for individual patients, the idea that war experiences were inflicting psychological damage on men—both predisposed and healthy—and causing even good soldiers to commit all sorts of offenses, including the ultimate crime of desertion, had grown to enormous proportions and had found acceptance at the top echelons of power as well. The receptivity to this explanation hardly surprises given the close integration of psychiatric expertise into military affairs that had occurred over the past decades.[77]

Psychiatry's Flexibility

This recognition of a wide range of mitigating factors affecting responsibility for the commission of crimes by both allegedly unsuitable recruits and healthy men who had long been subjected to the deleterious effects of modern war led psychiatrists to exercise a high degree of flexibility in evaluating their patients and advising the courts. Of course, psychiatrists made ample use of the two options formally open to them: declaring a patient responsible or not responsible for deeds according to Paragraph 51. Yet, they did not limit themselves to the legal binary that often appeared insufficient compared with the intricate realities of the cases they observed. Most basically, psychiatrists further expanded their options by determining some soldiers "likely" to fit the conditions of Paragraph 51 or "only relatively" to fit the determination of fully responsible.[78] They also more fundamentally altered the options available to them. Though it has been noted that psychiatrists failed to successfully lobby for creating the third, official category of "diminished responsibility" for determinations of mental soundness, the reality in practice is that such an outcome of examinations frequently appeared in the expert testimony in the form of highlighting various mitigating circumstances and ultimately recommending a milder judgment, even in cases where Paragraph 51 status was denied.[79] Furthermore, while the majority of attestations left their recommendations to issues of full, diminished, or no accountability for the deeds in question, some psychiatrists also attempted to further tailor their expert opinions to the situation by promoting the easing of punishment via reprieves, as exemplified in some of the cases discussed above. In short, recognizing the limits of the existing army (versus the army that could be curated in peacetime) as well as the tremendous wartime strains on all men, psychiatrists overwhelmingly promoted milder punishments for deserters deemed to be suffering from psychiatric conditions of all kinds, an approach they suggested was not only more justifiable but also more efficient in the long run.[80]

Unsurprisingly this questioning of the hard, legal binary also meant psychiatrists had to contend with their own medical dichotomy between being healthy and being mentally ill (*geisteskrank*). While the clear separation may have worked well in earlier times, the increasing focus within psychiatry on less grave but nonetheless pathological, "grey zone" conditions in the decades leading up to the war meant doctors had to soften this dichotomy by adding nuance in a variety of ways.[81] No longer merely a question of being healthy (*gesund*) or suffering from a mental illness (*Geisteskrankheit*)—in the nineteenth-century connotation of the word this signified the more serious types of sickness like schizophrenia or psychosis—the proliferation of border conditions that psychiatrists increasingly claimed to be within their purview as doctors meant many patients might be neither. Hence, when speaking about soldiers suffering from conditions like nervousness, hysteria, or psychopathy, doctors frequently had to emphasize that although such patients were not afflicted by a mental illness as commonly understood, they nonetheless suffered from a pathological condition that ruled out considering them healthy men. To distinguish being in some way "sick"—the plain adjective (*krank* or *krankhaft*) was used to describe the minds and mentalities of soldiers suffering from border conditions—yet not suffering from a (serious) mental illness, psychiatrists had to repeatedly qualify the term *Geisteskrankheit* to accurately convey a situation that the existing terminology did not fit. Thus, men diagnosed with a border condition were sick but not afflicted with a "true" (*echt*), "actual" (*eigentlich*), "proper" (*richtig*), or "definite" (*ausgesprochen*) *Geisteskrankheit*.[82] At the same time, they were clearly "not healthy," which meant in some cases they might be declared unaccountable due to their mental condition.[83] Practically, this led to oddities in record keeping, especially in forensic cases where the staff attempted to be as detailed as possible in the determination. For example, hospital staff labeled the outside of certain patient files with the determination "not mentally ill," but the internal label—which usually matched in other contexts—had a specific diagnosis listed. Or, the diagnosis line might include both the specific condition and the added note in parentheses "not mentally ill."

Space for Dissent

While examining how Germany dealt with desertion reveals more about the conceptions of various military authorities and psychiatrists, that some deserters had more ideological motivations questioning the very war effort itself can nonetheless be gleaned from the extant records, despite the difficulties inherent in these sources.[84] Consider again, for example, the case of Otto B., whom the authorities sent to Tübingen for observation and ultimately received a recommendation for a reprieve from sentencing.[85]

Although the attending physician concluded that the soldier was accountable, he diagnosed Otto B. as a degenerate, evidenced in part by the patient's "vivid, imaginative activities." Noted in the file but hardly a point of considerable significance in the testimony as anything other than evidence of the soldier's mental quality were the contents of these activities: "terrible fantasies" that "the uniform is a straightjacket; the treatment of people in the field is bad" and that "the German people are not fighting for their existence but for big capital." Speaking about such thoughts to his comrades in the army only made them think he was "crazy." Instead, Otto left because he "[could] no longer watch the misery."

Likewise, consider again the case of Jakob S.[86] The attending physician and hospital staff went to great lengths to document what they deemed the completely inappropriate and even despicable behavior of the soldier, who was ultimately diagnosed as a psychopath. Part of the evidence collected in the file is a copy of a poem found scribbled in the deserter's hospital room that included lines such as "We are not fighting for the Fatherland; We are also not fighting for God; We are only fighting for the rich and in so doing we poor go kaput."[87] Yet the poem never functioned in the patient file as anything more than one of many symptoms of Jakob's degeneracy. Indeed, the attending physician did not even consider it worthy of mention in his expert testimony. Of course, one might note that perhaps such statements played a role in the physician's ultimate handling of the case that went so far as to charge the soldier with simulation. At the same time, however, even these ideological concerns—which may or may not have been known by those involved beyond the hospital walls—did not prevent the authorities from expressing surprise at the psychiatrist's blunt recommendation and asking for a reconsideration. Ultimately, it is unknown what fate befell Jakob S.

The files are littered with hints that point to ideological underpinnings of other desertions. The patient file for accused deserter Georg S., for example, includes reference to "a revolt" that he and a couple of other men took part in.[88] The notes in another deserter's file make mention of that man's anger over "how badly he is being rewarded for sacrificing himself for the Fatherland."[89] Heinrich B. similarly complained that the clear disregard for soldiers sacrificing everything during the war could be taken as an indication of how badly the government would treat such men after it was all over.[90] Though one cannot be sure of the motivations in any one instance, the evidence of larger ideological issues underlying a variety of forms of disobedience and dissent, including desertion, is hard to deny.

Regardless of the reasons behind any one desertion, the involvement of military psychiatry brought more, not less, leniency to the process. Deserters were commonly referred for psychiatric observation, and the very act of desertion itself was viewed as a potential sign of a psychological problem. Consequently, psychiatrists frequently provided the courts with recommendations for partial or complete relief from punishment, a mildness also based in part on the recognition that wartime conditions increasingly made it expectable that soldiers would at times flee from service. Indeed, these considerations spurred many psychiatrists to expand their input options beyond the basic dichotomies to provide nuanced accounts of mitigating circumstances. In other words, not only did the majority of shell-shocked soldiers not experience the ruthless, brutal treatment so often highlighted in the portraits of military psychiatry during World War I, as chapter 2 has shown, but even men committing the crime of desertion—an essential challenge to compliance with military discipline and war efforts—would generally have been spared such an ordeal. That psychiatrists often considered the offender's own constitution and degeneracy to be at the heart of the crime did not change this. In a system that already treated deserters with surprising moderation under regular procedures that played out in the military courts, the further intervention of psychiatrists frequently lessened or completely eliminated any sentences given out.[91] In cases of doubt, psychiatrists often erred on the side of forbearance, following the principle of "*in dubio pro reo*," as Meier noted, or siding with the accused when uncertain.[92] Indeed, this tendency is probably what made the authorities question the doctor's certainty in declaring Jakob S. to be a simulator responsible for his crimes.[93]

Not only did deserters escape the harsh punishments imposed earlier in Germany, such as running the gauntlet, but men caught for this crime in World War I commonly fared better than elsewhere. Jail sentences were typically longer in other countries. Factors that could be considered mitigating in Germany, such as the common issue of inebriation in connection with desertion, were in and of themselves cause for punishment elsewhere, meaning more, not fewer, consequences for the soldier in question. While executions do not reveal everything, the ratios among the nations punishing soldiers for desertion with the ultimate sentence—death—are instructive as well.

Often noted is the discrepancy between Britain and Germany. Britain not only sentenced more men to death for desertion (2,004 vs. 48) but also carried out far more executions (269 vs. 18). One might further add the lesser noted numbers of executions for desertion in Austria-Hungary, which amounted to 430. Even Canada executed more men (22) for deserting than Germany did. Compared with France, which executed only 4 men for desertion during World War I, the German system still appears mild when considering that the French carried out approximately 500 death sentences for related crimes, at least some of which could likely have been subsumed under desertion had the legal codes of the two militaries not categorized certain actions differently. Of course, the caveats about specifically harsher treatment for ethnic minorities under military justice raised by Jahr and, especially, Ziemann may be valid, but such differential treatment has not left traces within the psychiatric records. Indeed, harsher treatment would likely have meant that minority deserters were less frequently sent for psychiatric observation.[94]

The numbers become even more divergent and miniscule on the World War I side when drawing out the comparison to the way German deserters were treated during World War II. Though the exact number of deserters executed by the Nazi regime as punishment for their actions during the war is not known, estimates range between fifteen thousand and eighteen thousand. Based on such numbers, the Third Reich executed over eight hundred to perhaps a thousand times as many deserters, hardly suggesting a major turning point down the path to Nazi inhumanity was made during World War I. Indeed, that is particularly the case for military psychiatry. Compared with their moderating role in desertion cases in the first war, military psychiatrists made determinations of non compos mentis more sparingly in the second. Furthermore, even psychiatric illnesses substantiated by expert testimony often played little role in mitigating the extent of sentencing under the Nazi regime, a clear rejection of the previous precedent both militarily and legally speaking. While terms of degeneracy were undoubtedly used by psychiatrists in both wars, the conceptions held and conclusions drawn from the same terms were nonetheless quite different.[95]

Why was dissent in the form of desertion medicalized more so in Germany—a development undoubtedly linked to the greater mildness with which authorities handled it—than in other countries, which primarily criminalized it? Some of the relevant factors, apparent in larger prewar developments, have been noted in chapter 1 and will be discussed more extensively in chapter 4: the integration of psychiatry into the military, especially for curating conscripts; the direction of psychiatric thought particularly as it extended into border areas and linked nonmartial behavior with abnormality; and the development of legal precedents in a rule-of-law state.[96] More intentional motives on the part of the military might be highlighted as well. While purposefully delegitimizing soldiers who deserted likely played some role, it is unlikely that this was as central to medicalizing deserters as it was to doing the same to explicit conscientious objectors.[97] After all, though the authorities clearly recognized the efforts of conscientious objectors to spread their beliefs and even feared some in the general public might become open to such ideas, they did not generally express the same concerns about deserters. While the relatives of conscientious objectors usually supported them in their convictions, for example, members of deserters' families were likelier to tell them to go back to their posts. Even when trying to persuade German troops to lay down their arms and surrender, Allied military propaganda clearly avoided any suggestion that it was promoting desertion for fear of the backlash instigating a crime of such "reprehensibility" would incite in its target audience. If looking for intentional reasons behind medicalizing desertion, a more valuable outcome of the process was likely to deflect any potential criticism from falling on the military. After all, desertion had long been linked to military mismanagement and the mistreatment of troops. Concern that military leaders could not adequately manage the troops and maintain discipline was the last thing needed in the midst of a grueling war. By making desertion about individual pathology and not military management or morale, medicalization helped prevent such a scandal.[98]

While this process may have muted potential criticism of the military surrounding desertion, it also provided soldiers with greater space for agency and expression of dissent.[99] After all, desertion posed a fundamental challenge to the legitimacy of the war effort.[100] Of course, not all desertions were suffused with a more pointed "ideological" intent.[101] Indeed, the majority likely were not. Yet, some undoubtedly were. The precise ratio will never be known. Regardless of the motivations, which were often intentionally obscured, courts frequently handed out light jail sentences. When psychiatrists got involved, they usually introduced more leniency into the process. Furthermore, the statistics reported in the psychiatry studies published at the time suggest that many deserters were declared unfit for further service. Among those pronounced fit, some were deemed suitable only for service on the home front. Even those ultimately bound for the field again might receive a recommended delay in their reposting.[102] Especially since German soldiers did not have a legal way of opting out of the war or of declaring one's self ethically opposed to it that would allow a reprieve from serving and fighting, these potential outcomes of a failed attempt at desertion probably looked like viable options. Indeed, even the authorities realized the potential double bind their methods for dealing with desertion could put them in.[103] What one deserter may have viewed as a humiliating ordeal for a regrettable attempt to sneak off, another may have seen as a circuitous route to a nonetheless desired end: not fighting anymore.

Chapter 4

Conscientious Objectors

Objects of Examination and Subjects with Agency

In September 1917 a battalion doctor contacted the head of the local psychiatric clinic that was helping with the treatment of soldiers in Strasbourg to refer a patient, a man named Sennes N.[1] On the referral form the troop doctor noted only the complaints of "slight excitability" and "frequent headaches," which makes the transfer seem somewhat peculiar, especially that far into the war. German resources had already become scarce, and headaches had to have ranked low on the list of psychiatric problems to be addressed.[2] Indeed, the physician at the clinic concluded that there were no "objective findings" to account for the symptoms. Yet, both the battalion doctor and the clinic physician agreed that Sennes N. had something very, very wrong with him. As the former undoubtedly knew when he put in for the transfer and the latter quickly found out upon the intake interview of the patient, infantryman Sennes N. was outright refusing to perform his service in the military. He had become a conscientious objector, one of a group of individuals that this chapter argues grew to be more significant than the literature has supposed and fared much better in the German system of medicalization than scholars have suggested.

The clinic physician, Dr. Rosenfeld, had ample opportunity to observe and converse with his patient over the next three and a half weeks. During this time, Rosenfeld characterized Sennes N. as "suffering from excessive affectation" that left him prone to believing in various "fictions" and "[unrealistic] ideas for improvement of the world," of which refusal to serve (*Kriegsdienstverweigerung*) was the latest. In particular, the infantryman had "gradually developed an incorrectible notion of the value and rights of the individual and of the war" that was driving his latest actions. That Rosenfeld not only disagreed with his patient's ideas but also thought them complete nonsense could further be seen from a subsequent comment that Sennes N. was "not to be dissuaded from the supposed rightness" of his principles, with the word "supposed" added to the record later to stress the physician's complete dismissal of such beliefs. Yet, the doctor continued, the unwilling infantryman showed himself unafraid to stand his ground, even if it meant he would be "put in front of a firing squad" for it.

At the same time, Rosenfeld could not find anything wrong with his patient beyond the soldier's beliefs surrounding his refusal to serve and his passionate defense of his position. The file did include reference to a "nervousness" that both of the soldier's parents suffered from, though Sennes N. himself had been healthy up to that point. Indeed, as the physician's meetings with his patient revealed, Sennes N. had been well enough and willing enough to serve in the army before, both during peacetime and into the first months of the war. Only the need to recuperate from an unfortunate grenade injury to the hand precipitated Sennes N.'s initial departure from service in late 1914. Still capable of working, however, Sennes N. found himself in much the same situation as countless other former soldiers discharged from service after being wounded: he continued to aid the national effort by assuming a position in the war industry at home. In particular, he was employed in a workshop in Strasbourg that made and repaired pieces of artillery. Not terribly fond of the work, however, Sennes thought about joining up again. He considered becoming an airman, an idea possibly sparked by the much-publicized success of flying ace Manfred von Richthofen. Richthofen, more commonly known as the Red Baron, had just published his account *Der Rote Kampfflieger* (*The Red Fighter Pilot*) earlier that year.[3]

While it is unclear whether Sennes N. ever read Richthofen's account (though it is hard to imagine he would not have been aware of the famous flying ace's exploits), another book did explicitly appear on the former soldier's reading list: Bertha von Suttner's *Die Waffen nieder!* (*Lay Down Your Arms!*).[4] Although Suttner represented a more traditional, pre-1914 pacifism whose proponents largely accepted the necessity of fighting in World War I, her antiwar novella did not spare readers the horrors of military conflict.[5] Interest in such reading materials might have been what Rosenfeld was referring to when he noted that even early on Sennes N. "had spent time on fictions" and other unreasonable ideas.

As Rosenfeld's notes suggest, it was his patient's thoughts about becoming an airman combined with the awareness of war's human costs reflected in both his own experiences and his reading choices that ultimately moved Sennes N. in a completely different direction regarding military service. Instead of thinking about the service to Germany and the glory that might await him, Sennes N. revealed to the physician that he could not help thinking about all the people who would be affected by his actions. In particular, the artillery worker felt burdened by the idea of bombs being dropped from planes on countless innocent people below. Such aerial bombing began in 1914, and both sides increasingly used it—with little accuracy and material effect but nonetheless creating dread among populaces—throughout the war. Indeed, June 1917 saw the fruition of Operation Türkenkreuz, a daytime bombing raid that inflicted almost six hundred casualties in the heart of London, making it the most lethal of the war against Britain. Given the widespread celebration of the successful mission in Germany, it is likely Sennes N. would have heard much about the operation and its human devastation.[6] By July 1917 at latest, and after much consideration, the former soldier ultimately decided that his thinking "had come so far": he could no longer support the war.

Despite again noting that beyond this issue the soldier was "not psychologically peculiar," Rosenfeld likely found yet another piece of the infantryman's refusal to serve as indicative of an underlying problem with his patient: Sennes N. had deliberately brought about this entire confrontation. Instead of feeling relief that he had not been called up to service again since being wounded in 1914, Sennes N. informed the army enlistment office in Strasbourg in July 1917—just as he finally concluded that he could no longer support the war in any way—that he "wish[ed] to be a soldier again" and requested an assignment. He asked only that he be given eight to ten days to get his affairs in order before having to report. Of course, Sennes N. had no desire to rejoin the army and no intention to follow the order that he ultimately did receive, which was to report to duty on August 31. Instead, he used the ample time provided by the enlistment office before the start of his service to write two letters. The first letter went to the local police chief; in it, Sennes N. indicated his refusal to serve and, hence, that he would be turning himself in at the station. The second letter went directly to Georg Michaelis, the recently appointed chancellor of Germany, who would hold the post for only a few months.[7] Rosenfeld considered these letters significant enough indicators of his patient's psychological problems that he had copies included in the file and even mentioned in his observations of Sennes N.'s mental state that the patient really believed writing a letter to the chancellor could make a difference, a fact the physician likely took as an inflated sense of importance and a pathological level of hubris for the lowly infantryman. Indeed, it was without any irony that Rosenfeld commented on what he found to be his patient's complete "one-sidedness" that left him unable to see the validity of any other viewpoint.

Aside from Rosenfeld's assessment of his patient's mental health, the letters written by Sennes N. before entering the hospital indicate that the physician had accurately captured the situation in terms of the events and underlying beliefs leading up to the soldier's admission to the psychiatric clinic in Strasbourg. Sennes N.'s letter to the chancellor further clarified his decision as well as his reasons and his intentions going forward. As the infantryman put it, his decision not only meant he refused to follow the order to report for duty, but he would also reject doing "every action supporting the war," whether that came in the form of "direct or indirect" participation. For an artillery worker, the meaning was clear: Sennes N. would no longer produce supplies integral to waging the war. The reasons for his rejection stemmed from his belief that war was "murder." "It is my conviction," he further explained, "that a person stands above all material things, that the right to existence of each person is equal." In Sennes N.'s mind, no order to use or even merely produce weapons meant to kill people could trump the universal human right to exist. He expressed hope that the chancellor would see the reason of his arguments, as they would be of benefit to everyone. Barring that outcome, Sennes N. concluded, the government would be signaling that it "was determined to stand by this barbarism" of war and would have to figure out what to do with him. For his part, Sennes N. would not change his mind. Instead, he hoped for his day in court, when the soldier intended to defend himself and his views for all to see. Only after this would he be able to live openly and "according to his belief."

Of course, Michaelis did not put an end to the war in response to Sennes N.'s letter or to any other calls for peace, including the Reichstag Peace Resolution that passed by almost a two-thirds majority in July 1917 with the support of Social Democrats, Progressives, and the Center Party, whose leader Matthias Erzberger had introduced it. The National Liberals, Conservatives, and High Command all remained committed to a victorious outcome of the war, a position held all the more staunchly as the Russian Empire was in the midst of the revolution. There is no indication that the chancellor ever responded to Sennes N.'s letter or made any specific recommendations concerning the particular handling of the recalcitrant soldier. Especially with the mutinies that racked the military in late 1918 more than a year away, soldiers like Sennes N.—who simply refused to follow the order to fight anymore—were not a common occurrence by any means and certainly posed no major threat to Germany from the standpoint of manpower loss itself. Even Peace Resolution proponents, to be sure, did not suggest anything like what Sennes N. was attempting; their proposal aimed to end the war by quickly negotiating a mild settlement void of territorial gains and indemnities that all belligerents could accept. Until such time, troops were to continue fighting.[8]

The newly reenlisted infantryman did turn himself in to the police station on September 12, intentionally waiting for almost two weeks after he was supposed to report for duty to signal a clear violation of orders. The police held him until the local military authorities picked him up. Merely a week later, however, instead of staring down a firing squad or even sitting in the brig, Sennes N. found himself quickly transferred to the local psychiatric clinic and under the watchful eye of Dr. Rosenfeld. Indeed, there is no indication the soldier had even been charged for his refusal to report and serve, as he was not in the psychiatric clinic for court-ordered observation—the usual status of a patient if he was also facing a potential trial and sentencing—but for the noted excitability and headaches. At the end of the patient's three-and-a-half-week stay, Rosenfeld released Sennes N. as "permanently fit for work duty" on the home front. Unlike many other men who were labeled similarly, however, Sennes N. was not suffering from a form of hysteria according to the doctor.[9] Instead, the diagnosis read "psychopathy."

As with many other psychiatric terms, the meaning of psychopathy was shifting and at times had a far broader usage than is common in today's parlance. Not specifically associated with violent proclivities or criminality, however, the term did often suggest an antisocial tendency on the part of the individual diagnosed as a psychopath. A late nineteenth-century explicator of the concept, Julius Koch linked it to conditions where an element of a person's morals—be that interpreted either in the ethical sense or more along the lines of views and feelings—was distinctly abnormal but the individual was otherwise mentally sound. While Koch did attempt to clarify that such "psychopathic inferiorities" (*psychopathische Minderwertigkeiten*, the term he proposed) could apply to quite specific deficiencies in otherwise good people, the close connections among his research, law breaking, and the rise of criminology made stigma difficult to avoid. By the time of World War I, Emil Kraepelin's eighth and last edition of *Psychiatrie: Ein Lehrbuch* used psychopathy as a larger term that included a number of personality problems, some of which—like the *Gesellschaftsfeinde* (literally, enemies of society)—continued to be associated more specifically with antisocial tendencies, while others were not.[10] The term would increasingly move away from focusing only on antisocial behaviors around this time, and specialists such as Adalbert Gregor—an Austrian-born psychiatrist who nonetheless spent his adult life practicing medicine throughout the German Empire, including during World War I—provided more open-ended, neutral definitions like that in his 1914 *Lehrbuch der Psychiatrischen Diagnostik*: psychopathy was "a departure of the personality from the psychophysiological average type that is detrimental to the individual or to the community . . . that manifests itself in quantitative and qualitative anomalies of complex psychological functioning."[11] Regardless, the negative connotation remained. Books such as Birnbaum's *Die Psychopathische Verbrecher*, which highlighted the connection between psychopathy and criminality, did little to help lessen the undesirable associations with the diagnosis.[12] Eugen Bleuler, another contemporary psychiatrist researching the topic, found that the term "psychopath" had largely become an "insult," though many patients who fit his definition of the phenomenon were, ethically speaking, "top notch" according to him.[13] As with so many psychiatric diagnoses then and now, what was intended as a scientific categorization in some cases became in reality a clearly malicious label in others.

Even having Sennes N.'s entire medical record available leaves open the question of the exact connotation Dr. Rosenfeld had in mind when using the term "psychopathy" to diagnose his patient. His notes are largely devoid of potentially more telling commentary on the soldier beyond the doctor's clear rejection of the soldier's refusal to serve as even potentially a comprehendible belief. Perhaps the only indication of some animus toward his patient is Rosenfeld's final recommendation for what to do with Sennes N. upon release: "employment in the war industry!" While such recommendations of employment and trying to use all available hands for the war effort when not engaged in actual fighting were common, as has been amply shown in the case of male hysterics, his use of an exclamation point stands out.[14] Indeed, in his recommendation Rosenfeld specifically noted the armory in Strasbourg, where Sennes N. had been employed. Sending the soldier back to the very same factory that he clearly said he could no longer work in—as opposed to leaving the particulars open or even recommending a job that Sennes N. could potentially have found acceptable, such as placement as a much-in-demand medical orderly—then punctuating his recommendation with an exclamation point suggests a certain insult added to injury beyond attention to mere wartime exigencies. Unfortunately, all extant records remain silent on whether Sennes N. returned to work at the armory, managed to gain another posting elsewhere that he found unobjectionable, or ended up in conflict with the authorities over this same issue again upon his release from the hospital.

What is clear from Sennes N.'s file, however, is that Rosenfeld saw psychopathy as a fitting diagnosis because of its ability to cut both ways. As Koch had conceptualized it—or, more specifically, his term "psychopathic inferiority"—the diagnosis filled a need for a category to describe issues that "do not represent mental illnesses, but . . . do not leave their bearer in full possession of his mental normality and capacity," and this understanding of psychopathy's liminal position regarding illness gained wide acceptance.[15] For Rosenfeld, then, psychopathy allowed him to square the circle of diagnosing a patient that was completely ordinary in all respects beyond his rejection of military service, a stance Rosenfeld found so incomprehensible that he could not consider any person espousing it to be "normal." Hence, Sennes N. was not actually insane, but at the same time he was not really of sound mind either. Rosenfeld further stressed just how unsound a moral sentiment the soldier's refusal to serve was by going beyond his initial diagnosis in the patient file and reporting to the authorities that Sennes N. suffered from "psychopathy of a severe degree."

It is unknown how many other men refused service for reasons of conscience, whether they were politically motivated, drawn from the doctrines of specific religious groups, or simply based on a more general sense of the war's immorality, as Sennes N.'s were. As noted in the introduction, the topic of conscientious objection has largely been overlooked in the scholarship, present at most in small asides or anecdotes as part of more specialized literature on, for example, certain religious minorities or political outsiders like anarchists. Even sympathetic contemporaries both outside of Germany and within who attempted right after the war to piece together the stories and fates of these men in an effort at celebration and commemoration had difficulty. Information was scarce; even direct inquiries to various authorities often led to few answers. Cases of objection became known to those searching for answers through the word of mouth of personal acquaintances or simply by chance.[16]

What stood out as clear even from the start to those researching the fate of conscientious objectors in Germany was the rather distinct handling they received, as such men were almost always medicalized. Helene Stöcker, a well-known activist in both the women's and peace movements, explained that Germany had also had conscientious objectors, but unlike elsewhere "such cases were mostly dealt with in that one sent the refusers to a psychiatric hospital for observation of their mental state and, depending upon the situation of the case, either released [them] as of unsound mind or kept them there."[17] She further explained in a subsequent report coauthored with fellow activists Martha Steinitz and Olga Misar that they could find no verifiable case of a conscientious objector being executed, as people had sometimes feared.[18] Even those individuals who ultimately ended up with jail sentences instead of indeterminate hospital stays had usually gone through periods in psychiatric institutions.[19]

Given the scarcity of information available on German conscientious objection, early sympathizers often spent significant time recounting the efforts of their British counterparts, whose refusals of military service were far better known both then and now. When Britain began conscripting men into the armed forces in March 1916, the Military Service Act that had passed a few months earlier included provisions for exemptions on several grounds, one of which was conscientious objection. The actual determination of eligibility for such an exemption fell to one of thousands of local tribunals set up in communities throughout the country. Normally, they were staffed by a mixture of local notables, ordinary citizens, and military representatives. Decision appeals could be made at dozens of higher-level tribunals, with a final verdict possible at the central Military Service Tribunal in Westminster. Nonetheless, a wide variability characterized the decisions, and tribunals frequently proved less than sympathetic arenas for men refusing service. Of the over 16,000 men who applied for exemption as conscientious objectors, most were excused only from more direct activities like combat duty. Instead, many accepted roles in noncombat corps, acting as medics, for example. Others were assigned to work in certain civilian sectors. Only 350 men received full exemptions for their conscientious objection to the war. Approximately 6,000 men were jailed for refusing to serve as ordered, though the majority ultimately brokered deals resulting in postings that both the authorities and the men themselves found workable. Only approximately 1,300 men—in addition to the 350 who received complete exemption—held out, refusing to undertake any compulsory service in support of the war.[20]

Nonetheless, even the lower count (anywhere from 1,300 to 1,650) of Brits who espoused absolute opposition to aiding the war effort dwarfed the isolated cases that were known in German circles, which numbered in the dozens (and the subsequent scholarship has done little to expand on that information). Hence, a certain level of idolization of their British counterparts could be found in these early reports from Germans sympathetic to conscientious objection. Stressing the idea of strength in numbers, such authors attempted to present their readers with what German objectors had clearly been lacking during the war itself: support. Always interested in international cooperation for obvious reasons, peace activists like Stöcker and Armin Wegner, who was intimately involved in the founding of the antidraft society Bund der Kriegsdienstgegner immediately after the war's end, saw no problem in lauding the work of colleagues in Britain, though such praise for those in a nation that had just a few years earlier counted as enemy number one for much of the German public likely did not help pacifism's appeal during Weimar.[21]

Certainly, this chapter does not suggest that the actual numbers of conscientious objectors in Germany reached levels similar to the over sixteen thousand who stepped forward in Britain during World War I. Indeed, the possibility of exemption and the tribunal system came about in part because the idea of conscientious objection had a greater presence in prewar Britain than in Germany. While this is no place to rehash the debates of the *Sonderweg* (concerning to what extent Germany took a fundamentally different and illiberal path to the modern era), nor should the militarism of the *Kaiserreich* be overstated, it is clear that martial values played a role in the way in which German objectors were treated.[22] At the same time, so did even more rudimentary facts like geography: as an island nation, Britain—whose enemies were at arm's length—could more easily forgo systematic conscription, which was introduced only two years into World War I.[23] Indeed, the emergence of more recognizable conscientious objection activities in certain places before and during World War I owes much to the lack of universal service in the armed forces. It should hardly surprise that countries like Britain as well as the United States, where objectors were also more notable, did not have universal conscription before the war, for example. And while they certainly shared a common heritage that placed stock in liberal and democratic governance, they also tended to have higher numbers of individuals belonging to religious minorities that rejected military service as a rule, such as the Quakers or the Jehovah's Witnesses, which were begun in Britain and the United States, respectively.[24] It is interesting to note in connection that Russia, which had serious deliberations weighing an exemption for conscientious objectors in the years before World War I, had a notable number of religious minorities (Doukhobors, Stundists, and Mennonites, who, unlike most remaining in Germany, still rejected conscription) opposed to military service, though it did not have a liberal political system.[25] At the same time, France had no such exemption for conscientious objectors to speak of, and the hostility to refusal of military service was so prominent that some have even spoken of a "French exceptionalism" for this issue.[26] In short, no one overarching factor—whether it be militarism or otherwise—can explain why Germany did not have the same history of conscientious objection before and during the war as a country like Britain did.

Yet, in recognizing that there was a system for formal exemptions in part because there were more objectors in Britain when conscription began, one should also recognize that the reverse is likely true. The existence of a formal tribunal system that could offer exemptions probably contributed to the number of objectors. Some of those men discussed in earlier chapters who expressed dissent in less direct manners, such as desertion, would likely have gone through a tribunal hearing had such an option existed. Whether that option would have actually played a role in precipitating their explicit refusal to serve or would merely have meant a willingness to self-identify and be counted is unclear. Either way, it would have certainly made the relative number of objectors in Germany compared with a country like Britain closer than dozens to thousands.

Other factors beyond smaller numbers have also contributed to the lack of research on the conscientious objectors who did exist in Germany during World War I. One already noted has been the high emphasis on the brutality of military psychiatry in the field more generally.[27] Another of importance is the subsequent history of conscientious objection and pacifism more generally. Given the rise of Nazism and another disastrous war only a couple of decades after the end of World War I, the significance of pacifism before 1945 has been questioned.[28] Even in the British case where conscientious objection was the most successful, the outbreak of World War II "distort[s]" how historians evaluate the extent of its purchase within society up till then, as the preeminent scholar of English pacifism Martin Ceadel notes.[29] Even as devoted an activist as Stöcker, who worked tirelessly to advance pacifism and conscientious objection more specifically during Weimar, remained largely silent on such activities in her memoir, a void that is hard not to connect to the sense of failure and disenchantment she likely felt after living long enough to see the world embroiled in war again.[30]

On an even more basic level, the location of much of the relevant information has also contributed to the neglect. Instead of collected on tribunal lists, for example, most of the cases of German conscientious objectors are buried deep in and among tens of thousands of individual medical records, if the psychiatric files have even survived till now.[31] Yet another problem in using such medical files is that some individuals whom one would have little doubt today labeling as conscientious objectors were not afforded the term anywhere in their records, which would have made locating them somewhat quicker. Contemporary physicians might reference the "symptoms" (refusal to serve and the patient's moral qualms) but at the same time never use the term *Kriegsdienstverweigerer*, the closest word for conscientious objector in German. Instead, psychiatrists could refer to the patient's "paranoia," with the issue of refusal to serve being little more than the minutiae of the disorder in their view.[32]

Current-day scholarship is also burdened with terminological difficulties. The variability of meanings behind "pacifism," especially when considering its historical development, has already been noted.[33] Even when using the term in its more recent and narrow sense to refer specifically to conscientious objection, one is still met with the diffuseness of that term as well. While a more detailed discussion of conscientious objection is beyond the scope of this study, a few of the most central issues concerning its boundaries must be noted. Though the earliest examples of conscientious objection were fueled by religion and frequently associated with certain sects, the validity of political or other secular beliefs as grounds for a refusal to serve has widely been recognized now both theoretically and legally. Indeed, nonreligious grounds for conscientious objection were already accepted in the process set up in Britain during World War I, for example, though in reality they were often less sympathetically judged. Another frequent issue concerning the boundaries of conscientious objection is what exactly is being opposed or exempted. In the strictest sense, it includes only combat service during wartime. In broader formulations it also includes opposition to activities indirectly supporting war or any service required in lieu of military enlistment even during peacetime. Finally, another major element of delineation is whether such an objection must be universally espoused or can be selectively applied to specific conflicts, a possibility that has also recently been recognized legally but actually has roots going back as far as theoretical treatises in medieval Europe. Importantly, the distinction between conscientious objection and an espousal of nonviolence more generally that eschews all physical altercations should also be noted.[34]

This study uses an inclusive definition of conscientious objection. All forms of conscience—whether they be religious, political, intellectual, or more generally moral—are included among the objectors in this chapter. Likewise, rejection of not only combat duty but also auxiliary service in the support corps or civilian sector that buttressed the war effort is included. Practically, however, most cases involve complete rejection of military service or even civilian service that would help aid in destruction and death. This stems from the large majority of objectors who refused only combat service but expressed a willingness to function in support positions like medics being handled informally, often by being granted a transfer. Compromises for religious minorities had long existed, such as the privileges granted to Mennonites by Frederick the Great in 1780—and subsequently applied to other religious minorities like the Quakers—excluding them from Prussian conscription. By the time of the North German Confederation the terms had changed, but Mennonites and certain other religious minorities were still guaranteed exemption from combat duty, a compromise that continued into the *Kaiserreich* in certain states.[35] Hence, most extant cases in the files are those involving individuals who in the British case would likely have been considered "absolutists" for their refusal of all types of service, another important consideration when comparing the relative numbers in each country.[36] Furthermore, a clear objection to World War I and refusal to continue fighting will be the basis for inclusion in this chapter. Those cases in which objection to the war more generally as the basis for not serving was likely but remained unclear or implicit have largely been included in previous chapters, especially the one on desertion.

At the same time, proof of a wholesale objection to any and all wars is not necessary to be included among the conscientious objectors here. On the one hand, the records do not always provide information on the objectors' views concerning further wars. On the other, actual universal rejection of military action appears to be a minority position generally. Often objectors can to varying degrees understand military service in other contexts. Even as devoted a proponent of radical pacifism and conscientious objection in the 1920s as Stöcker implicitly accepted the need for military action to stop the Axis powers during World War II. It was a practical realization not unlike that made by Albert Einstein, another famous supporter of conscientious objection, in the face of Nazi aggression. The well-known pacifist Ernst Friedrich, who was sent for psychiatric observation after refusing to serve during World War I, nonetheless chose to fight alongside the French against Germany in the early 1940s. Indeed, the individual histories of objectors on both sides of World War I suggest an opposition to fighting that could in certain cases be overridden, especially when the conscience in question was political and not religious in nature.[37] Two sailors brought up on charges by the military for failure to man their posts in early February 1918, for example, had been connected to flyers asserting "Down with the war!" but also stressing the importance of ensuring the Russian Revolution's success, realizing a German republic, and supporting the fight for workers everywhere. Though the ultimate goals may have been "peace, freedom, and bread," it is hard not to see this as an acceptance of far more than merely a linguistic class war given the circumstances at the time.[38] Similar sentiments were uttered by an American conscientious objector imprisoned in the Midwest during World War I: "If I should live in Russia at the present time I would find it difficult to constrain myself from fighting to defend a Socialist Nation, but as the U.S. has not reached that height, I have no such feeling."[39]

The Symptomology of Conscientious Objectors

From what is known about Wilhelm H., another man who refused to serve during World War I, the twenty-year-old soldier likely would have espoused a universal objection to all wars given his categorical rejection of killing.[40] In January 1917, the soldier was sent to the psychiatric field hospital in Cambrai for suspected paranoid psychosis, a concern that arose after he explicitly refused to obey any more orders. According to the initial reports from the staff there, others who had served with Wilhelm H. long knew of his unwillingness to fire on enemy soldiers, even though he had been in the field since August 1914. He was moved to the position of telephonist, but even this support role became unacceptable to his conscience. In March 1916, he applied for a transfer to the medical corps, which was granted. But by the beginning of 1917, Wilhelm H. had reached a point where he no longer felt any service, "that meant service with a weapon as well as everything that directly stood in support of it," could be undertaken. All this was in direct conflict with the "commandment of God and the most sacred duty of humans not to murder," a strong, categorical rejection that left little room for doubt. Of course, as a member of the Bible Student movement—some of whose adherents later came to be better known formally as Jehovah's Witnesses, a label that was sometimes used during World War I as well—Wilhelm H. believed that 1918 would usher in Christ's second coming, bringing eternal peace that would make questions of conscientious objection moot.[41]

The field hospital staff confirmed the suspicion that Wilhelm H. was suffering from paranoid psychosis. Given such a serious diagnosis, the soldier quickly found himself on a transport home to a military hospital in Düren, where he was admitted on February 19. Yet, after more than a month, this hospital also judged Wilhelm H. simply too seriously ill to treat. Foreseeing a very long hospital stay in the man's future, the staff doctors transferred Wilhelm H. onward to the Heil- und Pflegeanstalt in Düren, a civilian mental institution that was also tasked with treating soldiers, where he arrived on March 29. In the two months since the soldier had refused any further service in support of the war, little had changed in doctors' perceptions of his condition. As the earlier field hospital notes indicated and Düren military hospital's handling of the case confirmed, the soldier was "unshakably convinced of the correctness of his views, inveterate." They likely held little expectation that being treated in Düren's established mental hospital would yield better results, but at least Wilhelm H. would be in a place better suited to the long-term treatment of patients.

What had changed in the two months since the soldier's first admittance for examination, however, was his legal standing. As Wilhelm H. directly stated an unwillingness to further serve, the military charged him with refusal to obey orders. It was a foreseeable charge, at least in the sense that it largely reiterated the soldier's own declaration of his intentions. Indeed, refusal to obey orders (*Gehorsamsverweigerung*) frequently appeared as the charge in connection with conscientious objection cases. Given the variability of how such soldiers were treated—both legally and medically—charges of desertion, being AWOL, or even more serious crimes such as treason could come into play, that is assuming the authorities did not simply forgo all formal charges before a thorough psychiatric examination occurred.[42] In the case of Wilhelm H., his legal problems had already been resolved when the field doctor provided a report for the court that declared the soldier mentally ill and unaccountable for his behavior. At that point, all legal proceedings stopped, with the court satisfied that the matter now belonged to the realm of psychiatry.

Whether the order to send the refusing soldier for examination came from his superiors (as appears to be the case for both Wilhelm H. and Sennes N.) or the observation was court appointed (as it frequently was) to determine whether charges should be pursued, the utter incomprehensibility of conscientious objection and the underlying assumption that any man holding such ideas was quite possibly mentally ill remained the same for most everyone directly involved in these cases outside of the objector himself.[43] Speaking about conscientious objectors, the University of Bonn psychiatry professor Arthur Hübner felt it unnecessary to even entertain the validity of their ideas: "I do not particularly need to expand upon [the reasons] that these trains of thought do not stand up to criticism."[44] Citing reasons of conscience as the basis for refusing to serve sufficed to raise misgivings about the soldier's mental competence, a cause and effect that both physicians and objectors noted. This alone had "awakened doubts" of a soldier's sanity in the case of a court proceeding and subsequent psychiatric observation described by Wilhelm

Schmidt, a doctor at the University of Göttingen.[45] S. Fried, who would spend time in military prisons as well as a mental hospital for his repeated refusals to serve, reported after the war in Stöcker's journal *Die Neue Generation* that even his kind superior, who was "a soldier but also a human being," could not consider the objector's explanations as anything more than "craziness." It was perhaps this view of objection as craziness, as well as his kindly disposition, that led Fried's superior to drag his feet on the legal process, avoiding a harsher sentence.[46]

Similar to the greater tendency to see soldiers pegged for desertion as potentially unstable, the questioning of an objector's mental state was all the more automatic given the very explicit and deliberate manner in which such refusals were commonly stated. Robert Gaupp, who published on more cases of conscientious objection than any other physician did at the time, even remarked after analyzing several examples that "it was entirely characteristic that the military authorities as a rule first took the stance that a soldier who in view of the serious difficulties of our Fatherland decides to refuse service out of allegedly religious or moral grounds and stands by this refusal after notification of the seriousness of his awaiting punishment must be mentally ill."[47] So deep did the acceptance of war and martial values run that even many individuals in groups known for questioning the status quo in imperial Germany did not refuse military service in World War I. Frequently noted in this respect are the socialists—both the party and its many supporters throughout the populace.[48] Yet even more indicative is tacit acceptance among some anarchists that war needed to be waged in 1914.[49] Though, again, one should be careful not to assume a particularly German militarism at play, or that those who had been professed opponents of the government and status quo in other countries rejected military service either. Indeed, the same American conscientious objector noted above expressed his disappointment that other activists enlisted in the US army in 1917.[50]

Far more basic than even views of war or militarism, ingrained beliefs about appropriate gender roles and masculinity informed the actions of those involved. For men, that included soldiering.[51] It hardly surprises that a questionnaire—used aside from the war context itself as well—to test whether patients were oriented upon intake into a psychiatric hospital had an item asking what the role of a soldier was. The follow-up query was no less ambiguous in a country with universal conscription: "Does everyone have to become a soldier?" The assumed obviousness of the answer ranked up there alongside other questions like "Who was Christ?"[52] Indeed, if the patient himself was enlisted, "military conduct" could be referenced by the hospital staff as a marker of the patient's mental health, with no further explanation of what that might necessarily entail.[53] It is hard to imagine that such ideas about appropriate gender roles and manliness did not play a part—alongside economic and military exigencies—in various "treatments" proposed by some psychiatrists for anything from hysteria to conscientious objection. One can view the very specific recommendation to place Sennes N. back into the war industry despite his clear objections in this vein. If he could not completely fulfill his role as a man and fight, as norms of the time suggested, he might at least contribute to the upkeep and manufacture of the necessary weaponry.

Given that the charges had been dropped and a second set of doctors affirmed his diagnosis as a paranoid psychotic, Wilhelm H. appeared to have avoided both a prison sentence and being reposted in a job that he would have felt compelled to refuse when he was transferred to Düren's civilian mental institution at the end of March 1917. Instead, a very long hospital stay seemed likely to be in his future. After two more months of examination, much of the specific findings and observations of the initial two hospitals was confirmed. Wilhelm H. continued to reject any service in support of the war and cited as the reason his religious beliefs, which considered such acts "murder." Such ideas were actively discussed with his many visitors and in a sizable amount of written correspondence, something already noted at an earlier hospital. His Bible remained his constant companion, and he read extensively from it. Often he drew on it for quotes that he offered to other patients and hospital staff in trying to convince them of his viewpoint. And on that point he was relentless. The notes from the various hospitals repeatedly emphasize the inability of Wilhelm H. to understand the fault in his thinking; he was "firmly convinced," "fully convinced," and "rock-solidly convinced." His convictions were "inexorable" and "incorrigible," and no treatment seemed to bode success in remedying this. He persisted, despite the unsurprising assessment that his explanations for his refusal made no sense. As the attending physician at the civilian hospital saw it, this unwillingness to listen to reason and the bungled but unyielding attempts to convince others of his viewpoint despite the consequences indicated Wilhelm H.'s openness to a "sort of martyrdom." He would not shy from doing prison time if it came to that.

Of course, there is an unsurprising truth to all of these factors. Those who came out clearly as conscientious objectors during World War I in Germany had to be confident in their belief as well as clearly willing to suffer grave consequences for it. That they also attempted to convince others of their viewpoint makes sense as a commonality shared by many of them given their choice to explicitly and categorically state their objection as opposed to being more circumspect in their reasons, as many expressing dissent were. More telling of the way in which conscientious objection was medicalized, however, is the particular slant that contemporary psychiatrists brought to these indications. Indeed, the basic symptomology of conscientious objectors examined by psychiatrists is remarkably consistent, even before such cases were widely published on. Though one cannot discount that there may have been nonpublic discussions among physicians about this topic that was undoubtedly seen as significant, the consistency suggests that the files tell us as much about the beliefs of the physicians involved in treating conscientious objectors in these cases as they do about the specific patients' symptoms.[54]

Beyond merely being firm in their beliefs, those refusing service held convictions that frequently became interpreted as nothing short of hubris. Not merely convinced, such men allegedly placed an unwarranted confidence in their faculties of reason, as the numerous comments juxtaposing their unwavering commitment to objection alongside those undercutting their judgment suggest. Wilhelm H.'s explanations were bungled. Sennes N. was plagued by "poor judgment," shown not only by his conscientious objection but also in his belief that a lowly soldier writing the chancellor was acceptable. An orderly in Tübingen felt the need to record another objector named Felix D.'s air of "superiority" in connection to his beliefs, even though the staff member considered the patient as possessing a "simplicity and low-brow nature" in reality.[55] Indeed, once psychiatrists began publishing on such cases of conscientious objection, some explicitly noted the frequency of hubris. Beyond the specific content of their ideas, those refusing to serve showed themselves to be of questionable judgment in their "overestimation of self" in the grand scheme of things, as Hübner put it. Johann Jörger, a Swiss-based psychiatrist who nonetheless became involved in German scholarly discussions, also noted the frequency with which such men possessed a "self-confidence and a great self-esteem" that could just as well be called "vanity" in its excessiveness.[56]

An abnormal level of excitability and fervor often went hand in hand with the hubris noted by doctors. Alongside Wilhelm H.'s being "talkative" to a fault on the subject of his beliefs, there was Sennes N.'s repeated episodes of getting "excited" and showing "excessive affectation" about his ideas, for example. A common theme among the psychiatric observations of those refusing service, excitability often took on an even more heightened form according to some psychiatrists. The reserve military hospital physician S. Loeb published his case notes from the examination of thirty-three-year-old corporal A. Kr., a soldier who refused to allow himself to be vaccinated as well as to serve any longer. In his notes, Loeb described Corporal Kr.'s "fanatical" expression as he "propagandized" for his beliefs.[57] Indeed, in the summaries of the two cases of soldiers refusing service that he had examined, the University of Breslau professor Georg Stertz—who had trained with several leaders in the field of psychiatry, such as Nonne, Bonhoeffer, and Alzheimer—included references to "heightened excitability" and "increased emotional excitability," concluding that both patients were "fanatics." Given the extremely short, paragraph-long synopses he published, Stertz must have judged these factors highly significant.[58] Here again it is hard not to also read into this the underlying gender norms, with such references to these soldiers' excitability presented as a breach of manly composure giving way to feminine hysterics and even childlike impetuousness.[59] One conscientious objector named Ernst B. even received the diagnosis "infantile personality," owing to his "childlike, undeveloped nature," an estimation that had much to do with his fervent refusal to "bear a weapon or to go off to war."[60]

Unsurprisingly, the combination of hubris and excitability tending to fanaticism meant the last symptom psychiatrists frequently noted in connection with objectors was a desire for martyrdom. Rounding out his profile of objectors, Hübner followed up immediately on the "overestimation of self" with the subsequent observation: "Unfortunately it happens not seldom that a very animated temperament, even an abnormal emotional excitability and the tendency in the broadest way to propagandize for the settled upon trains of thought, is connected with the already described characteristics, so that these sick individuals feel themselves to be martyrs to their ideas."[61] Adolf Hoppe, another psychiatrist who published on two men he treated in Cologne, similarly noted its role, as he related "the obstinance with which our patients hold onto their convictions, their incorrigibility, their frank and definite obsession with [creating a] fuss and martyrdom."[62] The term "martyr" had already been used repeatedly in unpublished patient files of objectors treated before the subject was widely reported on. The files of Sennes N., Wilhelm H., and Felix D. all included explicit use of the term. Most other files alluded to it. The physician observing Friedrich G. concluded that his patient considered himself "'called' to stand against the war" regardless of the consequences, for example.[63] While invoking martyrdom might be most easily understood in the cases where the soldier cited religious grounds, the terminology appeared more generally, even in cases where nonreligious reasons were the cause. Moreover, unlike whatever importance may have been attached to the martyrdom of early Christians or of more recent men of belief, the implication in these psychological profiles always suggested the complete insensibility of conscientious objectors' actions, a false path when defending and dying for Germany was the reasonable alternative.[64]

In the assessment of his symptoms, then, not much had changed for Wilhelm H. after another two months in the civilian hospital in Düren. Nor had he had a change of heart about his own beliefs. Nonetheless, after a total of four months of examination and treatment the soldier was released as "not mentally ill." Much like Dr. Rosenfeld could not find anything wrong with Sennes N. other than his incomprehensible refusal to serve, the staff in Düren observed that aside from his conscientious objection, Wilhelm H. was "orderly," "diligent," and even "nice." Indeed, earlier reports had also noted that he was otherwise "oriented" and "orderly." Yet while the first two hospitals had considered his conscientious objection more defining and demonstrative of a serious mental illness, the attending physician at the last one ultimately found his otherwise normal behavior more indicative.

Hence, the official determination listed on the outside of Wilhelm H.'s file was "not mentally ill." It was an explicit clarification that drew on the common usage of mental illness in the contemporary literature as referring more narrowly to those conditions of a graver nature like psychosis and that was most likely made with an eye toward the potential legal consequences should Wilhelm H. choose to continue his refusal to serve.[65] In this sense, the soldier could be held accountable for his actions. Yet, the internal label, which almost always matched the external one in the patient files at Düren, offered a different diagnosis: "psychopath: convinced conscientious objector." Given the extent and gravity of the soldier's beliefs resulting in an unwillingness to fight for his country even in recognition of the serious consequences that it could have for Germany as well as for him individually, the psychiatrist did not consider Wilhelm H. to be well. Much like Sennes, Wilhelm was relegated to the grey zone of neither being insane nor being of completely sound mind.

Difficult Diagnoses and Psychiatry's Limits

Psychiatrists examining conscientious objectors often relied on the determination of psychopathy because they recognized the difficulty of establishing on which side of the line demarking (serious) mental illness these patients fell. Several of the case files include a variety of evidence on this point. Sent for court-ordered observation in Tübingen, another soldier refusing to serve, also named Wilhelm H. (not to be confused with the Wilhelm H. treated in Düren), received the diagnosis of "asocial psychopathy," which the attending physician Dr. Stockmayer felt the need to clarify as "not [a condition] in the sense of a definite mental illness."[66] At the same time, the psychiatrist recommended that the courts consider his patient to have a soundness of mind that was "considerably diminished" for the purposes of determining responsibility for his actions. Still not satisfied that he had expressed just how fine a line there was between being considered mentally ill and not being considered mentally ill in this case—as well as the difficulty of determining which side Wilhelm H. should ultimately fall on—Stockmayer added that he could not certify that his patient fit the conditions of Paragraph 51 in the Reich Penal Code, which allowed for punishment to be avoided in cases of mental unsoundness.[67] While the Wilhelm H. in Tübingen received a diagnosis littered with qualifications, and the Wilhelm H. treated in Düren got different diagnoses from different doctors, the sole physician undertaking the court-ordered observation of Friedrich G. could not even decide on one diagnosis himself, so the soldier's file label read "extremely abnormal and eccentric personality. Mental illness (?) hebephrenia," the latter a form of schizophrenia.[68]

Not merely an uncertainty expressed in patients' notes meant only for staff eyes or even revealed in private correspondence among physicians, the difficulty in determining whether men refusing to serve—despite knowing the desperate circumstances Germany was in and the serious charges that could be filed against them—were truly mentally ill was a discussion held openly in the medical journals and presentations of the time. Most of the specialists involved raised the point. Horstmann, for example, detailed his observation of an objector in which he disagreed with the first evaluation. At the same time, he admitted that most psychiatrists likely would not have overturned the original declaration of the patient as being of unsound mind. Instead, it was largely a matter of perspective and personal opinion: "In each case here it deals with the examination of questions that can for good reasons be answered differently by different parties."[69] Loeb likewise concluded the determination largely rested on the individual doctor's interpretation, as "there is no sharp dividing line" between those with mental illnesses and others who merely exhibited extreme eccentricity.[70] Not surprisingly, Birnbaum summarized the diagnosis process in such cases as "always especially tricky."[71]

Among the conscientious objectors identified for this study whose medical details are known from the original archival patient files or from the (at times verbatim) publications of the notes in medical journals of the time (a total of thirty-two men), the diagnoses are almost evenly divided between those finding the individuals were not mentally ill and those indicating they were.[72] It is not surprising that given the noted difficulty of making such a diagnosis, Wilhelm H. (from Tübingen) was not the only case in which the result was "split," designating the man to be free from serious mental illness but so mentally abnormal otherwise that the soldier could be considered only partially responsible for his actions under the law. Of course, even among the patients found not mentally ill, there were few who were "normal." Almost without exception they were categorized as psychopaths, and regardless of the attempts to rid the label of its derogatory connotations, they were often present. On the other side of the divide, the men found to be mentally ill all received diagnoses on the psychosis spectrum of the period, either a form of schizophrenia such as *dementia paranoides* or a more generalized diagnosis of paranoia, a term that in the psychiatric lingo of the time indicated the espousal of any delusion, whether persecutory or not.[73] As Kraepelin defined it, suffering from paranoia meant believing in a "lasting, unshakeable, delusional system," despite the individual retaining otherwise normal emotional and mental faculties.[74] Instead of conscientious objection merely being judged abnormal, problematic, and wrong—as in the case of psychopathy—it was considered even further separated from reality and more constitutive of the affected person's overall outlook, a "delusional peace idea" around which an entire life was ordered.[75] At the extreme end of the diagnoses, of course, was schizophrenia. Here, beyond finding the beliefs to be delusional, the diagnosis suggested greater impairment overall in the patient's faculties as well as a potential presence of hallucinations. Given the number of objectors who cited religious convictions for their refusal to serve, it is unclear how many diagnoses tipped in favor of schizophrenia upon learning that the patient heard the "voice of God" telling him not to fight, as one such soldier examined in Tübingen did.[76] Of course, on top of recognizing the difficulty of choosing between one and the other, physicians also left open the possibility that a case of psychopathy could develop into paranoia, and that paranoia could develop into a form of schizophrenia with time.[77] Regardless of the diagnosis, however, physicians emphasized the objector's inability to recognize what everybody else acknowledged to be beyond doubt: Germany was in need, and men were meant to serve as soldiers.

In his groundbreaking—and still most comprehensive to date—article, the historian Peter Brock was, on the one hand, correct to divide the responses between those finding German conscientious objectors "sane" and those seeing "some sort of mental disorder" as the root of their behavior.[78] On the other hand, his attempt to divide the doctors into the two camps was less fruitful.[79] Most of the physicians involved recognized the fuzzy nature of the border between the two designations in these cases.[80] While a dogged opposition may have characterized the debates over war neurosis between men like Oppenheim, on the one side, and Gaupp and Nonne, on the other, no such clear divisions or camps formed around the diagnoses of men refusing to serve, probably linked in part to the vastly fewer examples of this compared with soldiers suffering from shell shock.[81] Moreover, several of the physicians involved who worked on more than one case made determinations that placed patients on both sides of the mental illness divide.

Take Gaupp, whom Brock portrayed as "the outstanding figure in our first group of psychiatrists," in other words those who considered "most of the COs [conscientious objectors] as sane."[82] Yet, Gaupp had a sample size of eleven men—likely the largest number of objectors examined by one physician—and found five to be mentally ill.[83] That Brock acknowledged Gaupp found a "few CO's" to be ill was correct, but this did not accurately put into perspective that those few really meant about half, or 45 percent, given the small sample size.[84] Moreover, Brock indicated that relying on the published evidence that he consulted did not allow for even speculation as to whether the men declared mentally ill may indeed have been sick.[85] Yet, upon tracking down in the archives some of the actual patient files for the cases Gaupp published on, it seems likely that the biggest factor contributing to the diagnoses of serious mental illness in those five cases may indeed have been the basic incomprehensibility of a belief in conscientious objection.[86] Consider more fully the details of the Ernst B. case already noted. Just days before his eighteenth birthday, the soldier found himself in the Tübingen reserve military hospital under Gaupp's care after refusing to perform any military service. According to Gaupp's own expert report that he filed, Ernst B. "espoused a Christian worldview of pacifist nature that completely forbids him from undertaking war activities. . . . He would rather land in jail or suffer death than be a soldier," an assessment corroborated by the ego documents in the file. The young soldier belonged to a religious minority and had been taught these beliefs by his father, who was also a member of the group. Indeed, it was this fact that led Gaupp to conclude that Ernst B.'s beliefs "had been steered down the wrong track. One can speak of an 'induced religious delusion.'" Nowhere else in the notes did any medical staff member in Tübingen list any symptoms suggesting mental illness. Instead, what was clearly detailed was Ernst B.'s fervor and membership in a group of several people who believed exactly as he did. Indeed, there was reference to two other members of the same group who had been subject to psychiatric examination after they had refused to serve, though the ultimate findings were not noted. For Gaupp, the patient's young age certainly played a role, as the finding of "infantile personality" indicates. But the reason Ernst B. was not responsible for his actions was because he was mentally ill, suffering from a religious delusion. And the reason his belief was diagnosed as a delusion was because it was on the "wrong track" of conscientious objection, in other words a viewpoint Gaupp—like most of his contemporaries—simply could not accept as a valid option.

Perhaps the one physician among those associated with the treatment of conscientious objection in the contemporary literature who can be linked to an a priori position regarding the sanity of conscientious objectors is Josef Peretti, director of the Heil- und Pflegeanstalt Grafenberg.[87] While Peretti penned only one article on his experience treating soldiers refusing to serve—and that included just two or three men, depending on where one draws the line—the director of the Heil- und Pflegeanstalt Grafenberg diagnosed all of the individuals involved as suffering from paranoia. Given that his sample size involved only three cases, however, more telling for determining how he viewed objectors is the lack of difficulty he expressed in seeing mental illness as the root of these soldiers' behavior. Unlike almost all other physicians involved in these cases, he indicated little doubt about his findings.[88] Yet, this likely reveals as much about Peretti's approach to issues of mental competence more generally as it does about any particular approach he had to conscientious objection. Examining all the expert opinions filed for soldiers throughout the war concerning mental incompetence coming from the hospital he directed reveals that patients there were more frequently found to fit the requirements of Paragraph 51 of the Reich Penal Code than at other institutions. This applies to all types of infractions that landed the patients in the hospital for observation as well as to all types of diagnoses that were given to them. Very little appears to have been specific to declaring conscientious objectors as mentally ill from paranoia and incompetent.[89]

Furthermore, one should clarify that whether a patient refusing to serve was deemed mentally ill or competent did not correspond neatly to whether a given psychiatrist was likewise sympathetic or hostile to the soldier's plight, issues that Brock at times conflated as well in his categorization into two groups.[90] Even though he completely rejected their convictions, Gaupp showed himself to be sympathetic to objectors in multiple instances, a compassion uncorrelated to his determination of their illness. It was a response likely linked to his own acquaintance before the war with a medical student who, as an Adventist, went on to refuse performing any service on Saturdays and faced legal troubles because of this.[91] Schmidt emphasized that while objectors would have to face the consequences of their actions once found sane, to assume that anyone who thought completely differently was automatically mentally ill risked overlooking "that all great steps forward of our intellectual life were begun by personalities who were every bit the match in singularity of mind and resolute dogmatism as these religious fanatics. Merely success proved them right. If they had not succeeded over time, they would certainly stand there in the analysis of posterity where these people [conscientious objectors] appear in the general estimation."[92] Revealing himself most open to the possibility that conscientious objection might have some validity, if only for a time far in the future, Schmidt shied away from labeling the objectors psychopaths and simply concluded that they were "abnormal, in that they deviate from the common thinking, [but] they are not pathological." Cognizant of the extent to which values easily seeped into medical determinations in the case of psychiatry, he cautioned against the harm done by declaring them mentally ill and "dragging [their beliefs] through the mud," an injury far greater than any prison sentence.[93] Horstmann similarly noted the problem with relying too much on the incomprehensibility of conscientious objection when diagnosing a patient. After all, he concluded, if one were to use that as a criterion of insanity, "then entire sects of a pacifistic direction must be judged in the same way."[94] Yet, he understood this meant severe punishment for the soldier, an outcome that elicited some "compassion" from him.[95] At the same time, doctors like Hübner and Hoppe also believed conscientious objectors could be free from mental illness and legally competent. Instead of feeling conflicted about sending them off to be tried and given long jail sentences, however, both psychiatrists expressly warned against any sympathy for such men.[96] Indeed, Hoppe attempted to make his own argument against conscientious objection, complete with quotes from the Bible in support of his position, and chastised those who entertained the idea that refusing to serve might not inherently be "in the wrong or a crime."[97]

Rather than dividing doctors into two camps concerning the sanity of objectors, it is more productive to emphasize that while there may have been a minority of doctors who appeared to categorically reject that any man who espoused conscientious objection could be sane, most physicians involved acknowledged that at least some of the men might not be mentally ill, even if they could hardly be considered "normal." While it is impossible to determine all the factors influencing specific diagnoses and recommendations, the case files offer the general impression that physicians were attempting to make careful and considered determinations in cases involving conscientious objection, reflected in the quite open discussions of their difficulties in the journals of the period or their willingness to disagree with previous attestations about a given patient's mental competence.[98] Take, for example, the case of Friedrich G. As noted, the psychiatrist involved could not even decide on one diagnosis. Indeed, as the military reserve psychiatric station set up at the University of Heidelberg functioned only as an observation site—after which patients would quickly be transferred to other appropriate institutions based on their particular disorder—the lack of a settled diagnosis is significant, suggesting the need for a second opinion.

Moreover, one can reconstruct the "clues" that likely led the attending psychiatrist to suspect schizophrenia in Friedrich G.'s case. In addition to Friedrich G.'s espousal of conscientious objection, the doctor cataloged a list of "uncommon inclinations and interests," among which he included the soldier's abstinence from alcohol and vegetarianism. While some psychiatrists did come out in favor of temperance, including prominent practitioners like Eugen Bleuler, doctors were divided on that movement and were even more so against vegetarianism, as many physicians believed protein requirements for healthy living to be much higher and referred to vegetarians as "fanatics."[99] Regardless, it is clear that the doctor examining Friedrich G. found such ideas "eccentric" at the very least. He also found the manner in which the soldier spoke about his decision to become an objector notable: "Conspicuous are the various comments that draw attention to the fact that he feels himself 'called' to stand against the war," with the quotation marks around the word "called" indicating the psychiatrist may potentially have seen these as hallucinations. Undoubtedly of importance in his overall evaluation was Friedrich G.'s history of treatment in a sanatorium for anxiety, a condition so marked that he was declared unfit for field service in the military in 1913. The point here is not to try to determine whether Friedrich G. was or was not mentally ill, nor to deny that his conscientious objection was the most alarming "symptom" to the examining psychiatrist. The point is to draw attention to what was likewise true for the time: suspecting schizophrenia was not completely unreasonable by contemporary medical standards.

Certainly, that is not to suggest that the evaluations of objectors were correct, fair, or free of value judgments. Yet, that was an issue the psychiatrists themselves were keenly aware of (and continues to play a role in the field to this day).[100] University of Halle's Karl Pönitz, for example, warned against psychiatrists plying "value psychology," a tendency he saw increasing during the war.[101] Regardless of how much the profession as a whole enjoyed the greater status achieved by making itself integral to the functioning of the military and legal processes as part of its expanding area of competence at the end of the long nineteenth century, a pivotal position heightened all the more by the role of psychiatry in a "war of nerves" more generally, many physicians recognized that some issues were simply beyond their purview.[102] This was particularly true in the case of conscientious objection, as many of the soldiers cited grounds based in religion.[103] In essence, the doctors realized they were being tasked with determining "when religious beliefs are to be described as delusional," a question they repeatedly placed beyond their expertise, at least until psychiatry had further progressed on such issues.[104] This recognition of the limits of their own profession was indicated not only by the fact that approximately half the men were turned back over to the military to handle either legally or administratively, but also quite explicitly by doctors, such as one who concluded about an Adventist refusing to serve: "The question of how to deal with such cases is not a medical affair."[105] It echoed a more general sentiment expressed by Liebermeister in the medical journal for military doctors that suggested a stop had to be put to the constant "nonsense" of transferring soldiers to hospitals who really needed "disciplinary or legal" but not medical treatment.[106]

Indeed, the efforts to make well-considered determinations and the openness with which psychiatrists recognized the difficulties inherent in conscientious objector cases likewise call into question interpretations of German psychiatrists during World War I as little more than obedient accomplices to the larger needs of the state and military.[107] It is not that most psychiatrists did not recognize the sensitive nature of these cases; almost all did. Gaupp, for example, specifically forbid Felix D. from discussing his beliefs that would "incite other soldiers or deter them from being obedient."[108] Horstmann called such beliefs "infectious."[109] Hübner concluded that the conscientious objectors' hubris to try to influence decisions of national importance made them "downright dangerous to the state."[110] Yet, while these larger considerations for societal and national security may have determined the diagnoses of some psychiatrists—the case of Hans Paasche's institutionalization comes to mind—the level of open discussion, contention, and variability of outcomes suggests the claim cannot be made for the profession as a whole. While conscientious objectors were almost universally medicalized—in other words, first sent for psychiatric observation—there was no wholesale locking up of these men in mental institutions to neatly dispose of them as this might seem to suggest. Moreover, not even all "mentally ill" conscientious objectors were kept, with some simply being discharged from the hospital and the military (as not fit for service) into civilian life, as young Ernst B. was.[111]

Furthermore, regardless of whether the objectors were judged sane, the patient files (granted, a limited set) give little indication that these men were subjected to a particularly harsh or brutal regimen in the hospital, contrary to what one might assume given their stated beliefs. Indeed, aside from the dismissive attitude to conscientious objection and the loaded characterization of the soldiers as suffering from hubris, overexcitability, and pointless martyrdom in connection with this belief, much of the rest of the notations are surprising for their level of evenhandedness. There is no larger trend of attempting to paint these patients in the worst light possible as has been suggested more generally.[112] Alongside the undeniably negative comments about some of these men, one likewise finds notations about patients being "diligent, orderly, and nice" or of "good intelligence . . . [and] diligent and useful," despite the complete rejection of everything having to do with their conscientious objection specifically.[113] Felix D. even felt "touched that the sisters [female nursing staff] were so friendly to him, although they certainly [did] not approve of his ideas."[114] The kind treatment shown to the soldier continued even after Felix D. confessed that he could no longer keep his promise to remain silent on his views while in the hospital.

Such evenhandedness and compassion more generally may even suggest that some medical authorities had a certain level of esteem for individual objectors. This did not necessarily negate the belief that those refusing service were also completely wrongheaded, both logically and psychologically. While they may not have found objectors' motivations comprehensible, however, some psychiatrists betrayed what might be best termed grudging respect for the resoluteness of their patients in the face of the potentially severe consequences. If the files commonly characterized this willingness to martyr oneself as a misguided waste, it was nonetheless a recognition that objectors were willing to sacrifice everything for their beliefs if need be. Indeed, it is notable that psychiatric records make detailed reference to the statements of objectors who declared a willingness to die for their beliefs. Such commitment left an impression.

Read in another light, these statements may likewise have been important to objectors as a way not only to express their resoluteness but also to ward off any claims of cowardice. As soldiering was intimately tied up with masculinity and contemporaries linked to femininity a variety of issues (from hysteria to conscientious objection) that kept men from fighting, the willingness to stay the course despite difficulties and even die for one's convictions could be seen as a way in which objectors attempted to lay claim to some of the more generally accepted ideals of masculinity, such as self-control and composure, but put to very different ends. Though the sources do not allow for a more definitive analysis on this issue, the interpretation would be in keeping with some of the latest research on masculinity during World War I, which stresses the existence of competing strains and counterefforts to define manliness during a time of turmoil.[115]

The Impetus for Medicalization from Above and Below

Of course, none of this should be taken to mean that psychiatry during World War I did not play a role in propping up the military and the state. It did, as has frequently been suggested. While psychiatrists may not have played that role by obediently declaring all objectors insane, there is no getting around the delegitimization of these men and their beliefs as well as the quelling of any larger discussion of these issues during the war by merely putting these soldiers routinely through psychiatric observations. Indeed, this was likely one of the main reasons why the German authorities chose to medicalize issues of conscientious objection and many other issues of dissent: it was effective. Making the issue primarily one of psychiatry and sanity automatically shifted the focus from the larger idea of conscientious objection to the individual and his particular psychology. After all, even if the soldier was judged to be mentally competent, psychiatrists commonly labeled objectors as psychopaths anyway. Either way, political protest became neutralized as individual pathology, a taint that was hard to escape.[116] Memorializing fellow pacifist Hans Paasche, for example, Magnus Schwantje declared the need to make a case for the sanity of the man to be "superfluous," but then nonetheless went on to do exactly that because of how opponents might use the fact that the conscientious objector had been declared incompetent under Paragraph 51.[117] Even the conscientious objector himself was not immune to questioning his sanity when sitting in a mental hospital.[118] As Schmidt had noted, such "dragging through the mud" was far worse than any prison sentence.[119] Indeed, one might note it was more effective too. That so little was known during and after the war about even the conscientious objectors who did fully declare themselves as such is proof itself.

This hushing up of such men and their ideas was exactly what the state and military authorities intended. Indeed, much effort went into obtaining such silence, as authorities viewed public opinion as particularly vulnerable to such "infectious" ideas. In addition to the general censoring of daily reportage on issues like battle outcomes, for example, the authorities monitored public meetings as well as the activities of certain individuals deemed of concern. Among others, ideas of conscientious objection were to be silenced. If anything, refusals to fight were highlighted in the newspaper as problems of the enemy's failing nerve. Even imprisoning objectors seemed risky, as this would result in their day in court and, if convicted, the public martyrdom that so many of these soldiers gravitated to. Certainly, that would generate far more unwanted attention than these men's psychiatric observation in a mental facility. Furthermore, while most people dismissed conscientious objection as flat out wrong and incomprehensible—after all, this underlying attitude was also one of the initial reasons such men were medicalized—the authorities did fear the potential for a certain level of sympathy for conscientious objectors, at least as the war dragged on.[120]

Indeed, in one of the cases that seems more clearly to fall in the realm of a politicized diagnosis, authorities opted multiple times not to bring charges against Hans Paasche, though this was likely as much out of concern for his prominent connections as it was out of concern for the live wire of the soldier's conscientious objection.[121] Paasche was the son of Reichstag vice president Hermann Paasche and was well known in pacifist circles, receiving invitations to speak alongside people such as Stöcker and parliamentarian Eduard Bernstein.[122] After Paasche's actions could no longer go unchecked—one of the final straws appears to have been mailing antiwar cards to several people in 1916—he was finally charged with treason, yet given ample time to dispose of evidence and check himself into, not surprisingly, a sanatorium. Ultimately, a 113-page psychiatric evaluation that was described by biographer Werner Lange as nothing short of "fanciful" allowed the case to be settled by Paasche's long-term admission for psychiatric treatment, where he remained until revolting soldiers freed him during the November Revolution. Correspondence between the military and court authorities makes clear, however, that the institutionalization was a form of "military protective detention" preventing the objector from further spreading his ideas.[123]

Alongside the underlying assumptions of society about the role of men and the military at the time as well as the desire to delegitimize and silence the soldiers involved, the larger historical context in Germany also has to be considered to understand why conscientious objection was primarily medicalized instead of criminalized as it was elsewhere. Some of these reasons were discussed in chapter 1, but they bear repeating here. German science was preeminent in the world, a cause for pride both at home and abroad. This included medicine and psychiatry more specifically. Despite the oft-noted insecurity of the profession compared with other branches of medicine, psychiatry had steadily extended its purview to several other areas of German society by 1914. Importantly, one was the legal field. Dating back to the sixteenth-century provision that regulated punishment in many of the

German lands, criminals were not punished if they were of unsound mind when the crime was committed. With increasing professionalization of doctors more generally and psychiatrists more specifically over the nineteenth century, such determinations increasingly relied on expert testimonies after medical examination of the charged individual. Indeed, the use of medical experts by German courts exploded on the eve of World War I to include six hundred cases in which doctors were called on to provide an opinion. It was not only the court system that increasingly sought the input of the medical community but also other state institutions. The social welfare system developed under Bismarck meant an increased demand for medical care but also linked significant decisions—this time not on court cases but on pension payouts—to medical testimony. It was a development that ultimately fed into another area where psychiatry expanded, the military, with questions about "railway spine" and traumatic neurosis turning into debates over shell shock and hysteria. One need only consider the rhetoric surrounding World War I as a "war of nerves" to see the extent to which the military as well as many other areas had steadily become medicalized by 1914.[124]

Finally, like so many other psychiatric patients during the war, the objectors were not merely objects of a system either in their "treatment" or in their medicalization in the first place, despite commonly being portrayed as such.[125] A notable reason why conscientious objectors frequently ended up under psychiatric observation is because they—or their advocates and allies—used medicalization as a tactic at some point.[126] Discussing ways in which the military could further clamp down on crimes such as cowardice and "outright refusals to obey orders," the charge often associated with conscientious objection, the Ministry of War already noted in 1916 the more general problem of soldiers' "clever exploitation" of a variety of legal tactics to complicate their court cases and, just as importantly, prevent themselves from being sent back to duty.[127] Though it does not mention court-ordered psychiatric observation specifically, it almost certainly was implied as part of the problem given the frequency with which such expert opinions were increasingly being sought by this point. Indeed, throughout the cases involving soldiers refusing to serve one frequently finds that the psychiatric observation, regardless of whether it was officially ordered by a court, was something also sought by family members of the man in question. In the case of the two sailors who left their posts and were found with flyers asserting "Down with the war!" the father of one of the men pleaded with the court for leniency, explaining, "We parents and relatives [of the charged man] seriously doubt he committed his offence in full conscience and consideration." He further noted they found his son's behavior on his last visit home concerning.[128] It was a not so thinly veiled effort to get the court to consider ordering psychiatric observation of the man. In the case of Felix D., it was also the father who demanded his son be examined. Whatever questions the sailor's family may genuinely have had about his mental state—after all, they probably also found his beliefs incomprehensible—the blatant attempt to use the psychiatric system as a tactic for avoiding, lessening, or at least delaying punishment is clear in the case of Felix D., as the soldier's father shared the same beliefs as his son. The mother of another conscientious objector, Erwin Cuntz, called on a family friend who happened to be a respected psychiatrist to intervene on her son's behalf after he was charged. It was clear, however, that Cuntz did not want such help, writing to his mother, "If I was in the war, you could not run behind me and plead, 'Herr Frenchie, don't shoot at my son.' I ask you, be somewhat more composed and don't make me a laughingstock by such undignified behavior."[129] He likely realized the damage that being declared mentally unsound would inflict on his cause and was also probably embarrassed at what he felt was his overprotective mother's actions. Nonetheless, Cuntz did undergo psychiatric observation in Bonn, though he was ultimately released after two weeks.[130]

While Cuntz himself opposed using the tactic, other objectors did not. After being acquitted of the charge of refusing to obey orders by his use of a legal technicality, a process that dragged out the case for almost half a year till October 1917, dissenter Wilhelm Pieck noted in his diary on the eighteenth of that month the tips he had picked up for future run-ins, including "to report sick." Indeed, he turned to this tactic the next day when during his general medical exam he reported "severe, *nervous*, back pains," a complaint that already tilted things in the realm of psychiatry. Pieck did not test this tactic further, as he deserted not long after.[131] The committed socialist and war opponent Artur Zickler did, however. He reported sick, testing "what happens when one thinks: I don't have to if I don't want to?"[132] Not surprisingly, he soon found himself in a psychiatric hospital for observation. Upon being found sick and told he had to remain there for treatment, Zickler concluded, "I saw that my case was not unfavorable, that my results read 'hallucinations, agitated state, and impaired consciousness,' all things that outstandingly possessed the ability to crush my military career," which was exactly what he wanted.[133] Indeed, Zickler was sure to play along during his stay, such as in one case when he realized the doctor expected him to pass out, so he "did him the pleasure" of fainting.[134] Paasche's decision to flee to a sanatorium before being arrested and undergo psychiatric observation—a tactic that at various points he, his lawyer, his father, and his mother all appear to have played some role in—also clearly made use of the willingness to medicalize conscientious objectors, a move that undoubtedly relieved authorities in this high-profile case.[135] As some scholars have suggested in research examining other aspects of the medical system, here, too, medicalization must be viewed as a process promoted both from authorities above and from patients below.[136]

While not overlooking both the generally delegitimizing aspects of such treatment and the more specific deleterious effects on the individual men in question, the medicalization of conscientious objection had advantages not only for the authorities but also for many of those men refusing to serve.[137] In addition to the "agony . . . of living alongside the mad" for twenty weeks, Zickler also got a discharge from the army and was not required to do any further service during the war.[138] Cuntz remained for only two weeks, after which time the authorities felt it better to let the matter drop, not calling him up again as had been planned.[139] While the attending doctors specifically recommended a couple of the conscientious objectors be put to work in munitions factories, others were merely sent home or allowed to stay on as an employee in the very hospital where the observation occurred. That was the deal Gaupp worked out for Felix D. upon his discharge from the hospital in May 1917. For his part, Felix D. so appreciated what the psychiatrist had done for him that he continued to write letters to Gaupp even after the war and until at least Christmas of 1921, when he inquired as to whether he might work in the clinic again.[140] While some like Paasche felt sidelined by their time in psychiatric care, others appeared to find life in the hospital a workable solution that allowed them to avoid military service and carry on activities they found important, like Bible study and visits with coreligionists.[141]

Although the records remain silent on how several objectors fared after being released from the hospital, some men did serve jail time. While a comprehensive comparison with the treatment of conscientious objection in other countries is beyond the scope of this work, a brief consideration of even these cases featuring jail time fails to indicate that the German system was more brutal or "rigged" to the benefit of the authorities than others. Despite the frequent positive references to the system in Britain that accommodated the strength of objection there, as Ceadel notes, those men who were on the noncompromising end of the spectrum as absolutists—certainly the best group to compare with the German cases that were uncovered—commonly suffered jail sentences as well. (The American system also sentenced to prison many soldiers who completely refused service, as even recognized conscientious objectors still had to perform noncombat duty.)[142] Far from decent conditions, the internment proved so harrowing that several British objectors died, ten while in custody and fifty-nine shortly after being released. Most others simply received alternative service, a process that occurred in Germany as well, although informally.[143] Indeed, as Michael Noone Jr. has asserted, understanding the formal legal situation is as important as understanding how the actual cases are handled, with the latter process often making allowances not strictly protected by written law.[144]

Long jail sentences were common in the Russian Empire, and later under the Soviets objectors were often executed. France likewise imprisoned a sizable number of objectors, who usually resorted to desertion as their only real option, and shot others.[145] Although speaking more generally of the military justice and medical systems in Europe during World War I, Ben Shepard certainly has a point when asserting that German soldiers were in many ways treated "kindlier," a conclusion evident in the striking disparity of military death sentences carried out in total: 48 German, 307 British, and 700 French executions.[146] It is a comparison all the more astounding considering that the German military mobilized millions more men than Britain or France did. If one were to compare not just spatially but temporally, the numbers and consequences for conscientious objection under the Nazi regime are even grimmer. Criminalized instead of medicalized, conscientious objectors routinely found themselves in camps. Death sentences were handed out in the thousands, with the formalities of judges and lawyers largely dispensed with.[147] On the other hand, even Schmidt, the physician most sympathetic to conscientious objection during World War I in his writings, noted the "extensive mildness of our modern [imperial German] military justice system," a leniency he attributed in part to the willingness of the courts to consider psychiatrists' testimony as potentially mitigating.[148] However terrible the delegitimization, depoliticization, and consequent silencing of many conscientious objectors and their beliefs were by the medicalization of dissent during World War I, the *Kaiserreich* was still a country of laws even during wartime, something the Nazi regime never was.

Becoming a Conscientious Objector

A final word should be said about being a conscientious objector. Though the distinction is commonly overlooked, one should speak more appropriately about a *process of becoming* a conscientious objector during World War I in Germany. A majority of the conscientious objectors who surface in the records had actually served without objection (though perhaps still with reservations) in one capacity or another during the war. Most men simply followed along when called up for service, regardless of what their politics had been before the war. Indeed, even committed pacifists of the prewar era largely heeded the call to enlist, as conscientious objection was not a defined position before 1914 among the various antiwar organizations. Whether this stemmed from a belief in the rhetoric surrounding 1914 as a "defensive war" or from the momentary nationalistic fervor that gripped many, even in the most surprising circles, at the start of World War I, it is clear that the reasons began wearing thin as the war continued. Just as importantly, the real horrors of mechanized warfare and the extent of the catastrophe that World War I would become increasingly came into focus as no end was in sight.[149]

For some conscientious objectors these realities came not from reports or newspaper articles but from firsthand experience, often on the front lines of the war. Paasche, for example, already had experience in the military during his service in colonial Africa, involvement that he regretted almost immediately upon his return to Germany. He joined the military again at the outbreak of war in 1914, at the same time becoming a member of the newly formed, more radical pacifist organization Bund Neues Vaterland. It was not until 1916, when he ultimately refused to follow orders and his pacifist activities could no longer be ignored, that Paasche was quietly discharged, a mild response likely linked to his connections.[150] Before becoming a conscientious objector, Pieck had been to the front and fought in the Battle of the Somme in 1916, one of the largest and bloodiest of the war. After recuperating from an operation, he also refused to serve any longer.[151] Friedrich G. had likewise served since 1914, though not at the front but, notably, in a position that required him to work closely with the multitudes of war wounded. By May 1916, however, Friedrich G. felt he was "no longer in the position to perform service."[152] Wilhelm H. had served since August 1914, the bulk of that time at the front (even though he refused to shoot at enemy troops), but by January 1917 he had "gradually" come to the realization that no service was acceptable.[153] Sennes N.'s process of becoming a conscientious objector was also described as "gradual," a realization that came in mid-1917 only after also serving at the front, being wounded, and experiencing additional years of war and work in an armory. Only then did he recognize "things had come to the point" where he had to take a stand.[154] While there were soldiers who had refused to serve from the moment they were conscripted—men like Felix D. or Ernst B.—they were in the minority.[155] Even men professing religious reasons for their objection often underwent a process of transformation to that endpoint, as they became increasingly unwilling to serve in noncombat positions that they had previously deemed acceptable, leading to complete refusal of any service. Bible Student Hero von Ahlften, for example, had been in the military since 1915 but became a conscientious objector only in 1917. The historian Detlef Garbe presents this in the light of a larger internal debate among Bible Students, but the trend of many members of this religious group increasingly refusing to serve at all by the middle of the war fits with the more general transition in Germany indicating conscientious objection during World War I should be viewed as a process for most men involved, regardless of their reasons.[156] This is in contrast to Britain, where objectors could apply for exemption from the beginning when service became mandatory in 1916, notably a time after all hopes of a quick and glamorous war had long dissipated.

Contemporary psychiatrists writing on the medical particulars of men observed for their refusal to serve also included evidence suggesting conscientious objection often came at the end of a process of transformation. Not only did the case histories they reprinted in the journals frequently indicate the soldiers involved had undertaken prior service in the military, but some doctors specifically noted the impact field service likely had on precipitating the refusals.[157] Hoppe went so far as to specifically cite "battle fatigue" as "fertile soil from which antiwar worldviews sprout," though he interpreted this more as a pathological reaction—much like other war-related illnesses—than as an understandable conclusion.[158] At the same time, he did not think these men were simply exhibiting "cowardice."[159] While most soldiers could work through any difficulties they had and continue fighting, a few could not. These men would allegedly become conscientious objectors.

However various doctors conceived of the exact connection between wartime service and objection, almost all of the physicians who wrote on the topic noted that such refusals were a product of the second half of the war.

Cases began commanding the attention of psychiatrists in 1917, which is when the bulk of the objections occurred, though the files indicate at least some of these individuals had begun refusing to serve months earlier in 1916. Gaupp even expressed his surprise at how little he heard about this topic before the beginning of 1917 and how much he heard after that.[160] The timing of the rise of conscientious objection cases should not be conflated with the often-noted breakdown of military discipline at the very end of World War I. The mutinies in places such as Kiel in October and November 1918, for example, came at the very end and in desperate reaction to continuing a war that was all but officially over. Certainly, the dissent expressed by the objectors discussed here was clearly related to the grim realities of war, as both the individual case histories and the overarching trajectory indicate. But the despair of late 1918 was not the anguish of 1916 or 1917, no matter how bad those years had been. Nor was the fear of being one of the last to die pointlessly in a war that was almost over the same as the refusal to be one of many more to serve in a war that seemed like it would never end.[161]

As this chapter has shown, the men who took principled stands of conscientious objection during World War I were not numerous, but they also were not as uncommon as the literature suggests. Either way, their medicalization reveals much about imperial Germany. Instead of reflecting a repressive system of military psychiatry and a disregard for the rule of law, the medicalization of conscientious objectors stemmed in part from the openness of a legal system to mitigating circumstances and the adherence to such processes even during wartime. This is not to overlook the manner in which state and military authorities delegitimized and depoliticized conscientious objection within this system, nor to suggest that such processes were ever fair. Yet, the sheer amount and openness of medical discussion over the difficulty and even limits of psychiatry in dealing with these cases indicates that the physicians involved did not simply act as obedient accomplices doing the bidding of the authorities. Indeed, far from brutally repressing conscientious objectors, medicalization was at times something the men themselves fostered, as it provided room to maneuver and space for resistance for even the most absolutist among them.

Epilogue

"Has the war destroyed the peace movement?" Activist Magnus Schwantje addressed this question head-on in the fall of 1914. After all, he reasoned, everyone was thinking that. Articles argued that pacifists must have finally realized they were wrong: the outbreak of the war made all talk of international agreements and arbitration to avoid armed conflict pointless. Indeed, many people began to consider pacifists, far from merely being "dreamers," as "fools" risking the safety of Germany with their dangerous ideas. Yet, unwavering in his beliefs, Schwantje claimed that the war had not destroyed the peace movement; instead, the cause was "directly strengthened by it." Accordingly, the war did not prove pacifist ideas wrong; it had shown just how necessary they were.[1]

At the time, the situation did not look good for the peace movement, as the fate of the article itself shows. First published shortly after the outbreak of the war, the article was subsequently confiscated by the government. As they had done with so many other pieces penned by pacifists, the authorities silenced the article under the censorship measures enacted during the war.

Not only articles but also entire organizations were shut down and individual activists were monitored between 1914 and 1918. Even many who had been active in prewar pacifism largely put such ideas on hold, at least for the duration of the war. Schwantje's article itself became legal to distribute again only in December 1918, as controls on "propaganda" were being relaxed.[2]

Yet, by the fall of 1919, when Schwantje republished the article, he had reason to stand by his earlier assessment, as he now commented on how it was opponents of the movement who understood just how right pacifists had been.[3] Activist Ernst Friedrich expressed a similar sentiment after the war when he claimed, "There was not one reasonable person in November 1918 who would not have said 'Never Again War!'"[4] While certainly these were exaggerations or oversimplifications, the war had indeed given the peace movement a fillip that was palpable during Weimar. Numbers can tell part of the story. The German Peace Society, which had numbered only around ten thousand members on the eve of the war, had slightly more in 1920 with eleven thousand members. While this amounted to only a modest increase—though slightly greater proportionally speaking if one considers the massive death tolls of the war that led to approximately two million military deaths and hundreds of thousands more in the civilian populace of Germany—the membership climbed further by 1924 to twenty thousand. Just two years later, the membership of the German Peace Society totaled thirty thousand or more. Even more notable was the rise of several other pacifist societies. The Peace League of War Veterans (Friedensbund der Kriegsteilnehmer) amassed a sizable membership rivaling that of the German Peace Society. Indeed, the German Peace Cartel, which was an overarching organization that included over twenty separate pacifist groups under its umbrella, represented approximately one hundred thousand people in 1928. Beyond attracting more members, pacifist ideas gained a relevance in postwar society that had largely been absent before 1914. Not only did more notables become involved during the Weimar period, but events such as the yearly Never Again War (Nie Wieder Krieg) demonstrations held on every August 1 to mark the anniversary of German entry into World War I attracted hundreds of thousands of people. Such demonstrations formed in countless cities throughout Germany. Hundreds of thousands of people signed documents circulating in some districts in 1927 that represented a promise to refuse military or civilian service in any future war.[5] What had largely been silenced during the war—or at best forced to continue as often little more than the subtext of an act of desertion or the individual instances of refusal that were quickly hushed up—gained wide expression in Weimar.

Unsurprisingly, postwar pacifism not only grew in size but also expanded in scope. Many of the newer peace organizations had a more left-leaning political orientation than the older, bourgeois pacifism of the prewar era. Even within the German Peace Society the shift was notable, as the organization now incorporated some members espousing a more radical pacifism. Indeed, conscientious objection became a point of discussion within pacifist organizations after the war, even if it did not necessarily become dominant in all of them. The organization most closely associated with conscientious objection was the League of Resisters to War Service (Bund der Kriegsdienstgegner), founded in 1919. One can see this leftward trend to more radical pacifism exemplified in the personal trajectories of individual pacifists as well. Take, for example, Schwantje. While he included an explicit distancing of pacifism from conscientious objection in the 1914 article, Schwantje had become involved with the complete rejection of service by 1919 and was actually one of the founding members of the League of Resisters to War Service. Stöcker, another early member of the league, shows the same progression in her views. Though as a woman she did not have to grapple with serving in the military directly, she was intimately involved in helping her partner maximize his chances of not being sent into the field during the war. As much effort as Stöcker put into trying to use any and all connections to ensure this, however, the issue of simply refusing service did not come up. Yet the former German Peace Society supporter who became a member of the more vigorous New Fatherland League during the war had by 1919 fully espoused the principles of conscientious objection, a belief in nonviolence that Stöcker continued to espouse for some time even after the rise of the Nazis and her flight to the United States in the early 1940s.[6] Especially for this more radically oriented pacifism that subscribed to the idea of refusing service, World War I had been a "breakthrough."[7] As in so many other areas of life, the events of 1914–1918 had fundamentally changed how people conceptualized not only war but also pacifism.

It was not merely the war in a more general sense that had contributed to this upswing. So many of the actors involved with pacifism after 1918 had been enlisted in the war itself, from better-known individuals like Paasche (freed from the mental institution he had been remanded to in the midst of revolution during November 1918) and Zickler (a prominent member of the

Peace League of War Veterans) to the many more veterans who joined organizations or marched in Never Again War demonstrations in masses. Jason Crouthamel has skillfully shown just how involved veterans could become in the Weimar-era struggles over the legacy of the war and, importantly, has linked this with pacifist activities. Not surprisingly, many of them had also been treated by military psychiatry during the war. Attempting to ensure that their service was neither belittled nor forgotten but recognized for the important insights it gave them into the realities of battle, these soldiers during Weimar loudly rejected the romanticized view of war as glorious and invigorating. Even more notable, some of these men continued their activities well into the Third Reich, stridently countering Nazi efforts to monopolize both the memory of World War I and the allegiance of its veterans for their own ends. Though the fate of pacifism certainly experienced a downswing in the last years of Weimar and during the Third Reich (only to reemerge stronger again in the Federal Republic), these notable voices of dissent against Nazism should certainly not be overlooked, especially given the all too few attempts to counter that regime.[8]

Of course, not all veterans were pacifists, though Benjamin Ziemann has demonstrated the great extent to which left-leaning veterans organizations—even if they were not explicitly associated with pacifism—generally espoused such principles and expressed them in their activities. What is more indicative of soldiers' behavior in Weimar is the highly active role veterans claimed in expressing dissent in many forms. In some cases that was indeed about rejecting glorified combat narratives and cautioning against future wars. Yet, especially for disabled veterans, a lot of their efforts focused on decrying a pensioning system that they believed was unfair and did not recognize their wartime sacrifices. Mentally traumatized veterans had an especially difficult time in this respect. Though, as this book has shown, the reality of wartime conceptions, treatments, and pensioning procedures meant the lion's share of men did not get the dismissive treatment so often discussed in the scholarly literature, some shell-shocked soldiers certainly did. It also hardly surprises in the aftermath of a catastrophic war and in the midst of destabilizing hyperinflation during Weimar that the issue of psychologically (and physically) disabled veterans took on a heightened level of importance propelling discussion to an even greater degree of polarization and vitriol. The dismissive pronouncements of some psychiatrists concerning hysterical men continued unabated after the war as well, and rhetoric hurt, even if it did not reflect the reality of how many people viewed such men or the size and frequency of pensions provided that tended to be more generous than in other countries. It is not hard to understand the disgust and betrayal many soldiers felt after the war. But veterans hardly just accepted such dismissive claims or low pensions.[9]

Indeed, the agency of soldiers—so evident in their Weimar-era activities—has been central to this study of dissent and its medicalization during World War I. After all, one of the main arguments of this book has been that soldiers even in the medicalized setting run by military psychiatrists and their contracted civilian counterparts never became powerless objects but instead found spaces for and ways of expressing agency and dissent. This was possible in part because, generally, the treatment given to veterans was not as dismissive or as brutal as the scholarly literature has assumed. For the majority of traumatized soldiers this meant—despite being blamed by some psychiatrists for their own sickness and viewed as discipline problems—their treatment often relied on rest and restoration that could offer significant respite from the horrors of war. For some soldiers who were sick, however, it could also provide opportunities to express dissent. While they did not choose their illness, they could still choose how to negotiate treatment regimens and hospital stays, which could serve multiple ends.

Soldiers clearly expressing more overt dissent in the form of desertion also found themselves increasingly relegated to the domain of military psychiatry. Here they encountered a system that frequently further mitigated the punishment meted out by military courts. To do so, psychiatrists not only challenged the binary choice of fully accountable or fully unaccountable offered by the law but also added nuance to their own dichotomy of healthy versus mentally ill. Even though the attention to inherent constitutional weaknesses and degeneracy was greater in this forensic realm, psychiatrists did not ignore the effects of unprecedented warfare on delinquency. Furthermore, they also often sought the solution to the exigencies of war and the supposed unsuitability of many recruits in treatment, moderating punishments, and lessening exposure to combat. This meant that, whatever reason individual soldiers had for their actions, desertion was a gambit for expressing dissent, and one that likely allowed not a few ideologically inclined opponents of the war to achieve their ends of not serving.

Soldiers at the farthest end of the spectrum of dissent who explicitly proclaimed their opposition to the war as conscientious objectors again encountered a system in which psychiatrists were generally far more attentive to arriving at the right determinations concerning mental soundness than merely dispatching such men to oblivion in psychiatric institutions. Confinement in a hospital could happen, though that often proved a better alternative to the tough jail sentences that formed the main method of dealing with objectors in other countries, like—notably—Britain. Furthermore, other German objectors merely received discharges and postings in the civilian workforce. Of course, the system worked in part to discredit such men by pathologizing them instead of recognizing, even if still rejecting, their principled stance. Yet, however successful that approach was to quelling the wider spread of conscientious objection during the war, it would not work for long. Indeed, that such spaces for the continued agency among individual soldiers existed within the medicalizing of dissent during the war proved integral to the burgeoning afterward of a pacifism that is far more recognizable by today's standards.

While an important topic in itself as it uncovers soldiers' agency and recovers wartime dissention within the military, both issues that have been underemphasized, the medicalization of dissent in World War I offers insights into larger questions within German history as well. Of particular note here is the nature of imperial Germany as a rule-of-law state. Whatever delegitimizing effects the medicalization of dissent had on the affected individuals and their values, it grew out of the protections offered to those deemed unaccountable for their actions and an increasing reliance on expert opinion in making these determinations. Far from such psychiatric observations exemplifying a quick path to confinement of those expressing dissent in some form, they are better understood as a reflection of the considerable attention given to legal procedures and precedents even in the midst of a long and costly war. Though certainly the potential for the abuse of such practices is clear, one should not disregard the reality of the way in which they were actually used in most instances between 1914 and 1918.[10] Especially considering the way in which German military authorities handled dissent compared with other belligerents at the time, the procedures and outcomes were not any harsher, and at times were actually more moderate. This leads to another larger issue in German history concerning the extent of the connections between both world wars. Yet, comparing the medicalization of dissent—whether perceived or actual—during World War I with how it was handled by the Nazis both before and during World War II produces an even starker contrast. Whatever the shortcomings of military psychiatry between 1914 and 1918, and there were many, they did not represent a decisive turn down the path into the depravity of the Third Reich. This was an unfortunate truth not a few World War I veterans treated by psychiatrists during the war would discover firsthand, as Nazi "experts" began their investigations into the health of the national community, a pursuit that quickly turned deadly.[11]

Notes

Introduction

1. All quotes and details of the Wilhelm W. case are from his patient file (treatment dates July 14 to August 8, 1917), still located in Haus 5, which is the former Bewahrungshaus (a section specifically for forensic patients) of the hospital (now named the LVR-Klinik Düren) that has since been converted into a museum. Special appreciation is extended to Dr. Erhard Knauer, former head of the hospital, for allowing me access to several files in the on-site museum.

2. *Sanitätsbericht über das Deutsche Heer (Deutsches Feld- und Besatzungsheer) im Weltkriege 1914/1918*, Band III (Berlin: E. S. Mittler & Sohn, 1934), 145.

3. John Frith, "Syphilis—Its Early History and Treatment until Penicillin and the Debate on Its Origins," *Journal of Military and Veterans' Health* 20 (2012): 49–58; Juliet D. Hurn, "The History of General Paralysis of the Insane in Britain, 1830 to 1950" (PhD diss., University of London, 1998).

4. On this development, see, for example, Richard Noll, *American Madness: The Rise and Fall of Dementia Praecox* (Cambridge, MA: Harvard University Press, 2011), chapter 3.

5. Consider the reports of harassment in the case file of Hermann R. (treatment dates October 29, 1914, to June 21, 1915), thought by others to be a "*Drückeberger*" (malingerer).

Archiv des Landschaftsverbandes Rheinland (ALVR), Düren Krankenakten, Box October 6 to November 4, 1914.

6. Given the variety of ways in which conscientious objection can be and has been used, chapter 4 will provide a more extensive discussion of the term.

7. Werner Lange, *Hans Paasches Forschungsreise ins innerste Deutschland: Eine Biographie* (Bremen: Donat, 1995).

8. These specific aspects of conscientious objection cases will be examined in chapter 4.

9. Flurin Condrau addresses some of the general literature on this issue as well as the underlying theories—like those of Foucault—behind it. "The Patient's View Meets the Clinical Gaze," *Social History of Medicine* 20, no. 3 (2007), especially 528–29. Julia Barbara Köhne likewise provides a brief overview. *Kriegshysteriker: Strategische Bilder und mediale Techniken militärpsychiatrischen Wissens (1914–20)* (Husum: Matthiesen, 2009), 84–91. See also, for example, Jonathan Andrews, "Case Notes, Case Histories, and the Patients' Experience of Insanity at Gartnavel Royal Asylum, Glasgow, in the Nineteenth Century," *Social History of Medicine* 11, no. 2 (1998): 265; Edgar Jones and Simon Wessely, "War Syndromes: The Impact of Culture on Medically Unexplained Symptoms," *Medical History* 49, no. 1 (2005): 76; or the conference (featuring several notable German historians of psychiatry) summary by Michaela Ralser, "Tagungsbericht: Psychiatrische Krankenakten als Material der Wissenschaftsgeschichte. Methodisches Vorgehen am Einzelfall, 17.05.2007—19.05.2007 Berlin" in *H-Soz-Kult*, June 10, 2007, https://www.hsozkult.de/conferencereport/id/tagungsberichte-1602.

10. Several specific texts that assert this general narrative will be discussed individually below.

11. Peter Brock, "Confinement of Conscientious Objectors as Psychiatric Patients in World War I Germany," *Peace & Change* 23, no. 3 (1998): 247–64. For example, Wolfgang Eckart's magisterial, almost six-hundred-page book *Medizin und Krieg: Deutschland 1914–1924* (Paderborn: Schöningh, 2014), 158–62, includes a summary of only one particular case of conscientious objection.

12. See, for example, the short section on World War I in Detlef Garbe, *Between Resistance and Martyrdom: Jehovah's Witnesses in the Third Reich*, trans. Dagmar G. Grimm (Madison: University of Wisconsin Press, 2008), 33–34.

13. For example, Ingrid Sharp, a Germanist specializing in war and peace studies focusing on World War I, also touches on these underlying causes in detailing the lack of attention to conscientious objection in Germany. "Life Was Even Tougher for the German Conscientious Objectors of World War 1," The Conversation, May 15, 2014, https://theconversation.com/life-was-even-tougher-for-the-german-conscientious-objectors-of-world-war-i-26715.

14. J. W. Graham, *Conscription and Conscience: A History, 1916–1919* (London: Allen & Unwin, 1922). For more information on Graham himself, see Joanna Dales, "John William Graham and the Evolution of Peace: A Quaker View of Conflict before and during the First World War," *Quaker Studies* 21, no. 22 (2016): 169–92.

15. Graham, *Conscription and Conscience*, 358.

16. Andrews concludes that this reluctance "has more to do with convenience than utility." See "Case Notes," 256. Maria Hermes also notes this reluctance stemming from practical difficulties. *Krankheit: Krieg: Psychiatrische Deutungen des Ersten Weltkriegs* (Es-

sen: Klartext, 2012), 21. Undoubtedly the practical difficulties are, in part, to blame: physicians' handwriting, for example, was just as terrible then as it is purported to be now. Yet, the underuse of patient files also stems from the above-mentioned concerns about what the files can actually tell us beyond the mind-sets of the physicians who wrote them. Either way, the inclusion of patient files in the German scholarship has been even slower than in other regions. See Ralser, "Tagungsbericht."

17. Put into context, however, the number is not particularly small, a point discussed in chapter 4.

18. Ester Fischer-Homberger, "Der Bergriff 'Krankheit' als Funktion aussermedizinischer Gegebenheiten: Zur Geschichte der traumatischen Neurose," *Sudhoff's Archiv* 54 (1970): 225–41.

19. Ibid., 239–41.

20. Ibid., 235–36.

21. Ibid., 235.

22. Peter Riedesser and Axel Verderber, *Aufrüstung der Seelen: Militärpsychiatrie und Militärpsychologie in Deutschland und Amerika* (Freiburg: Dreisam-Verlag, 1985), 19.

23. Ibid., 11–12, 17–18.

24. Ibid., 20. They do briefly mention conscientious objection in the post-1945 period. While addressing the interconnection among psychiatry, sickness, and dissent, they largely focus on this in relation to the November Revolution commencing in that month of 1918.

25. Ibid., 117.

26. Wolfgang Eckart, "Kriegsgewalt und Psychotrauma im Ersten Weltkrieg," in *Verletzte Seelen: Möglichkeiten und Perspecktiven einer historischen Traumaforschung*, ed. Günter Seidler and Wolfgang Eckart (Giessen: Psychosozial-Verlag, 2005), 85–105; Eckart, *Medizin und Krieg*, especially 136–62.

27. Eckart, *Medizin und Krieg*, 103.

28. Köhne, *Kriegshysteriker*, especially 19–22. A subsequent article by Köhne begins to chart a new direction, however, and will be discussed below: "Screening Silent Resistance: Male Hysteria in First World War Medical Cinematography," in *Psychological Trauma and the Legacies of the First World War*, ed. Jason Crouthamel and Peter Leese (Basingstoke, UK: Palgrave Macmillan, 2017), 49–79.

29. Cay-Rüdiger Prüll, "Die Bedeutung des Ersten Weltkrieges für die Medizin im Nationalsozialismus," in *Nationalsozialismus und Erster Weltkrieg*, ed. Gerd Krumeich (Essen: Klartext, 2010), 364.

30. Hans-Georg Hofer, *Nervenschwäche und Krieg: Modernitätskritik und Krisenbewältigung in der österreichischen Psychiatrie (1880–1920)* (Vienna: Böhlau, 2004), especially 326.

31. Prüll, "Die Bedeutung," 365–66.

32. Doris Kaufmann, for example, calls the episode "highly significant for the scientific legitimation and acceptance of some practices of later National Socialist population policy." "Science as Cultural Practice: Psychiatry in the First World War and Weimar Germany," *Journal of Contemporary History* 34, no. 1 (1999): 142.

33. On the "research controversy" over this issue, see Babette Quinkert, Philipp Rauh, and Ulrike Winkler, "Einleitung," in *Krieg und Psychiatrie 1914–1950*, ed. Babette Quinkert, Philipp Rauh, and Ulrike Winkler (Göttingen: Wallstein, 2010), 15.

34. Paul Lerner, *Hysterical Men: War, Psychiatry, and the Politics of Trauma in Germany, 1890–1930* (Ithaca, NY: Cornell University Press, 2003).

35. Ibid., especially 4–6.

36. Cay-Rüdiger Prüll, "Rationale Therapie oder Unmenschlichkeit? Die deutsche Psychiatrie und die Behandlung der Soldaten im Ersten Weltkrieg," *Praxis: Schweizerische Rundschau für Medizin* 89 (2000): 1073–1082.

37. Lerner, *Hysterical Men*, 3. Other scholars focusing on more general trends have also indicated that rough treatment of traumatized soldiers was a European-wide phenomenon. See Joanna Bourke, "Suffering and the Healing Profession: The Experience of Military Medicine in the First and Second World Wars," in *War and Medicine*, ed. Melissa Larner, James Peto, and Nadine Monem (London: Black Dog, 2008), 108–25.

38. Lerner, *Hysterical Men*, especially 138–39.

39. Ibid., 113–23.

40. Ibid., for example, 106, 161.

41. Ibid., 7.

42. Ibid., 71.

43. Ibid., for example, 64, 137.

44. Ibid., 4.

45. Philipp Rauh, "Die militärpsychiatrischen Therapiemethoden im Ersten Weltkrieg—Diskurs und Praxis," in *"Heroische Therapien": Die deutsche Psychiatrie im internationalen Vergleich, 1918–1945*, ed. Hans-Walter Schmuhl und Volker Roelcke (Göttingen: Wallstein, 2013), 29.

46. The first report came in the article "What the Patient Records Reveal: Reassessing the Treatment of 'War Neurotics' in Germany (1914–1918)," in *War, Trauma and Medicine in Germany and Central Europe (1914–1939)*, ed. Georg Hofer, Livia Prüll, and Wolfgang Eckart (Freiburg: Centarus, 2011), 139–59. Peckl's subsequent article (for the volume that included research from the larger project) presented more detail but largely related the same findings. "Krank durch die 'seelischen Einwirkungen des Feldzuges'? Psychische Erkrankungen der Soldaten im Ersten Welkrieg und ihre Behandlung," in *Krieg und medikale Kultur: Patientenschicksale und ärztliches Handeln in der Zeit der Weltkrieg, 1914–1945*, ed. Livia Prüll and Philipp Rauh (Göttingen: Wallstein, 2014), 30–89. The extant data and arguments have since been reproduced in work by Prüll and Rauh, who focused on different issues in the initial volume but were also partners in the larger project. See, for example, Rauh and Prüll, "Krank durch den Krieg? Der Umgang mit psychisch kranken Veteranen in Deutschland in der Zeit der Weltkriege," in *Psychische Versehrungen im Zeitalter der Weltkriege*, ed. Gundula Gahlen, Wencke Meteling, and Christoph Nübel (Chemnitz: Portal Militärgeschichte, 2015), https://doi.org/10.15500/akm.24.06.2015.

47. See, for example, Peckl, "Patient Records," 151, 154–55; Peckl, "Krank," 63, 78.

48. Peckl, "Patient Records," 157; Peckl, "Krank," 72, 76.

49. Peckl, "Patient Records," 15–17; Peckl, "Krank," 79.

50. Hermes, *Krankheit: Krieg.*

51. Ibid., 220–21.

52. See, for example, ibid., 450–54.

53. Ibid., 135, 138, 148, 155–56, 159, 212, 460, 465.

54. Ibid., 315, 332. Peckl's analysis largely sidesteps the issue of timing. Similarly, she also indicates the importance of not overrelying on diagnostic distinctions but oddly does that in some of her analysis. Most affirmative of Hermes's point on diagnostic fuzziness is Köhne's work, likely a result of her own inclusion of a few dozen patient files among her sources. Köhne, *Kriegshysteriker.*

55. Hermes, *Krankheit: Krieg*, 68.

56. Köhne, "Screening Silent Resistance," especially 53–55. While Köhne also uses the term "agency" to describe the actions of the soldiers, she notably offers a definition (74) that does not include reference to intentions or goals. This is a problematic omission, at least as it concerns understanding the soldiers as actors. For more on the extensive debate and literature around how to define this concept, see Mustafa Emirbayer and Ann Mische, "What Is Agency?," *American Journal of Sociology* 103 (1998): 962–1023.

57. Peckl does not address dissent directly but focuses on the lack of harsh treatment and the recognition that war experiences could contribute to trauma, a finding that will be discussed below. She sees this time for recuperation without harsh treatments and the general recognition by doctors that many of these men deserved pensions for their trauma as providing a certain level of protection to patients that has heretofore largely been overlooked. Hermes, on the other hand, does explicitly note dissent (especially in the much-neglected realm of desertion) and directly connects up the possibility that a diagnosis of mental incompetence could protect the soldier in question. See Peckl, "Krank," 87; Hermes, *Krankheit: Krieg*, 248, 341–58.

58. Hermes, *Krankheit: Krieg*, 135, 148, 210–14. Peckl's publications do not comment on this issue in particular. But the articles have been set in volumes that have more generally presented themselves as proponents of the continuity argument from one world war to the next. In the volume that presented the overarching findings of the project Peckl was part of, for example, Prüll and Rauh asserted, "Hence, this book describes the history of a continued brutalization of German military medicine." "Militär und medikale Kultur in Deutschland 1914–1945. Eine Einleitung," in Prüll and Rauh, *Krieg und medikale Kultur*, 28. A similar close connection is argued by Rauh and Prüll in "Krank durch den Krieg?"

59. See, for example, the sad case of Kaspar W. discussed in chapter 2.

60. Ann Goldberg portrays an even larger cast of actors who were watching and could potentially become involved as part of a growing public concern with psychiatric care that did not go unnoticed by even parliament. "A Reinvented Public: 'Lunatic Rights' and Bourgeois Populism in the *Kaiserreich*," *German History* 21, no. 2 (2003): especially 159–61, 170. See also Dirk Blasius, *"Einfache Seelenstörung": Geschichte der deutsche Psychiatrie 1800–1945* (Frankfurt am Main: Fischer, 1994), 88–90, 111.

61. See, for example, Kaufmann, "Science as Cultural Practice," 139.

62. Though Peckl does not stress these findings, she suggests that average military doctors understood the connection between wartime trauma and hysteria, a conclusion that indicates disagreement in this area among even the recent patient-file-based research. See "Krank," 88.

63. Francisca Loetz, "Medikalisierung in Frankreich, Grossbritanien und Deutschland, 1750–1850: Ansätze, Ergebnisse und Perspektiven der Forschung," in *Das europäische Gesundheitssystem: Gemeinsamkeiten und Unterschiede in historischer Perspektive*, ed.

Wolfgang U. Eckart and Robert Jütte (Stuttgart: Steiner, 1994), 130, 148–50; Eberhard Wolff, "Medikalisierung von unten? Das Beispiel der jüdischen Krankenbesuchgesellschaften," in *Zwischen Aufklärung, Policey und Verwaltung: Zur Genese des Medizinalwesens 1750–1850*, ed. Bettina Wahrig and Werner Sohn (Wiesbaden: Harrassowitz Verlag, 2003), 179–80, 190; Wolfgang Eckart and Robert Jütte, *Medizingeschichte: Eine Einführung*, 2nd ed. (Köln: Böhlau Verlag GmbH und Cie, 2014), 19, 175–76. All three works also have short discussions of different ways in which the term itself has been defined and applied. A further consideration of the uses and limits of the term "medicalization" will be undertaken in chapter 1.

64. Mark Harrison, "The Medicalization of War—the Militarization of Medicine," *Social History of Medicine* 9, no. 2 (1996): 267–76.

65. Roy Porter, "The Patient's View: Doing Medical History from Below," *Theory and Society* 14, no. 2 (1985): 175–98.

66. Condrau, "Patient's View." A more optimistic view of the work done on patient history, though still noting the limits as well as discussing the overarching impact theories stressing control have had on research, is Alexandra Bacopoulous-Viau and Aude Fauvel, "The Patient's Turn: Roy Porter and Psychiatry's Tales, Thirty Years On," *Medical History* 60, no. 1 (2016): 1–18. On antipsychiatry more generally, see Nick Crossley, "R. D. Laing and the British Anti-psychiatry Movement: A Socio-historical Analysis," *Social Science & Medicine* 47 (1998): 877–89.

67. Wolfram Wette, "Militärgeschichte von unten," in *Krieg des kleinen Mannes: Eine Militärgeschichte von unten*, ed. Wolfram Wette (Munich: Piper, 1992), 9.

68. Dorothy Porter and Roy Porter, *Patient's Progress: Doctors and Doctoring in Eighteenth-Century England* (Stanford, CA: Stanford University Press, 1989), 15, quoted in Eckart and Jütte, *Medizingeschichte*, 348; on soldiers, see Benjamin Ziemann, "Verweigerungsformen von Frontsoldaten in der deutschen Armee 1914–1918," in *Gewalt im Krieg: Ausübung, Erfahrung und Verweigerung von Gewalt in Kriegen des 20: Jahrhunderts*, ed. Andreas Gestrich (Münster: Lit, 1996), 100.

69. For an insightful overview of many key concepts and trends in the field, see Rachel Adams, Benjamin Reiss, and David Serlin, eds., *Keywords for Disability Studies* (New York: New York University Press, 2015). Also particularly enlightening of the approach taken by scholars in disability studies is the article by Susan Burch: "Disorderly Pasts: Kinship, Diagnoses, and Remembering in American Indian-U.S. Histories," *Journal of Social History* 50 (2016): 362–85.

70. Sander L. Gilman, "Madness," in Adams, Reiss, and Serlin, *Keywords for Disability Studies*, 118; Licia Carlson, "Institutions," in Adams, Reiss, and Serlin, *Keywords for Disability Studies*, 109.

71. Susan Burch and Kim E. Nielsen, "History," in Adams, Reiss, and Serlin, *Keywords for Disability Studies*, 95–97; Susannah B. Mintz, "Invisibility," in Adams, Reiss, and Serlin, *Keywords for Disability Studies*, 113. A work in the field of disability studies that also deals with conscientious objectors and psychiatric patients is Stephen J. Taylor's *Acts of Conscience: World War II, Mental Institutions, and Religious Objectors* (Syracuse, NY: Syracuse University Press, 2009). Here, the same emphasis on uncovering the histories of the overlooked and forgotten is at work, though in quite a different configuration. Unlike Germans in World War I, the American objectors were not medicalized

and institutionalized but allowed to work in psychiatric hospitals as civilians in lieu of military service.

72. An early foundational text on this topic is the work of Talcot Parsons, *The Social System* (1951; Abingdon, UK: Routledge, 1991), especially chapter 10. See also Eckart and Jütte, *Medizingeschichte*, 350.

73. On the psychiatrist Karl Bonhoeffer and "war reluctance," for example, see Eckart, "Kriegsgewalt und Psychotrauma im Ersten Weltkrieg," 95; on Max Nonne and "those refusing service," see Prüll, "Die Bedeutung des Ersten Weltkrieges," 367.

74. Blasius, *"Einfache Seelenstörung,"* 88–90, 111; Goldberg, "Reinvented Public," 175.

75. Quote from Riedesser and Verderber, *Aufrüstung*, 20; Elaine Showalter, *The Female Malady: Women, Madness, and English Culture 1830–1980* (New York: Pantheon, 1985), especially chapters 6 and 7; Eric J. Leed, *No Man's Land: Combat & Identity in World War I* (Cambridge: Cambridge University Press, 1979), chapter 5. Hermes also picks up this point in her analysis, *Krankheit: Krieg*, 353.

76. Both Wolfram Wette and Paul Lerner seem to be suggesting this odd echoing as well by their reference to Freud's similar explanations of wartime mental illness. Wette, "Militärgeschichte von unten," 24; Lerner, *Hysterical Men*, 7.

77. Ziemann, "Verweigerungsformen," 110–11. While Wette's article is extremely valuable for the emphasis it places on soldier agency, it is also telling that the entire issue of mental illness and dissent is discussed in only two paragraphs. Wette also notes simulation of mental illness as a method of dissent. "Militärgeschichte von unten," 25.

78. Eckart and Jütte, *Medizingeschichte*, 201.

79. Ziemann, for example, refers to those simulating mental illness as a "certainly appreciable part," though he offers no statistics. While he may have more of a point if considering cases from the very end of the war, at which time dissent grew so considerably to include even open mutiny, the most recent literature on wartime psychiatry (noted above) does not suggest that physicians were overly concerned with malingerers, nor do the actual patient files suggest this either. See Ziemann, "Verweigerungsformen," 110. Of course, the limits of important approaches like those of Showalter can easily be seen when considering the theoretical nature of their universal explanations and the reality of hundreds of thousands of cases of soldiers treated for nervous disorders during the war.

80. For a general overview of these trends, see Bacopoulos-Viau and Fauvel, "The Patient's Turn."

81. Along similar lines, Ann Goldberg's nuanced book "treats the patients and their communities as historical agents in their own right, not merely as the objects of hegemonic discourses." *Sex, Religion, and the Making of Modern Madness: The Eberbach Asylum and German Society 1815–1849* (New York: Oxford University Press, 1999), 8.

82. A small portion of the files are typed. In either case, one can see that even in a single document within one file multiple perspectives sometimes appear. Different doctors might add commentary in the margins, or an individual might even cross out and rewrite his own text. Sometimes the changes were minimal, but at other times the alterations could be significant.

83. Porter, "Patient's View," especially 183. Similarly, see Salina Braun's discussion: *Heilung mit Defekt: Psychiatrisches Praxis an den Anstalten Hofheim und Siegburg, 1820–1878*

(Göttingen: Vandenhoeck & Ruprecht, 2008), 32–37, 386–91; Allan Beveridge, "Voices of the Mad: Patient Letters from the Royal Edinburgh Asylum, 1873–1908," *Psychological Medicine* 27, no. 4 (1997): especially 900–01, 907; Martin Scharfe, "Briefe aus dem Irrenhaus: Selbstzeugnisse von Patientinnen aus der Frühzeit der Marburger Anstalt," in *Heilbar und nützlich: Ziele und Wege der Psychiatrie in Marburg an der Lahn*, ed. Peter Sander, Gerhard Aumüller, and Christina Vanja (Marburg: Jonas, 2001).

84. For an overview of scholarship that has drawn on patient files and ego documents extensively, see Eckart and Jütte, *Medizingeschichte*, 198–99; Bacopoulos-Viau and Fauvel, "The Patient's Turn."

1. Antecedents

1. August Fauser, "Über die Bedeutung der neueren Entwicklung der Psychiatrie für die gerichtliche Medizin," *Juristisch-psychiatrische Grenzfragen* 2 (1904): 73.

2. Ibid., 69.

3. Ibid., 75.

4. This division among the practitioners caring for the mentally ill in the nineteenth century will be discussed in more detail below. For an insightful account, see Eric Engstrom, *Clinical Psychiatry in Imperial Germany: A History of Psychiatric Practice* (Ithaca, NY: Cornell University Press, 2003).

5. Fauser, "Über die Bedeutung," 70.

6. Erwin Ackerknecht, *A Short History of Psychiatry*, 2nd rev. ed., trans. Sula Wolff (New York: Hafner, 1968), 82.

7. Ibid., 82.

8. Richard Noll, "The Blood of the Insane," *History of Psychiatry* 17 (2006): 406–9. While Fauser's work on finding a simple test for schizophrenia did not bear fruit, one must also view such efforts in the context of the real contemporary advances surrounding the understanding and treatment of general paralysis of the insane (GPI), resulting from late-stage syphilis, in connection with the development of the Wasserman Test (1906) and the drug Salvarsan (1909). Around the turn of the century, up to a third of all patients in psychiatric institutions suffered from GPI, a condition that many physicians suspected might be somehow linked to syphilis but that had no definitive cause known for many decades. See Kelley Swain, "'Extraordinarily Arduous and Fraught with Danger': Syphilis, Salvarsan, and General Paresis of the Insane," *The Lancet: Psychiatry* 5 (2018): 687–768; Ackerknecht, *Short History of Psychiatry*, 75.

9. Eric J. Engstrom, "Assembling Professional Selves: On Psychiatric Instruction in Imperial Germany," in *Psychiatrie im 19. Jahrhundert. Forschungen zur Geschichte von psychiatrischen Institutionen, Debatten und Praktiken im deutschen Sprachraum*, ed. Eric J. Engstrom and Volker Roelcke (Basel: Schwabe Verlag, 2003), 133; Heinz-Peter Schmiedebach, "Sozialdarwinismus, Biologismus, Pazifismus—Ärztestimmen zum Erstenweltkrieg," in *Medizin und Krieg: Vom Dilemma der Heilberufe 1865–1985*, ed. Johanna Blecker and Heinz-Peter Schmiedebach (Frankfurt am Main: Fischer, 1987), 96–99; Roy Porter, *Madness: A Brief History* (Oxford: Oxford University Press, 2002), 118. On "crisis" specifically, see Martin Lengwiler, "Psychiatry beyond the Asylum: The Origins of

German Military Psychiatry before World War I," *History of Psychiatry* 14, no. 1 (2003): 46. Engstrom also refers to a "crisis" in German psychiatry, though this particular reference to diagnostic difficulties is linked to an earlier decade. *Clinical Psychiatry in Imperial Germany*, 29.

10. Lerner, *Hysterical Men*, 15 (Ackerknecht quoted on page 17).

11. Here Engstrom and Roelcke are speaking specifically about the rise of psychiatry's standing and at the same time the increased criticism it faced, but the point is more generally applicable to the positives and negatives at the turn of the century. "Die 'alte Psychiatrie'? Zur Geschichte und Aktualität der Psychiatrie im 19. Jahrhundert," in Engstrom and Roelcke, *Psychiatrie im 19. Jahrhundert*, 23. A similar point is made by Schmiedebach, "Sozialdarwinismus," 99; and Ann Goldberg, "The Mellage Trial and the Politics of Insane Asylums in Wilhelmine Germany," *Journal of Modern History* 74, no. 1 (2002): 2.

12. Ackerknecht, *Short History of Psychiatry*, 29–34; Blasius, *"Einfache Seelenstörung,"* 15–19; Porter, *Madness*, 108; Engstrom, *Clinical Psychiatry*, 23.

13. Michael Viszanik, *Irrenheil- und Pflegeanstalten Deutschlands, Frankreichs, sammt der Cretinen-Anstalt auf dem Abendherberg in der Schweiz, mit eigenen Bemerkungen* (Wien: Verlag von Carl Gerold, 1845), 142-64 (quote from 143). On Siegburg, see also Blasius, *"Einfache Seelenstörung,"* 24–40; Fritz Dross, "'. . . die Gemüse könnten füglich irgendwo anders gereinigt werden'—Beobachtungen zur Geschichte der Anstalt als Irren- und als Krankenhaus," in *"Moderne" Anstaltspsychiatrie im 19. und 20. Jahrhundert—Legitimation und Kritik*, ed. Heiner Fangerau and Karen Nolte (Stuttgart: Franz Steiner Verlag, 2006), 55-9; Braun, *Heilung mit Defekt.*

14. Porter, *Madness*, 112; Engstrom, *Clinical Psychiatry*, 17; Goldberg, "Mellage Trial," especially 6; Hermes, *Krankheit: Krieg*, 83; Prüll, "Rationale Therapie," 1076. For the raw numerical data on institutions, patients, and beds, see Blasius, *"Einfache Seelenstörung,"* 64; Hans Ludwig Siemen, *Menschen bleiben auf der Strecke . . . Psychiatrie zwischen Reform und Nationalsozialismus* (Gütersloh: Verlag Jakob-van-Hoddis, 1987), 23–24. Siemen also notes that the increased numbers receiving care in institutions rose faster than the general population increase. Out of every 10,000, the number of people receiving care rose from 10.6 in 1880 to 35.8 in 1913.

15. Engstrom, "Assembling Professional Selves," 132; Blasius, *"Einfache Seelenstörung,"* 19, 22, 69–70; Porter, *Madness*, 97; Engstrom, *Clinical Psychiatry*, 54–65; Goldberg, "Mellage Trial," 18; Ackerknecht, *Short History of Psychiatry*, 29, 83 (on fashionability of nervousness); Goldberg, "Reinvented Public," 163. On "nervousness" in Germany, see also Joachim Radkau, *Das Zeitalter der Nervosität: Deutschland Zwischen Bismarck und Hitler* (Munich: Carl Hanser Verlag, 1998). For a somewhat different view, see Michael Cowan, *Cult of the Will: Nervousness and German Modernity* (University Park, PA: Penn State University Press, 2008).

16. Geoffrey Cocks and Konrad H. Jarausch, eds., *German Professions, 1800–1950* (New York: Oxford University Press, 1990), especially 9–11; Claudia Huerkamp, "The Making of the Modern Medical Profession, 1800–1914: Prussian Doctors in the Nineteenth Century," in Cocks and Jarausch, *German Professions*, especially 68–71; Charles E. McClelland, *The German Experience of Professionalization: Modern Learned Professions and Their Organizations from the Early Nineteenth Century to the Hitler Era* (Cambridge:

Cambridge University Press, 1991), 9–10; Engstrom, "Assembling Professional Selves," 118–19; Engstrom, *Clinical Psychiatry*, 6–7; Blasius, *"Einfache Seelenstörung,"* 53, 58; Goldberg, "Mellage Trial," 6, 13–14; Ackerknecht, *Short History of Psychiatry*, 29–30; Porter, *Madness*, 97.

17. Engstrom, *Clinical Psychiatry*, 4, 68–69; Volker Roelcke, "Continuities or Ruptures? Concepts, Institutions and Contexts of Twentieth-Century German Psychiatry and Mental Health Care," in *Psychiatric Cultures Compared: Psychiatry and Mental Health Care in the Twentieth Century*, ed. Marijke Gijswijt-Hofstra, Harry Oosterhuis, Joost Vijselaar, and Hugh Freeman (Amsterdam: Amsterdam University Press, 2005), 164; Blasius, *"Einfache Seelenstörung,"* 47.

18. Engstrom, "Assembling Professional Selves," 119; Engstrom, *Clinical Psychiatry*, 151; Albrecht Hirschmüller, "The Development of Psychiatry and Neurology in the Nineteenth Century," trans. Madga Whitrow, *History of Psychiatry* 10 (1999): 400; Porter, *Madness*, 139.

19. Hirschmüller, "Psychiatry and Neurology," 405–7; Porter, *Madness*, 145; Engstrom, *Clinical Psychiatry*, 69, 108; Lerner, *Hysterical Men*, 16.

20. Ackerknecht, *Short History of Psychiatry*, 63. Ackerknecht notes the terms originated with Karl Jaspers. On this shift, see also Engstrom, *Clinical Psychiatry*, especially 148–63.

21. For the most comprehensive and nuanced account of this entire process, see Engstrom, *Clinical Psychiatry*. See also Ann Goldberg, *Honor, Politics, and the Law in Imperial Germany, 1871–1914* (Cambridge: Cambridge University Press, 2010), 170; Huerkamp, "Modern Medical Profession," 69–71; Schmiedebach, "Sozialdarwinismus," 93; Hirschmüller, "Psychiatry and Neurology," 405; Engstrom, "Assembling Professional Selves," 149; Ackerknecht, *Short History of Psychiatry*, 60; Paul Weindling, "Bourgeois Values, Doctors and the State: The Professionalization of Medicine in Germany 1848–1933," in *The German Bourgeoisie: Essays on the Social History of the German Middle Class from the Late Eighteenth to the Early Twentieth Century*, ed. David Blackbourn and Richard J. Evans (New York: Routledge, 1991), 216.

22. The contemporary meaning and usage of the terms "psychopath" and "psychopathic inferiority" will be discussed further in chapter 4. See also Richard F. Wetzell, "Psychiatry and Criminal Justice in Modern Germany, 1880–1933," *Journal of European Studies* 39, no. 3 (2009): (for quote) 273, 277; Wetzell, *Inventing the Criminal: A History of German Criminology, 1880–1945* (Chapel Hill: University of North Carolina Press, 2000), 49–68; Goldberg, "Mellage Trial," 11; Ulrich Bröckling, "Psychopathische Minderwertigkeit? Moralischer Schwachsinn? Krankhafter Wandertrieb? Zur Pathologisierung von Deserteuren im Deutschen Kaiserreich vor 1914," in *Armeen und ihre Deserteure: Vernachlässigte Kapitel einer Militärgeschichte der Neuzeit*, ed. Ulrich Bröckling and Michael Sikora (Göttingen: Vandenhoeck & Ruprecht, 1998), 166–67; Heinz-Peter Schmiedebach, "Zum Verständniswandel der 'psychopathische' Störungen am Anfang der naturwissenschaftlichen Psychiatrie in Deutschland," *Nervenarzt* 56 (1985): 140–45.

23. On the use of the specific term "grey zone," see Bröckling, "Psychopathische Minderwertigkeit?," 167. More generally, see Wetzell, "Psychiatry and Criminal Justice," 277; Goldberg, "Reinvented Public," 161; Schmiedebach, "Socialdarwinismus," 94–99; Weindling, "Bourgeois Values," especially 198–200; Huerkamp, "Modern Medical Profession," 73.

24. Wetzell, "Psychiatry and Criminal Justice," especially 271–73; Wetzell, *Inventing the Criminal*, 40–46; Lengwiler, "Psychiatry beyond the Asylum," 41, 47; Goldberg, "Mellage Trial," 13; Doris Kaufmann, "Psychiatrie und Strafjustiz im 19. Jahrhundert: die gerichtsmedizinischen Gutachten der Medizinischen Fakultät der Universität Tübingen 1770–1860," *Medizin, Gesellschaft und Geschichte* 10 (1991): especially 25–32; Urs Germann, "'Entmündung der Fachjustiz' oder 'Reserveengel der Jurisprudenz'? Psychiatrische Deutungsmacht im Kontext justizieller Entscheidungsprozesse. Das Beispiel der gerichtspsychiatrischen Begutungspraxis im Kanton Bern 1885–1920," in Engstrom and Roelcke, *Psychiatrie im 19. Jahrhundert*, 224.

25. Eric Engstrom, "Topographies of Forensic Practice in Imperial Germany," *International Journal of Law and Psychiatry* 37, no. 1 (2014): especially 63, 65.

26. Ann Goldberg, "The Limits of Medicalization: Jewish Lunatics and Nineteenth-Century Germany," *History of Psychiatry* 7 (1996): 265–85. Another important and nuanced discussion of the continued relevance of nonmedical paradigms in understanding criminality can be found in Warren Rosenblum, *Beyond the Prison Gates: Punishment and Welfare in Germany, 1850–1933* (Chapel Hill: University of North Carolina Press, 2008).

27. Wetzell, *Inventing the Criminal*, especially 40. See also Wetzell, "Psychiatry and Criminal Justice," especially 283–85.

28. Kaufmann, "Psychiatrie und Strafjustiz," especially 29–32; (on Switzerland but with comparison to Germany) Germann, "Entmündung"; Lengwiler, "Psychiatry beyond the Asylum," 55–56; Goldberg, "Mellage Trial," 13. The cases reviewed for this book in which the ultimate judicial outcome is known also support this conclusion.

29. Lengwiler, "Psychiatry beyond the Asylum," 57. On the extent to which the debate over medicalization turns on issues of definition or how high the "bar" is set, see Wetzell, "Psychiatry and Criminal Justice," 283–85. Here one might note that the term at its most fundamental level indicates conceptualizing behaviors and concerns within a medical paradigm—in other words, as health issues under the purview of doctors. Whether this must imply a negative evaluation of the behaviors, the extent to which such processes are promoted from above or below, and the degree to which concomitant developments like professionalization of medicine are involved are all matters of definitional debate. Eckart and Jütte, *Medizingeschichte*, 347–48; Nicholas Abercrombie, Stephen Hill, and Bryan S. Turner, *The Penguin Dictionary of Sociology*, 3rd ed. (London: Penguin, 1994), 262; Peter Conrad, "Medicalization and Social Control," *Annual Review of Sociology* 18 (1992): 209–32; Sayantani DasGupta, "Medicalization," in Adams, Reiss, and Serlin, *Keywords for Disability Studies*, 120–21; Peter Conrad and Joseph W. Schneider, *Deviance and Medicalization: From Badness to Sickness* (Columbus, OH: Merrill, 1985); Emilia Kaczmarek, "How to Distinguish Medicalization from Over-Medicalization," *Medicine, Health Care and Philosophy* 22 (2019): 119–28, doi:10.1007/s11019-018-9850-1. For a different aspect of the debate surrounding medicalization, see the short discussion in the introduction.

30. Though overrepresented among antipsychiatry activists, these jurists must have been the exception among their own profession more generally given the overall numbers of the antipsychiatry movement. See Goldberg, "Mellage Trial," especially 10–15; and Goldberg, "Reinvented Public." For an even more expansive view of the antipsychiatry

movement that also includes information on other countries, see Schmiedebach, who makes the significant point that the name antipsychiatry is problematic, as most of the movement's criticism did not question the science of psychiatry itself, at times even pushing for greater dissemination of the specialized knowledge to general physicians, for example. "Eine 'antipsychiatrische Bewegung,' um die Jahrhundertwende," in *Medizinkritische Bewegungen im Deutschen Reich (ca. 1870-ca. 1933)*, ed. Mirtin Dinges (Stuttgart: Franz Steiner Verlag, 1996), especially 129–30, 133, 135–37. See also Blasius, *"Einfache Seelenstörung,"* especially 111–13; Engstrom and Roelcke, "Die 'alte Psychiatrie'?," 23.

31. Bröckling, "Psychopathische Minderwertigkeit?," 171. On the process in the military courts more generally, see Lengwiler, "Psychiatry beyond the Asylum," 54–57.

32. Kaufmann, "Science as Cultural Practice," 132.

33. Franz Lemmers, "Zur Entwickelung der Militärpsychiatrie in Deutschland zwischen 1870 und 1918," *Abhandlungen zur Geschichte der Medizin und der Naturwissenschaften* 69 (1994): 35, 42; Katarzyna Norkowska, "Der Dichter in der Uniform: Gottfried Benns Verhältnis zum Militär," in *Benn Forum: Beiträge zur literarischen Moderne*, ed. Joachim Dyck, Hermann Korte, and Nadine Jessica Schmidt (Berlin: De Gruyter, 2001), 115; Mark Harrison, "War and Medicine in the Modern Era," in *War and Medicine*, ed. Melissa Larner, James Peto, and Nadine Monem (London: Black Dog, 2008), 10–27; Harrison, "Medicalization of War," especially 270–74; Lengwiler, "Psychiatry beyond the Asylum," 42; Lengwiler, "Auf dem Weg zur Sozialtechnologie: Die Bedeutung der frühen Militärpsychiatrie für die Professionalisierung der Psychiatrie in Deutschland," in Engstrom and Roelcke, *Psychiatrie im 19 Jahrhundert*, 246; Quinkert, Rauh, and Winkler, "Einleitung," 12; John G. Lorimer, "Why Would Modern Military Commanders Study the Franco-Prussian War?," *Defense Studies* 5 (2005): 108–9.

34. Lengwiler, "Psychiatry beyond the Asylum," 42.

35. Ibid., 45.

36. On military psychiatry and recruitment, see the informative articles by Lengwiler: "Psychiatry beyond the Asylum," especially 49–54; and "Auf dem Weg zur Sozialtechnologie," especially 248–60. See also Günter Komo, *"Für Volk und Vaterland": Die Militärpsychiatrie in den Weltkriegen* (Münster: Lit Verlag, 1992), especially 45–50. On the contradictions between the universal conscription idea and reality, see also Ute Frevert, *A Nation in Barracks: Modern Germany, Military Conscription and Civil Society* (Oxford: Berg, 2004), especially 54–55, 71, 90–91, 179.

37. Harrison, "Medicalization of War," 272; Christian Kliche, "Die Stellung der deutschen Militärärzte im Ersten Weltkrieg" (PhD diss., FU-Berlin, 1968), especially 2, 5, 28, 41–42; Lengwiler, "Auf dem Weg zur Sozialtechnologie," 260; Lengwiler, "Psychiatry beyond the Asylum," 41–42, 47; Komo, *"Für Volk und Vaterland,"* 53; Kaufmann, "Science as Cultural Practice," 132; Riedesser and Verderber, *Aufrüstung*, 10.

38. Lengwiler, "Psychiatry beyond the Asylum," especially 47.

39. Ibid., 50–51; Frevert, *Nation in Barracks*, 40, 59–61, 154–55, 158; David Blackbourn, *The Fontana History of Germany, 1780–1918: The Long Nineteenth Century* (London: Fontana, 1997), 375–77; Isabel V. Hull, *Absolute Destruction: Military Culture and the Practices of War in Imperial Germany* (Ithaca, NY: Cornell University Press, 2005), 103–7; Wilhelm Deist, *Militär, Staat und Gesellschaft: Studien zur preussisch-deutschen Militärgeschichte* (Munich: Oldenbourg, 1991), 31; Benjamin Ziemann, "Militarism," in *The*

Ashgate Research Companion to Imperial Germany, ed. Mathew Jeffries (Farnham: Ashgate, 2015), 376–81; Rosenblum, *Beyond the Prison Gates*, 27, 132–39. Rosenblum also notes that such exclusions were often overturned, either because military service could be seen as rehabilitation or because of military exigency during wartime.

40. Hull, *Absolute Destruction*, 104.

41. Blackbourn, *Fontana History of Germany*, 376. Bettina Brand-Claussen and Maike Rotzoll have examined the extent to which military habits and ideals permeated the culture of psychiatric institutions as well. "Uniform und Eigensinn: Reflexe des Militarismus in psychiatrischen Anstalten des deutschen Kaiserreichs," in *Schlachtschrecken-Konventionen: Das Rote Kreuz und die Erfindung der Menschlichkeit im Kriege*, ed. Wolfgang U. Eckart and Philipp Osten (Freiburg: Centaurus, 2011), 229–53.

42. Even if one were to use the term "militarism," it would be more appropriate to speak of "militarisms"—suggesting a variety of ways in which emphasis was placed on the preeminence of the military that could and did cut in a multiplicity of directions, not always serving the interests of conservative elites, as Benjamin Ziemann has astutely argued. Ziemann, "Militarism," 378–81; Ziemann, "'Der Hauptmann von Köpenick'—Symbol für den Sozialmilitarismus im wilhelmischen Deutschland?," in *Grenzüberschreitungen oder der Vermittler Bedrich Loewenstein. Festschrift zum 70. Geburtstag eines europäischen Historikers*, ed. Vilém Prečan, Milena Janišová, and Matthias Roeser (Prague: Institute for Contemporary History of the Academy of Sciences of the Czech Republic, 1999), 262, 264; Frevert, *Nation in Barracks*, especially 3, 23, 52–57, 82–83, 90–91, 103, 106, 109, 154–55, 167, 173, 182–83, 196–97, 219–21; Blackbourn, *Fontana History of Germany*, 375, 378–79, 383–84. On the role of military values and the association with manliness, see also chapter 4.

43. Roger Chickering, *Imperial Germany and a World without War: The Peace Movement and German Society, 1892–1914* (Princeton, NJ: Princeton University Press, 1975), 39–43.

44. At the time, Königsberg was part of Prussia; today it belongs to Russia and is known as Kaliningrad. Dieter Riesenberger, *Geschichte der Friendensbewegung in Deutschland: Von den Anfängen bis 1933* (Göttingen: Vandenhoeck & Ruprecht, 1985), 7, 23, 33, 66–69, 73, 85; Helmut Kramer and Wolfram Wette, "Pazifisten im Visier der Justiz. Ein bedrückendes Kapitel der deutschen Geschichte des 20. Jahrhunderts," in *Recht ist, was den Waffen nützt: Justiz und Pazifismus im 20. Jahrhundert*, ed. Helmut Kramer and Wolfram Wette (Berlin: Aufbau-Verlag, 2004), 17; Karlheinz Lipp, *Pazifismus in der Pfalz vor und während des Ersten Weltkrieges: Ein Lesebuch* (Nordhausen: Verlag Traugott Bautz, 2015), 7; Christian Jansen, "Pazifismus in Deutschland. Entwicklung und innere Widersprüche (1800–1940)," in Kramer and Wette, *Recht ist, was den Waffen nützt*, 61–63; Helene Stöcker, "Kriegsdienstverweigerung" (orig. 1922), in *Die Friedensbewegung; ein Handbuch der Weltfriedensströmungen der Gegenwart*, ed. Walter Fabian and Kurt Lenz (Cologne: Bund, 1985), 120; Chickering, *World without War*, 13, 46–66, 74–75, 241, 262; Guido Grünewald, *Nieder die Waffen! Hundert Jahre Deutsche Friedensgesellschaft 1892–1992* (Bremen: Donat, 1992), 16; Wolfram Wette, *Ernstfall Frieden: Lehren aus der deutschen Geschichte seit 1914* (Bremen: Donat, 2017), 88; James D. Shand, "Doves among the Eagles: German Pacifists and Their Government during World War I," *Journal of Contemporary History* 10 (1975): 96.

45. Chickering, *World without War*, 38–39.

46. Interestingly, Ziemann notes that Fried, although he was born in Vienna, "felt" German. Benjamin Ziemann, "German Pacifism in the Nineteenth and Twentieth Centuries," *Neue Politische Literatur* 60, no. 3 (2015): 419; Chickering, *World without War*, 12, 38–39, 43, 46–66, 79; Brian Orend, "Kant's Just War Theory," *Journal of the History of Philosophy* 37, no. 2 (1999): especially 323–25; Iain Atack, "Pacifism and Perpetual Peace," *Critical Studies on Security* 6, no. 2 (2018): 207–20; Jansen, "Pazifismus," 61; Riesenberger, *Geschichte der Friedensbewegung*, 9, 17–18; Peter van den Dungen, "Achievements of Peace Movements," in *Twentieth-Century Peace Movements: Successes and Failures*, ed. Guido Grünewald and Peter van den Dungen (Lewiston, NY: Edwin Mellen Press, 1995), 16; Jürgen Schreiber, "Kriegsdienstverweigerung: Eine historische und rechtsvergleichende Untersuchung" (Doctoral diss., Universität Bonn, 1952), 50; Grünewald, *Nieder die Waffen*, 11.

47. Kramer and Wette, "Pazifisten," 16–17; Chickering, *World without War*, 31, 48; Guido Grünewald, *Zur Geschichte der Kriegsdienstverweigerung* (Essen: Deutsche Friedensgesellschaft, 1982), 8, 12; Dungen, "Achievements," 22; Karl Holl, "Why Do Peace Movements Fail?," in Grünewald and Dungen, *Twentieth-Century Peace Movements*, 5; Karl Holl, "Pazifismus," in *Geschichtliche Grundbegriffe: Historisches Lexikon zur politisch-sozialen Sprache in Deutschland*, Bd. 4, ed. Otto Brunner, Werner Conze, and Reinhart Koselleck (Stuttgart: Klett-Cotta, 1978), 767–72, 781, 786; Peter Brock, *Pacifism in Europe to 1914* (Princeton, NJ: Princeton University Press, 1972), especially 472; Karl-Heinz Stahnke, "Die Kriegsdienstverweigerung in der Literatur," *Jahresbibliographie der Bibliothek für Zeitgeschichte* 35 (1963): 510. For more on the shifts in the meaning of pacifism, see chapter 4.

48. For more on Mennonites and conscientious objection, see Benjamin Goossen, *Chosen Nation: Mennonites and Germany in a Global Era* (Princeton, NJ: Princeton University Press, 2017); for background on Quaker objections, see Claus Bernet, "Kriegsdienstverweigerung im 19. Jahrhundert: Ein Beitrag zum Klischee des Militärstaats Preußen," *Militär und Gesellschaft in der Frühen Neuzeit* 12, no. 2 (2008): 204–22; Hellmuth Hecker, *Die Kriegsdienstverweigerung im deutschen und ausländischen Recht mit Übersetzung der ausländischen Texte* (Frankfurt am Main: Alfred Metzner Verlag, 1954), 9–10; Günter Hahnenfeld, *Kriegsdienstverweigerung* (Hamburg: Decker's Verlag, 1966), 24–25; Grünewald, *Zur Geschichte der Kriegsdienstverweigerung*, 12; Goossen, *Chosen Nation*, 98; Brock, *Pacifism in Europe*, chapter 11; Bernet, "Kriegsdienstverweigerung im 19"; Bundesarchiv Freiburg (BAF) PH 2/729 "Heranziehung von Mennoniten u.a. Sekten zum Kriegsdienst.- Schriftwechsel."

49. Quote from *Die Friedens-Warte* 16 (1914), 307, quoted in Grünewald, *Nieder die Waffen*, 59. See also Chickering, *World without War*, especially 94, 122, 270–85; Ziemann, "German Pacifism," 419–21; Grünewald, *Zur Geschichte der Kriegsdienstverweigerung*, 12, 18; Grünewald, *Nider die Waffen*, 55–56, 58–59; Riesenberger, *Geschichte der Friedensbewegung*, 97–100; Jansen, "Pazifismus," 69; Shand, "Doves among the Eagles"; Lipp, *Pazifismus in der Pfalz*, 8–11; Roger Chickering, *Imperial Germany and the Great War, 1914–18*, 2nd ed. (Cambridge: Cambridge University Press, 2004), 13–16, 34, 46–50; Matthew Stibbe, *Germany, 1914–1933: Politics, Society and Culture* (New York: Routledge, 2013), 12; Rebecca Ayako Bennette, "Remapping the German Homeland: Germania and Cath-

olic Efforts to Mobilise Continued Support during the First World War," *Immigrants and Minorities* 35, no. 3 (2017): 238, 241.

50. For more on the idea of a "war of nerves," the massive numbers of traumatized soldiers during the war, the idea of shell shock as a form of dissent, and the agency some patients had to use illness to their own ends to avoid continued fighting, see chapter 2 and corresponding citations; on the use of expert psychiatric testimony in military court cases, the overwhelming medicalization of more explicit forms of dissent, and the effort to delegitimize such ideas, see especially chapters 3 and 4 as well as the cited literature.

2. Hysterics and Other Patients

1. Again, the account presented over the next few pages is largely standard across many different contributions to the literature. Several have already been mentioned in the introduction. See, for example, the extensive treatments of the topic by Paul Lerner, among others: Lerner, "From Traumatic Neurosis to Male Hysteria: The Decline and Fall of Hermann Oppenheim, 1889–1919," in *Traumatic Pasts: History, Psychiatry, and Trauma in the Modern Age, 1870–1930*, ed. Mark S. Micale and Paul Lerner (Cambridge: Cambridge University Press, 2001), 140–71; Lerner, *Hysterical Men*, especially chapters 2–4; Eckart, *Medizin und Krieg*, especially 138–56; Peckl, "Krank," 42–43; Kaufmann, "Science as Cultural Practice," 133–34. On the implications of the Accident Insurance Bill of 1884, see Greg A. Eghigian, "The German Welfare State as a Discourse of Trauma," in Micale and Lerner, *Traumatic Pasts*, 92–112. On phenomena like "railway spine" more generally, see Eric Michal Caplan, "Trains, Brains, and Sprains: Railway Spine and the Origins of Psychoneuroses," *Bulletin of the History of Medicine* 69, no. 3 (1995): 387–419.

2. There is a vast body of literature on this topic; many contributions are referred to here. More generally, see Ben Shepard, *A War of Nerves: Soldiers and Psychiatrists in the Twentieth Century* (Cambridge, MA: Harvard University Press, 2003). On Germany more specifically, see Bernd Ulrich, "Krieg als Nervensache," *Die Zeit*, November 22, 1991.

3. "Die Nerven der Feldgrauen," *Germania*, February 25, 1917.

4. See, for example, the advertisements in *Germania* on January 6, 1915; February 21, 1915; March 11, 1915; September 1, 1915; and October 5, 1915. Given the importance of nerves to German success, even Kaffee Hag pitched its decaffeinated brew as an accessible wartime aid (*Germania*, March 16, 1915).

5. On wartime censorship, see Chickering, *Imperial Germany and the Great War*, 46–50.

6. "Die Zunahme der Geisteskrankheiten in Frankreich durch den Krieg," *Germania*, February 10, 1915. On France as a foil, see Rebecca Ayako Bennette, *Fighting for the Soul of Germany: The Catholic Struggle for Inclusion after Unification* (Cambridge, MA: Harvard University Press, 2012), 167–69; Michael Jeismann, *Das Vaterland der Feinde: Studien zum nationalen Feindbegriff und Selbstverständnis in Deutschland und Frankreich, 1792–1918* (Stuttgart: Klett-Cotta, 1992); Berit Pleitner, *Die 'vernünftige' Nation: Zur Funktion von Stereotypen über Polen und Franzosen im deutschen nationalen Diskurs 1850 bis 1871* (Frankfurt am Main: Peter Lang, 2001).

7. George Mosse, *The Image of Man: The Creation of Modern Masculinity* (New York: Oxford University Press, 1996), especially 109–12; Sonja Levsen, "Masculinities," in *1914-1918-online. International Encyclopedia of the First World War*, ed. Ute Daniel, Peter Gatrell, Oliver Janz, Heather Jones, Jennifer Keene, Alan Kramer, and Bill Nasson, issued by Freie Universität Berlin, Berlin (updated January 7, 2015), doi:10.15463/ie1418.10531; Hofer, *Nervenschwäche und Krieg*, 41, 271–82.

8. Lerner, *Hysterical Men*, 7, 20–23, 52–54; Fischer-Homberger, "Der Begriff. 'Krankheit,'" 240–41; Peckl, "Krank," 49–50; Quinkert, Rauh, and Winkler, "Einleitung," 13; Schmiedebach, "Zum Verständniswandel," 145.

9. While Oppenheim's concept of traumatic neurosis was an obvious example of defining a disorder's etiology in both psychological and physical terms, the more general sense that conditions often arose from an interplay of mind and body issues could be seen in physicians' conceptions of other conditions common during the war as well. See Stefanos Geroulanos and Todd Meyers, *The Human Body in the Age of Catastrophe: Brittleness, Integration, Science, and the Great War* (Chicago: University of Chicago Press, 2018).

10. Lerner, *Hysterical Men*, 62.

11. Rauh, "Therapiemethoden," 32.

12. Lerner, *Hysterical Men*, 71.

13. Mosse, *Image of Man*, especially 109–12; Levsen, "Masculinities"; Hofer, *Nervenschwäche und Krieg*, 41, 271–82; Köhne, "Screening Silent Resistance," especially 50–51.

14. See especially chapter 5 in *Hysterical Men*. On the particular problem of visits home, see also 147.

15. Cay-Rüdiger Prüll, "Die Bedeutung," 367; Eckart, *Medizin und Krieg*, 147; Lerner, *Hysterical Men*, 52; Kaufmann, "Science as Cultural Practice," 142; Jörg Wagenblast, *Die Tübinger Militärpsychiatrie im Zweiten Weltkrieg* (Stuttgart: Franz Steiner Verlag, 2016), 30.

16. Lerner, "From Traumatic Neurosis"; Prüll, "Rationale Therapie oder Unmenschlichkeit?," 1077; Claudia Leins, "Robert Eugen Gaupp: Leben und Werk" diss., Tübingen, 1991), 244–48; Stefan Wulf, "Nonne, Max," in *Neue Deutsche Biographie*, vol. 19, ed. Historische Komission bei der Bayerischen Akademie der Wissenschaften (Berlin: Dunker & Humblot, 1999), 333–35. For the textbook, see Hermann Oppenheim, *Lehrbuch der Nervenkrankheiten für Ärzte und Studierende* (Berlin: Hirschwald, 1894).

17. Lerner, *Hysterical Men*, especially chapters 4 and 5.

18. Quote from ibid., 109. See also Rauh, "Therapiemethoden," 36; Komo, *"Für Volk,"* 78.

19. Lerner, *Hysterical Men*, 107.

20. On the French case and Deschamps, see Shepard, *War of Nerves*, 103–4. On the German side, see Lerner, *Hysterical Men*, 193–205. Investigations are also detailed in archival files concerning Robert Gaupp. Universitätsarchiv, Eberhard Karls Universität Tübingen (UAT) 308/42 "Gaupp" and 308/89 "Kriegsneurose (1914–1918)."

21. For very specific commentary to this end, some even in the most recent literature centered on patient files, see Hermes, *Krankheit: Krieg*, 148; Komo, *"Für Volk,"* 77–78, 87–89; Rauh, "Therapiemethoden," 31; Riedesser and Verderber, *Aufrüstung*, 12; Stefanie Caroline Linden and Edgar Jones, "German Battle Casualties: The Treatment of Func-

tional Somatic Disorders during World War I," *Journal of the History of Medicine and Allied Sciences* 68, no. 4 (2013): 631, 657; Fischer-Homberger, "Der Begriff 'Krankheit,'" 240; Lerner, *Hysterical Men*, 64–66; Ruth Kloocke, Heinz-Peter Schmiedebach, and Stefan Priebe, "Psychological Injury in the Two World Wars: Changing Concepts and Terms in German Psychiatry," *History of Psychiatry* 16 (2005): 55.

22. Even in Lerner's extremely nuanced and careful research—the most detailed treatment extant—the difference is recognized, but the larger importance of the distinction is not drawn out. The emphasis remains on the difference with Oppenheim's theories, not subsequent lack of unity among his opponents on significant issues: "With few exceptions, they attacked Oppenheim's theories, claiming that neurotic conditions were psychogenic (or ideogenic) in nature and thus had less to do with combat conditions than with fear, the longing for safety, or the desire for a pension, most likely to occur in constitutionally pre-morbid men. In other words, doctors had two diagnostic choices for war neurosis." Lerner, "Traumatic Neurosis," 157.

23. Gundula Gahlen, "'Always Had a Pronouncedly Psychopathic Predisposition': The Significance of Class and Rank in First World War German Psychiatric Discourse," in *Psychological Trauma and the Legacies of the First World War*, ed. Jason Crouthamel and Peter Leese (Basingstoke, UK: Palgrave Macmillan, 2017), 81–113. Susanne Michl's careful research also indicates notable exceptions, though her ultimate conclusions generally agree more with traditional accounts that look for consensus. *Im Dienste des 'Volkskörpers': Deutsche und französiche Ärzte im Ersten Weltkrieg* (Göttingen: Vandenhoeck & Ruprecht, 2007), 202–3, 268–69.

24. See, for example, the results in Prüll and Rauh, "Militär und medikale Kultur"; Rauh, "Therapiemethoden"; and Hermes, *Krankheit: Krieg*. Most recently, the standard narrative of consensus at the elite level was recounted by Philip Rauh in his talk "Die militärpsychiatrischen Therapiemethoden im Ersten Weltkrieg—Diskurs und Praxis," given in October 2017 at the conference "Nerven und Krieg: Psychische Mobilisierungs- und Leidenserfahrungen in Deutschland 1900–1933" at the Freie Universität Berlin.

25. For more on the cutting-edge forefront of war neurosis treatment during World War I, the importance of the "Baden System," and Gaupp's importation of that to Württemberg, see Lerner, *Hysterical Men*, chapter 5. Comparing the actual patient files from the observation station in Heidelberg with those in Tübingen, however, reveals differences in how each functioned in reality. The former sent patients along to other hospitals after quick observation and diagnosis, but the latter actually undertook the treatment of some soldiers as well.

26. G. Voss, "Zur Frage der 'Begehrungsvorstellungen' und ihrer Bedeutung für die Entstehung der Hysterie," *Medizinishe Klinik* 32 (1917): 863.

27. Ibid., 862.

28. Ibid.

29. Ibid.

30. Ibid.

31. Ibid., 863.

32. Ibid.

33. Ibid.

34. All quotes in this paragraph from ibid.

35. G. Voss, "Begehrungsvorstellungen und Hysterie," *Deutsche Militärärztliche Zeitschrift* 47 (1918): 35–36. For other works by Voss, see, for example, "Die Ätiologie der Psychosen," in *Handbuch der Psychiatrie*, part 3, ed. G. Aschaffenburg (Leipzig: Deuticke, 1915), 1–115; "Der Einfluss der sozialen Lage auf Nerven- und Geisteskrankheiten, Selbstmord und Verbrechen," in *Krankheit und soziale Lage*, ed. Max Mosse and Gustav Tugendreich (Munich: J.F. Lehmanns, 1913), 400–472. Appearing in the same journal focusing on military medicine, H. Böhmig's approval of the many healthy soldiers who suffered from hysteria used similarly positive language, calling them "strong farmboys." "Bericht der Nervenabteilung des Reservelazaretts I. Dresden," *Deutsche Militärärztliche Zeitschrift* 45 (1916): 173.

36. These scholarly overviews are particularly important sources as their intended purpose was to provide a sense of the latest trends and shifts in the academic community on war psychiatry. Karl Birnbaum, "Ergebnisse der Neurologie und Psychiatrie: 50. Kriegsneurosen und -psychosen auf Grund der gegenwärtigen Kriegsbeobachtungen," *Zeitschrift für die gesamte Neurologie und Psychiatrie: Referate und Ergebnisse (ZNPRE)* 12 (1916): 359–60.

37. Birnbaum, "Ergebnisse 50," 351.

38. Ibid., 354. For a comparison of wish complexes in the French and German medical literature, see Michl, *Dienste des 'Volkskörpers,'* especially 202–24, 268–72.

39. Karl Birnbaum, "Ergebnisse der Neurologie und Psychiatrie: 56. Kriegsneurosen und -psychosen auf Grund der gegenwärtigen Kriegsbeobachtungen," *ZNPRE* 13 (1917): 479.

40. It is important to note, as Lerner points out, that a more nuanced reading of Oppenheim also reveals the physician's recognition of psychogenic causes as well. Lerner, "Traumatic Neurosis," 157.

41. Karl Birnbaum, "Ergebnisse der Neurologie und Psychiatrie: 67. Kriegsneurosen und -psychosen auf Grund der gegenwärtigen Kriegsbeobachtungen," *ZNPRE* 18 (1919): 64.

42. Karl Birnbaum, "Ergebnisse der Neurologie und Psychiatrie: 49. Kriegsneurosen und -psychosen auf Grund der gegenwärtigen Kriegsbeobachtungen," *ZNPRE* 12 (1916): 19; Karl Birnbaum, "Ergebnisse der Neurologie und Psychiatrie: 58. Kriegsneurosen und -psychosen auf Grund der gegenwärtigen Kriegsbeobachtungen," *ZNPRE* 14 (1917): 202.

43. Birnbaum, "Ergebnisse 58," 202. Komo also notes this counter viewpoint. *"Für Volk,"* 84.

44. See, for example, a discussion of the *Diagnostic and Statistical Manual of Mental Disorders* criteria for post-traumatic stress disorder (PTSD) and controversial changes between the fourth and fifth editions. Matthew J. Friedman, Patricia A. Resick, Richard A. Bryant, and Chris R. Brewin, "Considering PTSD for DSM-5," *Depression and Anxiety* 28 (2011): especially 751, 755–56.

45. Karl Birnbaum, "Ergebnisse der Neurologie und Psychiatrie: 48. Kriegsneurosen und -psychosen auf Grund der gegenwärtigen Kriegsbeobachtungen," *ZNPRE* 11 (1915): 330.

46. Ibid.

47. Birnbaum, "Ergebnisse 50," 354.

48. Birnbaum, "Ergebnisse 58," 194, 203.

49. Hermes adds that the physicians she studied, in addition to rejecting the role played by war trauma more generally, also failed to recognize the fundamentally different nature of World War I. *Krankheit: Krieg*, 160.

50. Gustav Liebermeister, "Über den jetzigen Stand der Lehre von den Kriegsneurose," *Deutsche Militärärztliche Zeitschrift* 47 (1918): 322. On his investigation, see Lerner, *Hysterical Men*, 200–206.

51. Liebermeister, "Über den jetzigen Stand," 323.

52. C. von Hösslin, "Über Fahnenflucht," *Zeitschrift für die gesamte Neurologie und Psychiatrie: Originalien* (*ZNPO*) 47 (1919): 348.

53. Birnbaum, "Ergebnisse 50," 329.

54. Ibid., 329–31. For subsequent reference to acquired dispositions even after the Munich conference, see, for example, Birnbaum, "Ergebnisse 58," 202.

55. For example, Peckl indicates the patients in her data sample were diagnosed with hysteria and neurasthenia in roughly equal numbers. "Krank," 58–59.

56. On the connotations of the two diagnoses and gender implications, there is a vast literature. See, for example, Radkau, *Das Zeitalter der Nervosität*; Showalter, *Female Malady*; Köhne, *Kriegshysteriker*; Lerner, *Hysterical Men*, 62–64; Peckl, "Krank," 44; Hermes, *Krankheit: Krieg*, chapter 5; Hofer, *Nervenschwäche und Krieg*, especially 20–21, 39, 220–21, 229.

57. Further complicating the picture was the recognition that the exhaustion linked to neurasthenia could also be psychogenic, as well as the existence of diagnoses like hystero-neurasthenia. Birnbaum, "Ergebnisse 48," 333, 336, 348; Birnbaum, "Ergebnisse 50," 343–44; Birnbaum, "Ergebnisse 56," 469; Birnbaum, "Ergebnisse 67," 23; Max Levy-Suhl, "Psychiatrisches und Neurologisches aus einem Kriegslazarett," *Neurologisches Centralblatt* 23 (1916): 955; Shepard, *War of Nerves*, 9–10; Gahlen, "Significance of Class and Rank," especially 85, 87–88, 91; Peckl, "Krank," 45, 58–59, 74–75; Peckl, "Patient Records," 146.

58. Gahlen, "Significance of Class and Rank"; Peckl, "Krank," especially 72; Peckl, "Patient Records," 157; Hermes, *Krankheit: Krieg*, especially 333–34, 410.

59. All quotes and details of the Josef A. case are from his patient file (treatment dates July 19 to August 29, 1917), still located in Haus 5, which is the former Bewahrungshaus of the Heil- und Pflegeanstalt Düren (now named the LVR-Klinik Düren) that has since been converted into a museum. Appreciation is extended to Dr. Erhard Knauer, former head of the hospital, for allowing me special access to several files in the on-site museum. On the history of the hospital, see Erhard Knauer, Friedel Schulz, and Heinz Lepper, *125 Jahre Rheinische Kliniken Düren: gestern, heute, morgen: Von der Provinzialanstalt zur Fachklinik* (Cologne: Rheinland Verlag, 2003).

60. On the importance for etiologic interpretations of what was mentioned and ignored and even how the formulas were structured, see Köhne, *Kriegshysteriker*, 989–99; Hermes, *Krankheit: Krieg*, 164–65.

61. On the many terms related or equated (depending on the particular scholar's interpretation), see, for example, Eckart, "Kriegsgewalt und Psychotrauma," 85; Köhne, *Kriegshysteriker*, 73, 94; Lerner, *Hysterical Men*, 61–62.

62. For all quotes and details from the case of Georg D., see UAT 669/28470.

63. This was a common event recounted by soldiers. See, for example, Ernst Jünger, *Storm of Steel*, trans. Michael Hofmann (1920; London: Penguin, 2003), 98–99. See also Leo van Bergen, *Before My Helpless Sight: Suffering, Dying and Military Medicine on the Western Front, 1914–1918*, trans. Liz Waters (London: Routledge, 2016), 226.

64. Though this explanation is not as all-encompassing as has been suggested, it does likely have applicability in cases. See, for example, Rauh, "Therapiemethoden," 44.

65. Lerner, *Hysterical Men*, 61–62; Riedesser and Verderber, *Aufrüstung*, 11; Komo, *"Für Volk,"* 72. Also on the point that the continued use of diagnoses like these indicated recognition of the connection to wartime trauma, see Wagenblast, *Militärpscyhiatrie*, 31.

66. See, for example, Kaufmann, "Science as Cultural Practice," 133–34; Peckl, "Krank," 44–45.

67. On the role of individual style, see Peckl, "Krank," 71–72.

68. All quotes and details on Georg W. from UAT 669/28310.

69. Wilhelm N. (treatment dates April 16 to May 8, 1917), ALVR, Grafenberg Krankenakten, Box N-OP 1917. On the Grafenberg hospital, see Joachim Becker, "Die Geschichte des Rheinischen Landeskrankenhauses Düsseldorf-Grafenberg von 1876 bis 1918" (Med. diss., Universität Düsseldorf, 1978).

70. I would like to thank Prof. Dr. Maike Rotzoll for not only granting me access to these files at the Historisches Archiv der Psychiatrischen Universitätsklinik Heidelberg but also confirming this impression of the diagnostic synonymity at times.

71. All quotes and details for this case are from the Historisches Archiv der Psychiatrischen Universitätsklinik Heidelberg (HAPUH), "Reserve=Lazarett XVI, Die Psychiatrische Klinik zu Heidelberg, Patientenakten," Box Kr to [illeg], Friedrich K. (treatment dates December 4 to December 12, 1917).

72. Petra Peckl consulted the psychiatric records remaining in the military archives in Freiburg for soldiers in various *Lazaretten* during World War I (as a member of the larger project "Krieg und medikale Kultur. Patientenschicksale im Zeitalter der Weltkriege 1914–1945"). Her first report came in the article "What the Patient Records Reveal." Peckl's subsequent article (for the volume that included research from the larger project) presented more detail but largely related the same findings: "Krank durch die 'seelischen Einwirkungen des Feldzuges'?" As Peckl is apparently no longer working in academia, the extant data and arguments have since been reproduced in work by Prüll and Rauh, who focused on different issues in the initial volume but were partners in the larger project. See, for example, Rauh and Prüll, "Krank durch den Krieg?" Most recently, Rauh presented research from this set at the conference "Nerven und Krieg." Maria Hermes published her findings based on patient files from one city hospital in Bremen, the St. Jürgen-Asyl: *Krankheit: Krieg*. Linden and Jones have produced a third study based on patient files, though it tends more toward a report, with limited historiographic engagement: "Battle Casualties."

73. Hermes, *Krankheit: Krieg*, 315, 332; Peckl, "Krank," 88. Rauh suggested this argument again most recently at the conference "Nerven und Krieg."

74. Robert Gaupp, *Die Nervenkranken des Krieges: Ihre Beurteilung und Behandlung. Ein Wort zur Aufklarung und Mahnung unseres Volkes* (Stuttgart: Evangelischer Presseverband für Württemberg, 1917), 16, translated and quoted in Lerner, *Hysterical Men*, 204.

75. The files are all 1917 cases drawn randomly from the UAT 669/28400-600 range. Those included among the fifty-three (none of which are for officers) all either explicitly list the diagnosis on the main line as hysteria or include clear reference to hysteria in the paperwork. For example, 669/28669 is included though the diagnosis is "psychogenic episodes" as the end report detailing where the patient should be sent includes the description "psychogenic (hysterical)" for his condition. Similarly, the file 669/28645 has the main diagnosis line reading "nervous complains after burial" but includes elsewhere the diagnosis of "traumatic hysteria."

76. Linden and Jones provide a good overview of the variety of treatments in "Battle Casualties." See also Lerner, *Hysterical Men*, 113–14.

77. Though lack of pensions is still frequently tied to hysteria in the literature, Peckl's research on nonelite institutions has shown that pensions were still awarded to men treated there. Similarly, a good corrective on the granting of pensions more generally is Stephanie Neuner, *Politik und Psychiatrie: Die staatliche Versorgung psychisch Kriegsbeschädigter in Deutschland, 1920–39* (Göttingen: Vandenhoeck & Ruprecht, 2011). Gaupp's own papers for the *Reservelazarett* include a copy of the "Anhaltspunkte für die militärarztliche Beurteilung der Frage der Dienstbeschädigung oder Kriegsdienstbeschädigung bei den haufigsten psychischen und nervosen Erkrankungen," which indicates quite minimal requirements for declaring an infirmity to be attributed to the soldier's service. UAT 308/90 "Reservelazarett II."

78. Both Hermes and Peckl also found reliance on mild treatments and extensive stays for treatment in the nonelite cases they researched. They disagree, however, on whether doctors acknowledged the harmful effects of war, with Hermes concluding they did not. Hermes, *Krankheit: Krieg*, 148, 449, 450–51; and Peckl, "Krank," 63, 78, 88.

79. See, for example, UAT 669/28581; 669/28649; 669/28684. On rhetoric proposing denial of the comforts of home, see Lerner, *Hysterical Men*, 147; Michl, *Dienste des 'Volkskörpers,'* 208.

80. See, for example, UAT 669/28438; 669/28684.

81. All quotes and details for the Wilhelm B. case are from UAT 669/28438.

82. For an example of the unsympathetic and harsh treatment that could be handed out in Tübingen, see UAT 669/28664.

83. Jason Crouthamel, *The Great War and German Memory: Society, Politics and Psychological Trauma, 1914–45* (Exeter: University of Exeter Press, 2009), 44; Hermes, *Krankheit: Krieg*, 21–22.

84. UAT 669/28708.

85. For example, UAT 669/28496; 669/28522; 669/28442.

86. UAT 308/89, Letter from Gaupp to the *Sanitätsamt* in Stuttgart on September 23, 1918, concerning Liebermeister's lecture on war neurosis in January. On Gaupp's public defense of Liebermeister, see Lerner, *Hysterical Men*, 200–206.

87. For more on the man generally, see Claudia Leins, "Robert Eugen Gaupp: Leben und Werk" (Doctoral diss., Tübingen, 1991).

88. Karl Weiler, "Ein Jahr Kriegsneurotikerbehandlung," *Münchener Medizinische Wochenschrift* 66 (1919): 402. The reference to Lourdes not only reveals the efforts to portray psychiatric treatments as miraculous but also likely drew on the increased cachet of such sites as places of comfort during the war. On the increased draw of religiosity during

the war among soldiers and their families, see Alexander Watson, *Enduring the Great War: Combat, Morale and Collapse in the German and British Armies, 1914–1918* (Cambridge: Cambridge University Press, 2014), especially 93-98; Owen Davies, *A Supernatural War: Magic, Divination, and Faith during the First World War* (New York: Oxford University Press, 2018), especially 63–64, 141, 185–87.

89. Quinkert, Rauh, and Winkler, "Einleitung," 13; Ackerknecht, *Short History of Psychiatry*, 82; Peckl, "Krank," 33–34, 49–50; Ioanna Mamali, "'Das "naturwissenschafliche" Ideal': Von der Zwangsbehandlung zur NS-Erbgesundheitspolitik. Ferdinand Kehrer, 1915–1945," in *Heroische Therapien: Die deutsche Psychiatrie im internationalen Vergleich 1918–1945*, ed. Hans-Walter Schmuhl and Volker Roelcke (Göttingen: Wallstein Verlag, 2013), 255–56.

90. UAT 669/28771.

91. UAT 669/28669.

92. UAT 669/28498. On earlier attempts with work therapy, see Lerner, *Hysterical Men*, 57; Thomas Beddies, "'Aktivere Krankenbehandlung' und 'Arbeitstherapie': Anwendungsformen und Begründungszusammenhänge bei Hermann Simon und Carl Schneider," in Schmuhl and Roelcke, *Heroische Therapien*, 268–86.

93. UAT 669/28567.

94. UAT 669/28645.

95. UAT 669/28589.

96. UAT 669/28579.

97. "Gründsätze für die Behandlung und Beurteilung der sogennanten Kriegsneurotiker," *Deutsche Militärärztliche Zeitschrift* 47 (1918): 434; Otto Martineck, "Tagung der in der Kriegsneurotikerbehandliung tätigen Ärzte der Heeresverwaltung am 9. Oktober d.j., Kurzer Bericht," *Deutsche Militärärztliche Zeitschrift* 47 (1918): 405; Weiler, "Ein Jahr Kriegsneurotikerbehandlung," 403. Lerner also notes this view of treatment as inappropriate for psychopaths. *Hysterical Men*, 207.

98. On the figures, which range from over six hundred thousand more generally to estimations of war tremblers specifically at about two hundred thousand, see Eckart, *Medizin und Krieg*, 142; Hermes, *Krankheit: Krieg*, 14n6.

99. Kliche, *Die Stellung*, 7, 17–18, 25, 28, 41; Kaufmann, "Science as Cultural Practice," 132; Komo, *"Für Volk,"* 57; Lerner, *Hysterical Men*, 42; Peckl, "Krank," 354; Hermes, *Krankheit: Krieg*, 107; Becker, "Düsseldorf-Grafenberg," 145–50; Renate Goldmann, Erhard Knauer, and Eusebius Wirdeier, *Moderne, Weltkrieg, Irrenhaus: Bruche in der Psychiatrie, 1900–1930* (Essen: Klartext Verlag, 2014), 86–87.

100. Eckart, *Die Wunden heilen sehr schön: Feldpostkarten aus dem Lazarett 1914-1918* (Stuttgart: Franz Steiner Verlag, 2013), 40; Goldmann, Knauer, and Wirdeier, *Irrenhaus*, 42; Hermes, *Krankheit: Krieg*, 109; Becker, "Düsseldorf-Grafenberg," 146; Komo, *"Für Volk,"* 61; Knauer, Schulz, and Lepper, *Düren*, 42–45.

101. Such conditions are noted in many files. For some specifically mentioned here, see the case files in ALVR, Düren Krankenakten: Peter D. (treatment dates November 14 to December 6, 1914), Box November 5 to December 1, 1914; Leo S. (treatment dates March 13 to June 20, 1917), Box March 1 to March 27, 1917; Ernst H. (treatment dates January 23 to March 31, 1915), Box January 13 to January 29, 1915; Heinrich S. (treatment dates November 19, 1915, to June 2, 1916), Box November 7 to November 23, 1915;

Kaspar W. (treatment dates February 7, 1916, to January 22, 1917), Box February 7 to February 25, 1916.

102. Among others, see the file in ALVR, Düren Krankenakten: Max S. (treatment dates December 9, 1915, to November 30, 1916), Box November 7 to December 9, 1915. (Oddly, there are two boxes that both begin with November 7 and have partially overlapping dates in 1915.) For Grafenberg, see ALVR, Grafenberg Krankenakten, Johann M. (treatment dates September 21 to December 14, 1914), Box Mu-Pa 1914; Alfred B. (treatment dates August 14, 1915, to March 23, 1917), Box Be-Bl 1915; Jakob E. (treatment dates August 6, 1915, to January 12, 1916), Box E-Fim 1915. On Gaupp, see the letter from March 13, 1918, in UAT 308/42. Concerning psychoanalysis, the authorities did express interest in the therapy in September 1918, but the end of the war brought plans to introduce it more widely to an end. On the relatively minor role of Freud concerning the treatment of traumatized soldiers during the war, see Lerner, *Hysterical Men*, 9, 137, 164–66.

103. On staff efforts to make the most of their limited resources, see Goldmann, Knauer, and Wirdeier, *Irrenhaus*, 50.

104. Physical ailments are included in the files of PERS 9 "Krankenunterlagen von Angehörigen der Preußischen Armee, Preußischen Marine, Kaiserlichen Marine, Schutztruppen, Reichswehr, und Wehrmacht" at the Bundesarchiv Freiburg (BAF).

105. The quotes and details for this case are all drawn from the patient file of Kaspar W. (treatment dates February 7, 1916, to January 22, 1917), ALVR, Düren Krankenakten, Box February 7 to February 25, 1916.

106. With the need for men in the military, the support staff involved in patient care increasingly consisted of women. See the numbers in Becker, "Düsseldorf-Grafenberg," 147; Goldmann, Knauer, and Wideier, *Irrenhaus*, 87.

107. At the same time, there were cases of extraordinary care being shown for patients as well. Indeed, a remarkable case of forbearance and compassion for a seemingly unlikely candidate involved Gaupp and a conscientious objector he treated in Tübingen. See chapter 4.

108. In his extensively detailed account, Lerner includes references to many issues noted here, but he interprets them rather differently, as will be discussed below. See *Hysterical Men*, especially 175, chapter 7.

109. Josef W. (treatment dates September 15, 1914, to December 13, 1919), ALVR, Grafenberg Krankenakten, Box Wi-Z 1914.

110. Letters and other forms of open communication were clearly an important issue in this oversight, as patients in other cases sometimes had to sneak out letters to tell of their mistreatment. See Goldberg, "Reinvented Public," 170.

111. Karl W. (treatment dates November 4, 1915, to August 4, 1916), ALVR, Düren Krankenakten, Box October 26 to November 4, 1915.

112. The gendering of the patient likely stemmed not only from the idea of mentally ill soldiers as effeminate—here the connections to hysteria come to mind again—but also from the general tendency to infantilize and feminize psychiatric institution patients. See, for example, Goldberg, "Reinvented Public," 165.

113. Kaspar W. (treatment dates February 7, 1916, to January 22, 1917), ALVR, Düren Krankenakten, Box February 7 to February 25, 1916.

114. See, for example, the cases of Paul B. (treatment dates November 30, 1915, to June 6, 1916), ALVR, Düren Krankenakten, Box November 7 to December 9, 1915; and Paul W. (treatment dates February 19 to June 20, 1916), ALVR, Düren Krankenakten, Box February 7 to February 25, 1916.

115. Goldberg, "Reinvented Public"; Goldberg, "Mellage Trial"; Blasius, *"Einfache Seelenstörung,"* especially 19, 88–90, 111.

116. For a contrasting view suggesting that "doctors and patients did not seem to question the legitimacy" of brutal treatment, see Linden and Jones, "Battle Casualties," 652. The emphasis on increased consideration for those who sacrificed during the war could extend to widows and other family members of fallen soldiers as well. ALVR, Rheinische Prov. Heil-und Pflegeanstalt Bedburg-Hau (Kr. Cleve), File 23113 "Abgelehnte Aufnahme=Anträge."

117. Leo S. (treatment dates March 13 to June 20, 1917), ALVR, Düren Krankenakten, Box March 1 to March 27, 1917.

118. Georg B. (treatment dates December 19, 1915, to November 21, 1916), ALVR, Düren Krankenakten, Box December 11 to December 31, 1915.

119. Kaspar W. (treatment dates February 7, 1916, to January 22, 1917), ALVR, Düren Krankenakten, Box February 7 to February 25, 1916.

120. Hans-Georg Hofer, "Beyond Freud and Wagner-Jauregg: War Psychiatry and the Hapsburg Army," in *War, Trauma and Medicine in Germany and Central Europe (1914-1939)*, ed. Hans-Georg Hofer, Cay-Rüdiger Prüll, and Wolfgang U. Eckart (Freiburg: Centaurus, 2011), 69–70. Lerner includes it in part III of his book entitled "Aftermath: Hysteria, Trauma, Memory."

121. On Liebermeister or the Reichstag events, see Lerner, *Hysterical Men*, chapter 7.

122. Lerner, *Hysterical Men*, 195–96. Quote from Gaupp originally in *Nervenkranken des Krieges*, 2.

123. Hofer, *Nervenschwäche und Krieg*, especially 326. He addresses the German developments only briefly, but his analysis is highly insightful.

124. On Deschamps, see Shepard, *War of Nerves*, 103–4. On earlier and later psychiatric practices, see, for example, Ackerknecht, *Short History of Psychiatry*; Quinkert, Rauh, and Winkler, "Einleitung."

125. On the calls for more recognition of agency among patients in the historical scholarship, see especially Shepard, *War of Nerves*, xxi. Also see the additional literature in the introduction to this book.

126. All quotes and details for this case are from the file for Josef W. (treatment dates December 18, 1914, to April 3, 1916), ALVR, Düren Krankenakten, Box December 10 to December 30, 1914.

127. Ludwig O. (treatment dates November 4 to November 12, 1915), ALVR, Düren Krankenakten, Box October 26 to November 4, 1915.

128. Ernst H. (treatment dates January 23 to March 31, 1915), ALVR, Düren Krankenakten, Box January 13 to January 29, 1915. The soldier with whom he broke out was fellow patient Carl M.

129. Albert F. (treatment dates December 16, 1915, to June 6, 1916), ALVR, Grafenberg Krankenakten, Box E-Fim 1915.

130. UAT 669/28646.

131. All quotes and details from the file for Hermann R. (treatment dates October 29, 1914, to June 21, 1915), ALVR, Düren Krankenakten, Box October 6 to November 4, 1914).

132. Johann B. (treatment dates November 20, 1917, to December 18, 1918), ALVR, Galkhausen Krankenakten, Box B.

133. Birnbaum summarized a lot of the debates on malingering in the reports for the *ZNPRE* as well.

134. The case files include very few instances where simulation was suspected or alleged. Lerner also notes the relatively small actual impact of the simulation issue for treatment. *Hysterical Men*, 139. For the contrary interpretation, see Ziemann, "Verweigerungsformen," 110.

135. Riedesser and Verderber, *Aufrüstung*, 20; Showalter, *Female Malady*, especially chapters 6 and 7; Leeds, *No Man's Land*, chapter 5. Hermes also notes this point in her analysis. *Krankheit: Krieg*, 353.

3. Deserters

1. The quotes and details for this case are all drawn from the patient file of Jakob S. (treatment dates May 16 to August 8, 1917; August 14 to October 3, 1917), ALVR, Düren Krankenakten, Box April 25 to May 29, 1917.

2. Ziemann, "Verweigerungsformen," 110–11; Wette, "Militärgeschichte von unten." 25. For the infrequency of such accusations in treating shell shock, see chapter 2 as well as Lerner, *Hysterical Men*, 139. More generally, Hermes notes the small role simulation played in actual treatment concerns, including legal cases. *Krankheit: Krieg*, especially 237–68.

3. Alfred Storch, "Beiträge zur Psychopathologie der unerlaubten Entferung und Fahnenflucht im Felde," *ZNPO* 46 (1919): 356.

4. Max Kastan, "Die strafbare Handlungen psychisch-kranker Angehöriger des Feldheeres," *Archiv für Psychiatrie und Nervenkrankheiten* 56, nos. 2 and 3 (1916): 791; Birnbaum, "Ergebnisse 56," 520.

5. Examples can be found, for example, in the journal literature of the period: W. Horstmann, "Religiosität oder Wahn?," *ZNPO* 49 (1919): 218–42.

6. Bröckling, "Psychopathische Minderwertigkeit?," 166, 171; Ulrich Bröckling, *Disziplin: Soziologie und Geschichte militärischer Gehorsamsproduktion* (Paderborn: Fink, 1997), 231. On this development, also see chapter 1. Contemporary psychiatric journals also noted the preponderance of desertion cases among men sent for observation. See, for example, Birnbaum, "Ergebnisse 62," 67; Hösslin, "Über Fahnenflucht," 345.

7. The specific term "accommodation" was used by both Max Meier and Karl Pönitz, though other psychiatrists expressed the general sentiment as well. Meier, "Fahnenflucht und unerlaubte Entfernung im Krieg" (Doctoral diss., Universität Bonn, 1917), 41; Pönitz, "Psychologie und Psychopathologie der Fahnenflucht im Kriege," *Archiv für Kriminologie* 68 (1917): 261.

8. Christoph Jahr, *Gewöhnliche Soldaten: Desertion und Deserteure im deutschen und britischen Heer 1914–1918* (Göttingen: Vandenhoeck & Ruprecht, 1996), 17, 26; Ulrich

Bröckling and Michael Sikora, "Einleitung," in *Armeen und ihre Deserteure: Vernachlässigte Kapitel einer Militärgeschichte der Neuzeit*, ed. Ulrich Bröckling and Michael Sikora (Göttingen: Vandenhoeck & Ruprecht, 1998), 7–8; Benjamin Ziemann, *Violence and the German Soldier in the Great War: Killing, Dying, Surviving*, trans. Andrew Evans (London: Bloomsbury, 2017), 93; Bröckling, *Disziplin*, 196, 236–37; Ziemann, "Verweigerungsformen," 118; Wette, "Militärgeschichte von unten," 30.

9. *Sanitätsbericht über das Deutsche Heer*, 145.

10. Jahr provides detailed analysis and has several tables showing breakdowns of available numbers for units in Bavaria and Württemberg that he uses to estimate numbers for the entire German army. *Gewöhnliche Soldaten*, 149–61, 198–201. When considering both the field army and the units stationed within Germany, Jahr estimates there were 130,000–150,000 cases. See also Ziemann, *Violence and the German Soldier*, 99–100. On amnesty, see also BAF, RM 27-XV/48 "Gericht der 2. Marine-Inspektion.-Fahnenflucht.-Bestimmungen über das Verfahren gegen Abwesende"; BAF, PH 8-I/713 "Verfahrensakte."

11. Ziemann, *Violence and the German Soldier*, especially 106–8. As they include different assumptions in their calculations and different constituents under the broad category of "deserters" that they are quantifying, the comparison of Jahr's and Ziemann's numbers with each other as well as with the number of psychiatric cases in World War I can be undertaken in only the most general sense for illustrative purposes.

12. On the debate, see Jahr, *Gewöhnliche Soldaten*, 155–67; Ziemann, *Violence and the German Soldier*, especially chapter 7; Watson, *Enduring the Great War*, especially 40–41; Wilhelm Deist, "The Military Collapse of the German Empire," *War in History* 3, no. 2 (1996): 186–207; van Bergen, *Before My Helpless Sight*, 206.

13. Ziemann, *Violence and the German Soldier*, 108.

14. Jahr, *Gewöhnliche Soldaten*, especially 49, 81, 87, 155, 198–201, 248, 336; Christoph Jahr, "'Der Krieg zwingt die Justiz, ihr Innerstes zu revidieren,' Desertion und Militärgerichtsbarkeit im Ersten Weltkrieg," in Bröckling and Sikora, *Armeen und ihre Deserteure*, especially 196, 200, 202 (source of the quote), 204–21.

15. Ziemann, *Violence and the German Soldier*, especially 112–20 (quote from 120).

16. Ibid., 119. Though the content of the patient files for this study did not lend itself to in-depth analysis along the lines of perceived racial or ethnic differences, Hofer presents an illuminating analysis of the role these factors played in psychiatry in the diverse Hapsburg Empire. *Nervenschwäche und Krieg*, especially 329–38.

17. Jahr, *Gewöhnliche Soldaten*, 46, 50 (the source of the quote), 114–15; Jahr, "Der Krieg zwingt die Justiz," 189, 210; Ziemann, "Verweigerungsformen," 110–12; Ziemann, *Violence and the German Soldier*, 109.

18. Bröckling, *Disziplin*, especially 230–33; Bröckling, "Psychopathische Minderwertigkeit." Hermes also notes the potential for psychiatry to have a "protective function." *Krankheit: Krieg*, 350, 354, 358. Hofer does the same for the Hapsburg case. *Nervenschwäche und Krieg*, 262–66. For a general discussion of the idea of "sickness" and all the corresponding social "advantages and disadvantages" that such labeling creates, see Fischer-Homberger, "Der Begriff 'Krankheit,'" especially 240.

19. Hermes, *Krankheit: Krieg*, 241–45.

20. Bröckling, *Disziplin*, chapter 2, especially 74–75.

21. Ibid., chapter 3; Patrick J. Geary, *The Myth of Nations: The Medieval Origins of Europe* (Princeton, NJ: Princeton University Press, 2002), especially 23–29; Bröckling and Sikora, "Einleitung," 14; Ulfried Weißer, *Die Bundesrepublik Deutschland-ein Erfolgsprojekt* (Berlin: Frank & Timm, 2015), 53. On the prestige of the military in Germany as well as psychiatry's role in paring down conscription numbers, see chapter 1.

22. Again, these comparisons and further calculations are based on the detailed statistics and analysis provided by Jahr, drawing heavily on the available numbers for Bavaria and Württemberg. If anything, Jahr tends to downplay desertion and its consequences, even when at the levels noted here. *Gewöhnliche Soldaten*, 149–61, especially 155 for the increased rates between the years noted.

23. Pönitz, "Psychologie und Psychopathologie," 263. Both the contemporary psychiatric articles and the current scholarly literature discuss the array of reasons for desertion: Wilhelm Schmidt, *Forensisch-Psychiatrische Erfahrungen im Krieg* (Berlin: Karger, 1918), 1–13; Hösslin, "Über Fahnenflucht," especially 347–49; Jahr, *Gewöhnliche Soldaten*, especially 109, 134–42; Jahr, "Der Krieg zwingt die Justiz," especially 190–99; Ziemann, *Violence and the German Soldier*, especially 109–12. On nostalgia specifically, see Michael Roper, "Nostalgia as an Emotional Experience in the Great War," *Historical Journal* 54 (2011): 421–51. On the role of fear in wartime, as well as a larger debate about the concurrent importance of battlefield emotions such as guilt, horror, excitement, and even joy, see John Keegan, *The Face of Battle* (New York: Viking, 1976), 72; Dave Grossman, *On Killing: The Psychological Cost of Learning to Kill in War and Society* (Boston: Little Brown, 1995), 30, 54, 74–75; Joanna Bourke, *An Intimate History of Killing: Face-to-Face Killing in Twentieth-Century Warfare* (New York: Basic, 1999), 18, 31, 54, 362; Joanna Bourke, "The Emotions of War: Fear and the British and American Military, 1914–45," *Historical Research* 74 (2001): 314–30.

24. Again, the matter was discussed in the contemporary journal literature, such as in the articles cited in the previous note. For the scholarly discussion, see Jahr, *Gewöhnliche Soldaten*, 140–42; Ziemann, *Violence and the German Soldier*, 111–12; Hermes, *Krankheit: Krieg*, 241. On the difficulties of finding such motives, see Jahr, "Der Krieg zwingt die Justiz," 196, 198; Ziemann, *Violence and the German Soldier*, 109.

25. Meier, "Fahnenflucht und unerlaubte Entfernung," 9; Hösslin, "Über Fahnenflucht," 344–45; Kastan, "Die strafbare Handlungen," 792; Bröckling, "Psychopathische Minderwertigkeit," 165; Jahr, "Der Krieg zwingt die Justiz," 188; Jahr, *Gewöhnliche Soldaten*, 79. The pertinent phrase regarding the distinction read "with the intention to remove himself permanently." *Militär-Straftgesetzbuch. Vom 20. Juni 1872* (Berlin: Mittler and Son, 1883), 17.

26. Ziemann, *Violence and the German Soldier*, 105; Jahr, *Gewöhnliche Soldaten*, 43; Pönitz, "Psychologie und Psychopathologie," 262; Hösslin, "Über Fahnenflucht," 344–45; Schmidt, *Forensisch-Psychiatrische Erfahrungen im Krieg*, 2. For a rare case in which the individual admitted outright to the intention to desert, see BAF, RM 27-XIV/50 "Gericht der I. Marine-Inspektion in Kiel.- Untersuchung wegen Fahnenflucht und Raub."

27. The case of Wilhelm W. that was examined in the introduction exemplifies this potentially ambiguous border between classifying individuals more so among deserters or among conscientious objectors for the sake of analysis. This study has placed Wilhelm W. among the latter, because it appears his attempts to leave were only halfhearted and he

expressed his reservations and outright refusal to those in his company (even if he decided it best not to elaborate on them in the hospital). Furthermore, the language he uses in the letter to his sister is quite similar to that found in the statements of other conscientious objectors. The discussion of conscientious objection could make a cameo appearance in the contemporary journal literature on desertion; scholars of Germany also often mention objectors when discussing deserters, considering them together especially given the paucity of research done on the former. See, for example, Schmidt, *Forensisch-Psychiatrische Erfahrungen im Krieg*, 10; Ziemann, *Violence and the German Soldier*, 108; Bröckling and Sikora, "Einleitung," 10. Notably, Jahr considers them together as well but includes no section on German conscientious objection, only identifying objectors in Britain. *Gewöhnliche Soldaten*, 126–27. The particular definition of conscientious objector used in this study is discussed more in chapter 4.

28. Quoted at length in Ziemann, *Violence and the German Soldier*, 111–12. See also Jahr, *Gewöhnliche Soldaten*, 140.

29. An account provided by Wilhelm Pieck for the months leading up to his desertion in 1917 details his opposition to the war, which he suggests was known among his regiment. Bundesarchiv Berlin-Lichtenberg (BAB-Li), NY 4036/13 "Aufzeichnungen Wilhelm Piecks im Militärgefängnis Kattowitz." Whatever paper trail his desertion case itself made—if any, since he was never caught or tried for it—would not have been linked to this account, however, which is likely extant only because of the prominence Pieck ultimately gained. See also Fritz Erpenbeck, *Wilhelm Pieck: Ein Lebensbild* (Berlin: Dietz, 1951), especially 46–60; Deutscher Kulturbund, *Wilhelm Pieck* ([East] Berlin: Deutscher Kulturbund, 1960), especially 138; Norbert Haase, *Deutsche Deserteure* (Berlin: Rotbuch Verlag, 1987), 37.

30. Bröckling, "Psychopathische Minderwertigkeit," 171.

31. Meier, "Fahnenflucht und unerlaubte Entfernung," 12. See also 5–6.

32. Schmidt, *Forensisch-Psychiatrische Erfahrungen im Krieg*, 12. In her comparison of outcomes of military patients and civilian patients for a Bremen hospital, Hermes indicates that the former were also likelier to receive non compos mentis declarations than the latter.

33. Jahr, *Gewöhnliche Soldaten*, 115.

34. Hermes reports the large numbers of deserters in the Bremen hospital she studies as well, though she does not highlight the particular likelihood of such men being sent for observation compared with soldiers committing other types of crimes. *Krankheit: Krieg*, 345.

35. BAF, PH 22-II/730 "Festungs- und Hauptlazarett II Königsberg, Arrestanstalt und Psychiatrische Abteilung."

36. Schmidt, *Forensisch-Psychiatrische Erfahrungen im Krieg*.

37. H. Stoll, *Ergebnisse psychiatrischer Begutachtung beim Kriegsgericht* (Halle: Carl Marhold Verlag, 1918). Stoll presents the numbers in a rather complicated manner at the outset of his study, requiring the reader to sift through all 158 determinations to obtain more accurate percentages.

38. Hösslin, "Über Fahnenflucht," 344.

39. This corresponds closely to the findings of Weiler for the attestations he provided in Munich during the war. Though he did not report on the exact numbers of cases, he did

indicate that 55 percent of all attestations involved the crime of desertion. "Kriegsgerichtspsychiatrische Erfahrungen und ihre Verwertung für die Strafrechtspflege im Allgemeinen," *Monatsschrift für Kriminalpsychologie und Strafrechtsreform* 12/13 (1921/1922): 289.

40. This is especially the case when not considering the large numbers of deserters in mid to late 1918, who often were not caught or charged in the midst of military collapse, much less sent for psychiatric observation.

41. Meier, "Fahnenflucht und unerlaubte Entfernung," 9. See also Frevert, *Nation in Barracks*, 81.

42. All details and quotes for this case are from the treatment file for Willy J. (treatment dates March 10 to August 31, 1917), ALVR, Düren Krankenakten, Box March 1 to March 27, 1917. Conversely, noting a patient's "military conduct" could be shorthand for indicating health. See BAF, PERS 9 13819 (Box 01.01.1891 Sa-Schme), Wilhelm S. (intake date June 5, 1918).

43. Hermes offers some statistics that also suggest desertion itself was seen as an indication of mental illness. *Krankheit: Krieg*, 345. On the more general connection proposed between disobedience and mental disturbance, see Bröckling, "Psychopathische Minderwertigkeit," 171; Komo, "*Für Volk*," 89.

44. *Strafgesetzbuch für das Deutsche Reich* (Nördlingen: C. H. Beck'schen Buchdruckerei, 1871), 11.

45. Hösslin, "Über Fahnenflucht," 350.

46. Schmidt, *Forensisch-Psychiatrische Erfahrungen im Krieg*, 4.

47. More articles noted the breakdown between those considered responsible for deeds and those not, a determination that did not mean mental health, however.

48. Stoll, *Ergebnisse psychiatrischer Begutachtung*. The statistics are calculated by consulting the outcomes the physician reported for all patients he observed, separating out those that were being charged with the crime of desertion.

49. Meier, "Fahnenflucht und unerlaubte Entfernung," 136, table II.

50. Hösslin, "Über Fahnenflucht," 354–55.

51. Jahr, *Gewöhnliche Soldaten*; Jahr, "Der Krieg zwingt die Justiz"; Ziemann, *Violence and the German Soldier*, especially chapter 5. On variability related to a particular institution or physician, see also Peckl, "Krank," 71–72.

52. On contemporary understandings of epilepsy, see Emil Kraepelin, *Psychiatrie: Ein Lehrbuch für studierende und Ärzte*, 8th ed., Band III, Teil II (Leipzig: Barth, 1913), 1069–78. For diagnoses frequently given to deserters under observation, see, for example, Birnbaum, "Ergebnisse 67," 60; Birnbaum, "Ergebnisse 49," 79–80; Storch, "Beiträge zur Psychopathologie der unerlaubten Entferung und Fahnenflucht," 349–58; Pönitz, "Psychologie und Psychopathologie," 263; Schmidt, *Forensisch-Psychiatrische Erfahrungen im Krieg*, 1, 4; Meier, "Fahnenflucht und unerlaubte Entfernung," 21; Stoll, *Ergebnisse psychiatrischer Begutachtung*, 8; K. Boas, "Fahnenflucht und unerlaubte Entfernung im Kriege, von Max Meier," *Neurologisches Centralblatt* 38 (1919): 40–41; Karl Birnbaum, "Kastan, Die strafbaren Handlungen psychisch kranker Angehöriger des Feldheeres/ Stiefler, Forensisch-psychiatrische Beobachtungen im Felde" (review), *Archiv für Kriminologie* 69 (1918): 300–301.

53. The full title in the original French is *Traité des dégénérescences physiques, intellectuelles et morales de l'espèce humaine et des causes qui produisent des variétés maladives.*

Ronald Chase, *The Making of Modern Psychiatry* (Berlin: Logos, 2018), 39–45; Wetzell, *Inventing the Criminal*, 20. On the idea of degeneracy, see also Lerner, *Hysterical Men*, 19–23; Hermes, *Krankheit: Krieg*, 193–94.

54. Interestingly, Hermes notes that this term did not appear often in the case files she consulted in Bremen. *Krankheit: Krieg*, 198–99.

55. Wetzell, *Inventing the Criminal*, especially 46–52, 145. As Wetzell notes, the words "degeneracy" and "inferiority" tended to be used more before the war; during Weimar, "psychopath" became the preferred term. Hence, it is not surprising that in the midst of World War I one finds all of these words used commonly.

56. On degeneration as an explanation of "socially condemned behaviors," see the informative book by Wetzell, *Inventing the Criminal* (quote from 47).

57. All quotes are drawn from the case of Karl S. in UAT 669/28848.

58. Details for the case of Otto B. from UAT 669/28565. Emphasis in the original.

59. Details for the case of Julius G. from UAT 669/28794.

60. See the discussion of this development in chapter 1. See also Lerner, *Hysterical Men*, 55–56.

61. Meier, "Fahnenflucht und unerlaubte Entfernung," 18.

62. Ibid., 19. This sense that one could hardly expect anything else finds echo in many places, several noted in the text here. See also Georg Stiefler, "Forensich-Psychiatrish aus dem Felde," *Wiener Medizinische Wochenschrift* 69 (1919): 1416–20, 1472–74. Though Stiefler was practicing in Linz, his findings on desertion also made it into overviews of the literature in Germany during the war itself. Birnbaum, "Ergebnisse 56," 516–19.

63. Hösslin, "Über Fahnenflucht," 345.

64. All details and quotes for this case are from the treatment file for Nikolaus S. (treatment dates May 4 to June 15, 1917), ALVR, Düren Krankenakten, Box April 25 to May 29, 1917.

65. Chase, *Modern Psychiatry*, 39–45.

66. Hösslin, "Über Fahnenflucht," 351.

67. Ibid., 351–53.

68. Ibid., 354.

69. Meier, "Fahnenflucht und unerlaubte Entfernung," 17–18.

70. Storch, "Beiträge zur Psychopathologie der unerlaubten Entferung und Fahnenflucht," especially 365.

71. Ibid., especially 366.

72. Ibid., 349, 357.

73. Ibid., 367. In one sense, Pönitz did not go as far as Storch; the former did not so clearly indicate that completely healthy men might be led to desert by the strains of war. On the other hand, Pönitz went further by fundamentally questioning the division of men into valuable and less valuable or inferior, even as he himself employed it. Of men who deserted, the psychiatrist also recognized that some may have lived out civilian lives without any problems, concluding they should not be judged so harshly. Indeed, it caused him to comment that the "estimation of the social value of a man from time to time can come to completely different results" depending on the circumstances and what they call for. "Psychologie und Psychopathologie," 281.

74. Birnbaum, "Ergebnisse 56," especially 515–16. Given that Storch's article was not yet published and that Birnbaum does not mention his name, it can be concluded that Birnbaum was not merely reiterating the same study results. Max Kastan added yet another nuance to the discussion, suggesting a third category beyond healthy versus unhealthy that also played into understanding the connection between psychiatric disturbance and criminality in the army: an individual's social situation in civilian life. Whether one was young or old, for example, or single or the head of a family also impacted how one would psychologically fare during wartime and the likelihood of offending. "Die strafbaren Handlungen," especially 574–75.

75. Wilhelm S. (treatment dates November 4 to December 14, 1915, and May 26 to June 17, 1916), ALVR, Grafenberg Krankenakten, Box Se-Sti 1915.

76. Stein addressed the parliament in March 1917 and June 1918. Jahr, *Gewöhnliche Soldaten*, 300.

77. This also harmonizes with the willingness of courts—both civil and military—to largely accept the recommendations from psychiatrists in their ultimate juridical rulings, a development noted in chapter 1. See also, for example, Kastan, "Die strafbare Handlungen," 578.

78. See, for example, the breakdown offered in Hösslin, "Über Fahnenflucht," 354; Meier, "Fahnenflucht und unerlaubte Entfernung," 136, table II.

79. On the failure to create a third, official category, see, for example, Engstrom, "Topographies of Forensic Practice," 65; Wetzell, *Inventing the Criminal*, 80.

80. See, for example, the case of Julius G. discussed above. UAT 669/28794. Though differing in terms of how military psychiatry is characterized in its treatment of soldiers, this in many ways echoes the emphasis Paul Lerner has rightly put on the rationalization concerns of psychiatrists during World War I. *Hysterical Men*.

81. Bröckling, "Psychopathische Minderwertigkeit?," 167. On the expansion into border conditions, see also chapter 1.

82. On such attempts to clarify and nuance conditions despite the limits of the terminology, see Schmidt, *Forensisch-Psychiatrische Erfahrungen im Krieg*, 25; Meier, "Fahnenflucht und unerlaubte Entfernung," 13, 20, 41; Kastan, "Die strafbare Handlungen," 791. Similar attempts appeared in the actual patient files: Case of Franz B. (treatment dates November 23, 1915, to January 7, 1916), ALVR, Düren Krankenakten, Box for November 7 to November 23, 1915. Komo also includes an example that qualifies being "mentally ill" in the "narrow sense of the word." "*Für Volk*," 49.

83. On the explicit inclusion of men suffering from such conditions among the "not healthy," see, for example, Pönitz, "Psychologie und Psychopathologie," 264; Hösslin, "Über Fahnenflucht," 354; Birnbaum, "Ergebnisse 49," 80.

84. Indeed, much of the discussion of desertion under the Nazis revolves around this question of desertion as "resistance." Ziemann, *Violence and the German Soldier*, 93. On source limitations regarding motivations, see Jahr, "Der Krieg zwingt die Justiz," 196, 198; Ziemann, *Violence and the German Soldier*, 109.

85. Details for the case of Otto B. are from UAT 669/28565.

86. The quotes and details for this case are all drawn from the patient file of Jakob S. (treatment dates May 16 to August 8, 1917; August 14 to October 3, 1917), ALVR, Düren Krankenakten, Box April 25 to May 29, 1917.

87. Common to a lot of the antiwar propaganda of the time, such poems are also noted by Wilhelm Pieck. BAB-Li, NY 4036/13.

88. File for Georg S. (treatment dates November 27, 1914, to July 1, 1915), Haus 5, Düren Hospital.

89. Wladislaus S. (treatment dates February 16 to May 2, 1917, and May 3 to May 27, 1917) ALVR, Düren Krankenakten, Box January 27 to February 27, 1917.

90. Heinrich B. (treatment dates February 23 to August 11, 1916), ALVR, Grafenberg Krankenakten, Box Bri-C 1916.

91. On the military court procedures and outcomes, see Jahr, *Gewöhnliche Soldaten*; Jahr, "Der Krieg zwingt die Justiz."

92. Meier, "Fahnenflucht und unerlaubte Entfernung," 39–40. This is significant especially given that a notable expert like Evald Stier—author of the widely cited foundational work on military psychiatry and desertion—argued for less leniency in his prewar work: *Fahnenflucht und unerlaubte Entfernung: Eine psychologische, psychiatrische und militärrechtliche Studie* (Halle: Verlag Carl Marhold, 1905). See also Thomas Kraft, *Fahnenflucht und Kriegsneurose: Gegenbilder zur Ideologie des Kampfes in der deutschsprachigen Literature nach dem Zweiten Weltkrieg* (Würzburg: Königshausen & Neumann, 1994), 28.

93. See the opening case above.

94. While variations in how different minorities were considered did not leave an imprint in the archival files, there are occasional references to particular groups in public discussions, such as the clear anti-Jewish intent behind an article dealing with Adventists. "Religiöser oder militärischer Gehorsam?," *Deutsche Tageszeitung*, February 23, 1908, BAF, PH 2/729. In terms of numbers, there are sometimes small variances in the statistics cited for military executions in World War I. Bröckling, *Disziplin*, 74; Bröckling, "Psychopathische Minderwertigkeit," 165; Jahr, *Gewöhnliche Soldaten*, 18, 87, 336; Ziemann, *Violence and the German Soldier*, especially 112–20; Steven R. Welch, "Military Justice," in *1914-1918-online. International Encyclopedia of the First World War*, ed. Ute Daniel, Peter Gatrell, Oliver Janz, Heather Jones, Jennifer Keene, Alan Kramer, and Bill Nasson, issued by Freie Universität Berlin, Berlin (updated October 8, 2014), doi:10.15463/ie1418.10393. On the differences between German and Austro-Hungarian military law in punishing soldiers' inebriation, see Stoll, *Ergebnisse psychiatrischer Begutachtung*, 9–11. On the potentially harsher treatment of soldiers with psychiatric conditions in Britain, see Gerard Oram, *Military Executions during World War I* (Basingstoke, UK: Palgrave Macmillan, 2003), especially 64. Thomas Kraft notes the statistics for German death sentences not only during the war but also for the longer period of 1907 to 1932, during which time 1,547 death sentences were handed down, of which 337 were carried out. Hence, if one calculates the average rate of executions per month for both terms, the results indicate that death sentences were less likely to be issued during the war and less frequently carried out, perhaps reflecting the recognition of the many mitigating factors soldiers faced during the war. On the statistics, see Kraft, *Fahnenflucht und Kriegsneurose*, 22. For a rare example of an execution proceeding for desertion, see BAF, RM 121-I/906 "Gericht der I. Marinedivision.- Verfahren wegen Fahnenflucht."

95. Bröckling and Sikora, "Einleitung," 14; Welch, "Military Justice"; Detlef Garbe, "Radikale Verweigerung aus Prinzipientreue und Gewissensgehorsam: Kriegsdienstver-

weigerung im 'Dritten Reich,'" in *Ausübung, Erfahrung und Verweigerung*, ed. Andreas Gestrich (Münster: Lit, 1996), 148–51; Dieter Knippenschild, "Deserteure im Zweiten Weltkrieg: Der Stand der Debatte," in Bröckling and Sikora, *Armeen und ihre Deserteure*, 232. On a connection among imperial discussions of military discipline, degeneracy, and the Nazi era, see, for example, Bröckling, "Psychopathische Minderwertigkeit," 182. See also a more moderate position that leaves open the connections in Jahr, "Der Krieg zwingt die Justiz," 216.

96. See the relevant secondary literature on such developments cited in those chapters.

97. Other scholars have alluded to the role psychiatry played in delegitimizing dissent, though variation exists on whether the medicalization was pursued intentionally to "depoliticize" soldiers. Bröckling, *Disziplin*, 230–31; Riedesser and Verderber, *Aufrüstung*, 20, 126; Hermes, *Krankheit: Krieg*, especially 354, 358.

98. Jahr, "Der Krieg zwingt die Justiz," 197; Jahr, *Gewöhnliche Soldaten*, 109, 165, 189; Bröckling, "Psychopathische Minderwertigkeiten," 172; Bröckling, *Disziplin*, 230–31. On conscientious objectors' efforts to spread their ideas and the authorities' concern, see chapter 4.

99. As Jahr notes, soldiers could and did find ways to be not merely the "object" but also the "subject of action," even when at the bottom of the military hierarchy and in the midst of a grueling war; he also speaks of a "scope of action" afforded soldiers, despite real limits to this as well. *Gewöhnliche Soldaten*, 32–33, 95. Similarly, see Ziemann, "Verweigerungsformen," 100; Wette, "Militärgeschichte von unten," 24.

100. Bröckling and Sikora, "Einleitung," 10.

101. Ibid., 8.

102. See, for example, the statistical breakdown of these recommendations in Hösslin, "Über Fahnenflucht," 354–55; Meier, "Fahnenflucht und unerlaubte Entfernung," 136, table II.

103. See various concerns expressed in BAF, RM 43/1301 "Landesverrat und Fahnenflucht." See also Jahr, *Gewöhnliche Soldaten*, 196–98.

4. Conscientious Objectors

1. All information and quotes for this case are drawn from BAF, PERS 9, 13814 (Box 01.01.1891 Mül-N), Sennes N. (treatment dates October 5 to October 31, 1917).

2. On the problems associated with the shortage of human and material resources during the war affecting medical treatment, see chapter 2.

3. Manfred von Richthofen, *Der Rote Kampflieger* (Berlin: Ullstein Verlag, 1917). On the celebrity status of Richthofen, see Joachim Castan, *Der Rote Baron: Die ganze Geschichte des Manfred von Richthofen* (Stuttgart: Klett-Cotta, 2007), especially chapter 6.

4. Bertha von Suttner, *Die Waffen nieder! Eine Lebensgeschichte* (Dresden: Pierson, 1899).

5. See the treatment of pre-1914 pacifism in chapter 1.

6. Alan G. Simmonds, *Britain and World War I* (New York: Routledge, 2012), 162; Richard Overy, *The Bombing War: Europe 1939–1945* (London: Penguin, 2014), 20–21;

David Stevenson, *With Our Backs to the Wall: Victory and Defeat in 1918* (Cambridge, MA: Belknap Press of Harvard University Press, 2011), 186; Raymond H. Fredette, *The Sky on Fire: The First Battle of Britain, 1917–1918* (Tuscaloosa: University of Alabama Press, 2007), 60–64.

7. On Michaelis, see Christoph Regulski, *Die Reichskanzlerschaft von Georg Michaelis 1917: Deutschlands Entwickelung zur parlementarisch-demokratischen Monarchie im Ersten Weltkrieg* (Marburg: Tectum, 2003).

8. Wilfried Loth, *Katholiken im Kaiserreich* (Düsseldorf: Droste, 1984), especially 326–39; Chickering, *Imperial Germany and the Great War*, 161–62; David Welch, *Germany, Propaganda and the Total War 1914–1918: The Sins of Omission* (New Brunswick, NJ: Rutgers University Press, 2000), 161.

9. See chapter 2 as well as Lerner, *Hysterical Men*.

10. Wetzell, *Inventing the Criminal*, 48–49, 56, 60; Thomas Stompe, "Psychopathie—Geschichte und Dimensionen," *Neuropsychiatrie* 23 (2009): 3–4; Theodore Million, Erik Simonsen, and Morton Birket-Smith, "Historical Conceptions of Psychopathy in the United States and Europe," in *Psychopathy: Antisocial, Criminal, and Violent Behaviors*, ed. Theodore Million, Erik Simonsen, Morton Birket-Smith, and R. D. Davis (New York: Guilford Press, 1998), 7–28; Kraepelin, *Psychiatrie*; B. Schwarzwald, "Die Kriegsdelikte der Psychopathen," *ZNPO* 43 (1918): 215. For an examination of not only how the term developed historically but also how it came to have its present-day meaning, see the fascinating article by Greg A. Eghigian, "A Drifting Concept for an Unruly Menace: A History of Psychopathy in Germany," *Isis* 106, no. 2 (2015): 283–309.

11. Adalbert Gregor, *Lehrbuch der Psychiatrischen Diagnostik* (Berlin: Karger, 1914), 133.

12. Karl Birnbaum, *Die psychopathische Verbrecher: Die Grenzzustände zwischen geistiger Gesundheit und Krankheit in ihren Beziehungen zu Verbrechen und Strafwesen* (Berlin: Langenscheidt, 1914).

13. Eugen Bleuler, *Lehrbuch der Psychiatrie* (1916; New York: Springer, 1983), 557–58, quoted in Stompe, "Psychopathie," 4. See Stompe more generally on this point as well (4–5).

14. On hysterics and employment, see especially Lerner, *Hysterical Men*.

15. Julius Koch, *Die Psychopathischen Minderwertigkeiten* (Ravensburg: Otto Maier, 1891–93), 1, 13, 18, 110, quoted in Wetzell, *Inventing the Criminal*, 48. On this point more generally, see also Wetzell, 48–49; Wagenblast, *Die Tübinger Militärpsychiatrie*, 45; Eghigian, "Drifting Concept," especially 309.

16. Graham, *Conscription and Conscience*, 358–59; Johann Ohrtmann, *Die Bewegung der Kriegsdienstgegner: Ein schlichter Bericht von schlichtem Heldentum* (Heide: Riechert, 1932), 8; Marth Steinitz, Olga Misar, and Helene Stöcker, *Kriegsdienstverweigerer in Deutschland und Österreich* (Berlin: Die Neue Generation Verlag, 1923), 3; Brock, "Confinement of Conscientious Objectors," especially 247, 259n2. See also the relevant discussion in the introduction.

17. Stöcker, "Kriegsdienstverweigerung," 126. For a more recent reference that indicates the distinctness of medicalization in Germany, see Charles C. Moskos and John Whiteclay Chambers II, "Introduction: The Secularization of Conscience," in *The New*

Conscience Objection: From Sacred to Secular Resistance, ed. Charles C. Moskos and John Whiteclay Chambers II (New York: Oxford University Press, 1993), 12.

18. Steinitz, Misar, and Stöcker, *Kriegsdienstverweigerer*, 3.

19. The Weimar reports on conscientious objectors note several individual cases in which this happened. For more on the medicalization of conscientious objectors and these cases, see also Armin T. Wegner, *Die Verbrechen der Stunde—Die Verbrechen der Ewigkeit: Drei Reden wider die Gewalt* (Berlin: Verlag Neues Vaterland, 1922); Graham, *Conscription and Conscience*, 358–59.

20. Martin Ceadel, *Pacifism in Britain 1914–1945: The Defining of a Faith* (New York: Oxford University Press, 1980), especially chapter 4; Peter Brock, "Prison Samizdat of British Conscientious Objectors in the Two World Wars," in *Against the Draft*, ed. Peter Brock (Toronto: University of Toronto Press, 2006), 223–24; Graham, *Conscription and Conscience*, especially 68–70.

21. Indeed, Wegner refers to the victors of World War I as having "freed us from ourselves" in ending German militarism with the conditions of the Treaty of Versailles. *Verbrechen der Stunde*, 30. In addition to the other Weimar-era pieces noted here, see also Lilli Jannasch, "Die angelsächsische Bruderhand," *Die Weltbühne* 16 (1920): 428–30; Martha Steinitz, *Die englischen Kriegsdienstverweigerer: mit einem Anhang: Klassischer Pazifismus und Kriegsdienstverweigerung* (Berlin: Verlag Neues Vaterland, 1921).

22. Even noted opponent of the *Sonderweg* theory David Blackbourn mentions the important role of the military and martial values in nineteenth-century Germany. *Fontana History of Germany*, 374–85. For a recent overview of the *Sonderweg* with relevant literature from both sides, see Jürgen Kocka, "Looking Back on the Sonderweg," *Central European History* 51 (2018): 137–42. See also the discussion of the military in imperial Germany in chapter 1.

23. Ceadel, *Pacifism in Britain*, 24.

24. "Zum Weltfrieden durch Kreigsdienstverweigerung," *Die Neue Generation* 18 (1922): 376; Moskos and Chambers, "Introduction," 11–12.

25. Ohrtmann, *Die Bewegung der Kriegsdienstgegner*, 12; Graham, *Conscription and Conscience*, 365–68. On the developments within Mennonitism in Germany, including the long-term accommodation with full military service, see the eye-opening book by Goossen, *Chosen Nation*.

26. Moskos and Chambers, commenting on the work of Michel L. Martin in "Introduction," 17.

27. See especially chapter 2.

28. Wette, *Ernstfall Frieden*, 14.

29. Ceadel, *Pacifism in Britain*, 2.

30. Reinhold Lüttgemeier-Davin and Kerstin Wolff, "Einleitung: Helene Stöckers unvollendete Lebenserinnerungen," in *Lebenserinnerungen: Die unvollendete Autobiographie einer frauenbewegten Pazifisten, Helene Stöcker* (Vienna: Bohlau, 2015), 28.

31. From the number of files of objectors found in the archival holdings after reviewing approximately 2,200 individual cases, one might suggest a rough estimate putting the overall number of such men in Germany during World War I in the several hundreds.

32. The term *Kriegsdienstverweigerer* has come to refer to someone who refuses military service on the basis on conscience, but this is more a common connotation than inherent in the denotation of the word, as it is in the English version. Some individuals—both during World War I and afterward—have largely used it for its more basic definition, which simply refers to someone who refuses service with the reasons left open. See, for example, the usage and qualifications in this respect made by Hecker, *Die Kriegsdienstverweigerung im deutschen und ausländischen Recht*. The file of Georg W., who was treated in the university clinic in Freiburg, is an example of a particularly elusive case. Not included among the objectors in this chapter, as the record is too ambiguous, Georg W. was sent to the hospital because of "exaggerated piety" that made him completely unsuitable for service. Indeed, he was dismissed from the army on the basis of this alone and allowed to go back to his civilian job as a postman. While the file never explored the exact difficulties surrounding his religious beliefs, the fact that Georg had already secured the noncombatant position of telephonist further suggests he may have had reservations about military service. Universitätsarchiv, Albert-Ludwigs-Universität Freiburg (UAF), B0253/968. On the particular issues with using medical files as sources, see the relevant section in the introduction.

33. See chapter 1. See also Brock, *Pacifism in Europe*, 472; Ceadel, *Pacifism in Britain*, 9.

34. For good overviews of the theoretical boundaries and debates concerning conscientious objection, see Brock, *Pacifism in Europe*, especially 471–81; Moskos and Chambers, "Introduction,"especially 3–15. See also Hecker, *Die Kriegsdienstverweigerung im deutschen und ausländischen Recht*, 5, 13–14; Grünewald, *Zur Geschichte der Kriegsdienstverweigerung*, 18; Ulrich Linse, *Organisierter Anarchismus im Deutschen Kaiserreich von 1871* (Berlin: Duncker & Humblot, 1969), 363; Schreiber, "Kreigsdienstverweigerung," 20–22; Stahnke, "Kriegsdienstverweigerung," 510; Ceadel, *Pacifism in Britain*, chapters 2–4.

35. Hecker, *Die Kriegsdienstverweigerung im deutschen und ausländischen Recht*, 9–10; Grünewald, *Zur Geschichte der Kriegsdienstverweigerung*, 12; Goossen, *Chosen Nation*, 98; Brock, *Pacifism in Europe*, chapter 11; Bernet, "Kriegsdienstverweigerung."

36. On the term "absolutists" versus "alternativists," see Brock, *Pacifism in Europe*, 477.

37. Lüttgemeier-Davin and Wolff, "Einleitung," 27; Wette, *Ernstfall Frieden*, especially 264; Ulrich Linse, "Biographische Daten," in *Ernst Friedrich zum 10: Todestag*, ed. Andreas W. Mytze (Berlin: Mylet-Druck, 1977), 64, 68–69; Moskos and Chambers, "Introduction," 12–13.

38. See a legal case from April 19, 1918, in BAF, RM 121-I/908 "Gericht der I. Marinedivision.-Verfahren wegen Fahnenflucht und Kriegsverrat."

39. See Kroch Library Manuscript Collections, Cornell University, Fred Briehl Papers, Box 1, folder 15, letter from Fred Briehl to his partner Edna on March 7, 1918.

40. All details and quotes for this case are from the treatment file for Wilhelm H. (treatment dates March 29 to May 23, 1917), ALVR, Düren Krankenakten, Box March 28 to April 24, 1917.

41. For more background on the Bible Student movement, see Garbe, *Between Resistance and Martyrdom*, especially chapter 1.

42. The psychiatrist Georg Stertz noted the offenses normally were variations on *Gehorsamsverweigerung* but included those of insulting and questioning superior offi-

cers as well. "Verschrobene Fanatiker," *Berliner Klinische Wochenschrift* 56 (1919): 588. Not surprisingly, such charges were also grouped (alongside refusal to obey orders) under the same (sixth) section of imperial military law entitled "Strafbare Handlungen gegen die Pflichten der militärischen Unterordnung." See Wilhelm Brauer, *Handbuch des Deutschen Militärstrafrechts* (Erlangen: Enke, 1872), 123–44. While the charges of refusal to obey orders, desertion, and going AWOL (*Gehorsamsverweigerung, Fahnenflucht,* and *Unerlaubte Entferung*) were frequently noted in connection with dissent more generally and conscientious objection specifically, those linked to treason were the exception. See, for example, BAF, RM 43/1301 as well as the case of Hans Paasche discussed in this book.

43. On this incomprehensibility, see Brock, "Confinement of Conscientious Objectors," 257; Komo, "*Für Volk*," 89; Bröckling, *Disziplin*, 230–31; Gerd Krumeich, "Vorwort zur Wiederveröffentlichung," in *Krieg dem Kriege*, ed. Ernst Friedrich (Munich: Deutsche Verlags-Anstalt, 2004), iv; Bröckling, "Psychopathische Minderwertigkeit," 171. While objectors' views have often been met with skepticism, Erik-Jan Zürcher suggests the common people expressed far less disapproval of such ideas in the Ottoman Empire during World War I. "Refusing to Serve by Other Means: Desertion in the Late Ottoman Empire," in *Conscientious Objection: Resisting Militarized Society*, ed. Özgur Heval Çinar and Coşkun Üsterci (London: Zed, 2009), 50.

44. A. H. Hübner, *Über Wahrsager, Weltverbesserer, Nerven=und Geisteskrankheiten im Krieg: Vortrag gehalten in der Anthropologischen Gesellschaft zu Bonn* (Bonn: Marcus & Webers Verlag, 1918), 18.

45. Schmidt, *Forensich-Psychiatrishe Erfahrungen im Kriege*, 10.

46. *Die Neue Generation* 24 (1928): 66–68. The article is reprinted in Grünewald, *Zur Geschichte der Kriegsdienstverweigerung*, 37–38 (quote from 38).

47. Robert Gaupp, "Dienstverweigerung aus religösen (und politischen) Gründen und ihre gerichtärztliche Beurteilung," *Medicinisches Correspondenz-Blatt* 88 (1918): 168. Brock also discusses this incomprehensibility of conscientious objection as well as references this quote, in a somewhat different format, in "Confinement of Conscientious Objectors," 252, 257. The widely acknowledged "need of the Fatherland" frequently arose in psychiatric discussions questioning the choices of objectors. Karl Weiler, "Versorgung und weitere Behandlung der psychopathischen, hysterischen und neurotischen Kriegsteilnehmer," *Münchener Medizinische Wochenschrift* 67 (1919): 531.

48. Wette, *Ernstfall Frieden*, 75.

49. Linse, *Organisierter Anarchismus*, especially 313–20.

50. See, for example, Kroch Library Manuscript Collections, Cornell University, Fred Briehl Papers, Box 1, folder 12, letter from Fred to "Dear All" on February 11, 1918.

51. The literature on this topic is vast. See, for example, Karin Hausen, "Die Polarisierung der 'Geschlechtscharacktere'—Eine Spiegelung der Dissoziation von Erwerbs-und Familienleben," in *Sozialgeschichte der Familie in der Neuzeit Europas: Neue Forschungen*, ed. Werner Conze (Stuttgart: Klett, 1976): 363–93; Ida Blom, Karen Hagemann, and Catherine Hall, *Gendered Nation: Nationalisms and Gender Order in the Long Nineteenth Century* (Oxford: Berg, 2000); Mosse, *Image of Man*. In connection with German military psychiatry more specifically, see the works of Köhne, *Kriegshysteriker*; Hermes, *Krankheit: Krieg*, especially chapter 5.

52. Franz T. (treatment dates February 19 to August 12, 1915), ALVR, Düren Krankenakten, Box February 19 to March 31, 1915.

53. See, for example, BAF, PERS 9 13819 (Box 01.01.1891 Sa-Schme), Wilhelm S. (intake date June 5, 1918).

54. On the importance of physicians' preconceptions in constructing patient files, see the discussion in the introduction as well as Condrau, "Patient's View Meets the Clinical Gaze," especially 528–29; Köhne, *Kriegshysteriker*, 84–91.

55. UAT 669/28711 (treatment dates March 17 to May 30, 1917). Interestingly, this assessment was questioned by the attending physician, which was an uncommon occurrence.

56. Johann Jörger, "Über Dienstverweigerer und Friedensapostel," *ZNPO* 43 (1918): 133. The extent to which a patient's disagreement with the norms and beliefs of the attending medical staff commonly becomes pathologized as a symptom of sickness is discussed in detail in the enlightening article by Merrick D. Pilling, Andrea Daley, Margaret F. Bigson, Lori E. Ross, and Juveria Zaheer, "Assessing 'Insight', Determining Agency, and Autonomy: Implicating Social Identities," in *Containing Madness: Gender and 'Psy' in Institutional Contexts*, ed. Jennifer Kilty and Erin Dej (Cham: Palgrave Macmillan, 2018), 191–213.

57. S. Loeb, "Dienstverweigerung aus religiösen Gründen und ihre gerichtsärztliche Beurteilung," *Psychiatrisch-Neurologische Wochenschrift* 20 (1918): 192.

58. Stertz, "Verschrobene Fanatiker," 587.

59. On the disenfranchisement of women and children implied more generally by grouping them together as well as the view that they need to be protected by men, see Sharon M. Meagher and Patrice DiQuinzio, "Introduction: Women and Children First," in *Women and Children First: Feminism, Rhetoric, and Public Policy*, ed. Sharon M. Meager and Patrice DiQuinzio (Albany, NY: SUNY Press, 2005), 1–13; R. Charli Carpenter, "'Women and Children First': Gender, Norms, and Humanitarian Evacuation in the Balkans 1991–95," *International Organization* 57, no. 4 (2003): 661–94.

60. UAT 669/28709 (treatment dates October 9 to October 25, 1917).

61. Hübner, *Über Wahrsager*, 14.

62. Adolf Hoppe, "Militärischer Ungehorsam aus religiöser Überzeugung," *ZNPO* 45 (1919): 405.

63. Information for this case is drawn from the file of Friedrich G. (treatment dates January 30 to February 22, 1917), HAPUH, Patientenakten, Box Gauss-Glock. While some of the objectors uncovered in the archival patient files for this project are also recognizable as the patients reported on by physicians in the medical literature during and immediately after the war, Friedrich G. appears to be the only objector included in this study whose actual medical reports have subsequently been used in the present-day scholarship. See also *Medizin und Krieg* (158–62), where Wolfgang Eckart includes information on Friedrich G. but with some notably different interpretations and emphases.

64. On the importance of invoking early Christian martyrs and comparisons to standing against religious persecution during the *Kaiserreich*, see Bennette, *Fighting for the Soul of Germany*, especially chapter 4.

65. On the broader and more narrow usages of the term, see the discussion in chapter 3.

66. The information for this case is drawn from UAT 669/28748 (treatment dates May 12 to May 25, 1917).

67. *Strafgesetzbuch für das Deutsche Reich* (Nördlingen: C. H. Beck'schen Buchdruckerei, 1871), 11. See also discussions of Paragraph 51 in chapter 3.

68. Friedrich G. (treatment dates January 30 to February 22, 1917), HAPUH, Patientenakten, Box Gauss-Glock.

69. Horstmann, "Religiosität oder Wahn?," 218.

70. Loeb, "Dienstverweigerung," 194.

71. Karl Birnbaum, "Ergebnisse der Neurologie und Psychiatrie: 62. Kriegsneurosen und -psychosen auf Grund der gegenwärtigen Kriegsbeobachtungen," *ZNPRE* 16 (1918): 68.

72. This does not account for over a dozen additional cases of objection found in the archival files as well as published accounts that are not included in this tally because of, for example, lack of information concerning the diagnosis or the psychiatric observation never being completed.

73. On the early twentieth-century conceptions of these terms as well as Kraepelin's role at the time, see Noll, *American Madness*, chapter 3 as well as page 93; Richard Noll, *The Encyclopedia of Schizophrenia and Other Psychotic Disorders*, 3rd ed. (New York: Facts on File, 2007), 124–27, 302–3; Kenneth S. Kendler, "The Clinical Features of Paranoia in the 20th Century and Their Representation in Diagnostic Criteria from DSM-III through DSM-5," *Schizophrenia Bulletin* 43 (2017): 332–42; Heinz Schott and Rainer Tölle, *Geschichte der Psychiatrie: Krankheitslehren, Irrwege, Behandlungsformen* (Munich: Beck, 2006), 387–88.

74. Kraepelin, *Psychiatrie*, 1713.

75. Josef Peretti, "Erfahrungen über psycho-pathologische Zustände bei Kriegsteilnehmern," *Schmidts Jahrbücher* 84 (1917): 259.

76. Gaupp, "Dienstverweigerung aus religiösen (und politischen) Gründen," (1918), 168. Gaupp found this soldier to be mentally ill, as the patient heard the voice "distinctly." Yet in another case Gaupp did not find mental illness, clarifying that in his judgment the patient heard the voice of God "not with the human ear, but purely inwardly." UAT 669/28711, Felix D. (treatment dates March 17 to May 30, 1917).

77. Jörger, "Über Dienstverweigerer," 131; Schott and Tölle, *Geschichte*, 388.

78. Brock, "Confinement of Conscientious Objectors," 253. Brock largely ignored the subsequent issue: that even the "sane" patients were still diagnosed with psychopathy. Regardless, his article is still very informative and has been highly influential for the writing of this chapter.

79. Ibid.

80. A point Brock's own multiple qualifications to his overall framework seemed to acknowledge.

81. On the hysteria debate, see chapter 2 as well as Lerner, *Hysterical Men*.

82. Brock, "Confinement of Conscientious Objectors," 253.

83. Brock indicated that Gaupp had a sample size of thirteen, but this appears to have been a double counting by the historian of two patients that Gaupp wrote about both

when discussing his entire experiences with COs and separately, when discussing the two Jehovah's Witnesses. "Confinement of Conscientious Objectors," 253, 261n19.

84. Ibid., 258.

85. Ibid.

86. Gaupp did not provide enough specifics about the patients to make directly locating the records possible. Nonetheless, enough details were present to recognize patients he wrote about in journal articles when they appeared (by chance) in the extant archival files being reviewed.

87. Brock includes him as the most notable among the doctors in the second group that saw objection resulting from illness. "Confinement of Conscientious Objectors," 255.

88. Peretti, "Erfahrungen," 259–60.

89. This is based on a review of all military cases treated at the Heil- und Pflegeanstalt Grafenberg during the war, a collection including several hundred soldiers' files.

90. Brock, "Confinement of Conscientious Objectors," especially 256–57.

91. Gaupp, "Dienstverweigerung aus religiösen (und politischen) Gründen," (1918), 167.

92. Schmidt, *Forensisch-Psychiatrische Erfahrungen im Krieg*, 11.

93. Ibid.

94. Horstmann, "Religiosität oder Wahn?," 238.

95. Ibid., 239.

96. Hoppe, "Militärischer Ungehorsam," especially 401-05, 408–12; Hübner, *Über Wahrsager*, 19.

97. Hoppe, "Militärischer Ungehorsam," 401.

98. Brock also emphasizes this point. "Confinement of Conscientious Objectors," 258.

99. On alcohol abstinence and psychiatry in Germany, see Thomas Haenel, *Zur Geschichte der Psychiatrie: Gedanken zur allgemeinen und Baseler Psychiatriegeschichte* (Basel: Springer Basel, 1982), 39–40. On the debates and slow acceptance of vegetarianism in Germany, see Corinna Treitel, *Eating Nature in Modern Germany: Food, Agriculture, and Environment, c. 1870–2000* (Cambridge: Cambridge University Press 2017), especially 104–5. More generally, temperance and vegetarianism—as well as women's issues—appear to have been a common set of interests among German objectors not linked to a particular religious sect. A similar association applied in Britain. Ceadel, *Pacifism*, 84.

100. Dominic Sisti, Michael Young, and Arthur Caplan, "Defining Mental Illnesses: Can Values and Objectivity Get Along?," *BMC Psychiatry* 13 (2013): 346; John Z. Sadler, *Values and Psychiatric Diagnoses* (New York: Oxford University Press, 2004).

101. Pönitz, "Psychologie und Psychopathologie der Fahnenflucht,," 280.

102. On the rise of the profession, see Quinkert, Rauh, and Winkler, "Einleitung," 13; Peckl, "Krank," 33–34; Wetzell, *Inventing the Criminal*, 39–42. On the "war of nerves," see more generally Shepard, *War of Nerves*. On Germany more specifically, see Bernd Ulrich, "Krieg als Nervensache," *Die Zeit*, November 22, 1991.

103. See also Brock, "Confinement of Conscientious Objectors," 255–56.

104. Verein für wissenschaftliche Heilkunde, Königsberg, "Offizielles Protokoll," *Deutsche Medizinische Wochenschrift* 44 (1918): 645. The reported quote was made by E. Meyer during a talk entitled "Religiöse Wahnideen und Kriegsdienst." On the need for psychiatry to specifically focus on issues of religion in the future, see especially Horst-

mann, "Religiosität oder Wahn?"; Robert Gaupp, "Dienstverweigerung aus religiösen (und politischen) Gründen und ihre gerichtsärztliche Beurteilung," *ZNPRE* 17 (1919): 84–85.

105. M. Laehr, "Kriegsärztlicher Abend der Zehlendorfer Lazarette am 24. Juli 1918," *Neurologisches Centralblatt* 37 (1918): 704.

106. Liebermeister, "Über den jetzigen Stand," 325. Gaupp also included a copy of Liebermeister's article among his work papers. UAT 308/89.

107. "Accomplices" is the term used specifically by Riedesser and Verderber, but the implication is found throughout much of the literature (a lot of it noted in chapter 2) of German psychiatry during World War I, especially in connection with the issue of war neurosis and the shift to hysteria as a diagnosis. Riedesser and Verderber, *Aufrüstung*, 7. Notable opposition to this idea can be found in Hermes, *Krankheit: Krieg*, especially 268, 345–55. Nonetheless, Hermes underemphasizes the extent to which the authorities were helped, even by this less than uniform and submissive response from psychiatrists.

108. UAT 669/28711 (treatment dates March 17 to May 30, 1917).

109. Horstmann, "Religiosität oder Wahn?," 239. Here the language recalls the similar manner in which hysterical men were spoken of. See Lerner, *Hysterical Men*, especially chapter 5.

110. Hübner, *Über Wahrsager*, 20.

111. UAT 669/28709 (treatment dates October 9 to October 25, 1917).

112. See, for example, the commentary by Kaufmann—in this case on war neurotics specifically, but implied for wartime psychiatry more generally. "Science as Cultural Practice," especially 136–38.

113. Wilhelm H. (treatment dates March 29 to May 23, 1917), ALVR, Düren Krankenakten, Box for March 28 to April 24, 1917; Horstmann, "Religiosität oder Wahn?," 223.

114. UAT 669/28711 (treatment dates March 17 to May 30, 1917).

115. Mosse, *Image of Man*, especially 109–12; Levsen, "Masculinities"; Hofer, *Nervenschwäche und Krieg*, 20–21, 39, 41, 220–21, 229, 271–82; Ute Frevert, "Wartime Emotions: Honour, Shame, and the Ecstasy of Sacrifice," in *1914-1918-online. International Encyclopedia of the First World War*, ed. Ute Daniel, Peter Gatrell, Oliver Janz, Heather Jones, Jennifer Keene, Alan Kramer, and Bill Nasson, issued by Freie Universität Berlin, Berlin (updated October 8, 2014), doi:10.15463/ie1418.10409; Köhne, *Kriegshysteriker*; Lerner, *Hysterical Men*, 62–64; Peckl, "Krank," 44; Hermes, *Krankheit: Krieg*, chapter 5; Jason Crouthamel, *An Intimate History of the Front: Masculinity, Sexuality, and German Soldiers in the First World War* (New York: Palgrave Macmillan, 2014), especially 6–7, 9, 103. On the potential for conscientious objectors to redefine masculinity, see Daniel Conway, *Masculinities, Militarisation and the End Conscription Campaign: War Resistance in Apartheid South Africa* (New York: Manchester University Press, 2012), 32, 129.

116. Bröckling, *Disziplin*, 230–31; Riedesser and Verderber, *Aufrüstung*, 20, 126. On the larger history of psychiatry as a political tool, see Robert van Voren, "Political Abuse of Psychiatry—an Historical Overview," *Schizophrenia Bulletin* 36 (2010): 33–35. On the general connection between medicalization and depoliticization, see Conrad and Schneider, *Deviance and Medicalization*.

117. Magnus Schwantje, *Hans Paasche: Sein Leben und Wirken* (Berlin: Verlag Neues Vaterland, 1921), 19.

118. Felix D. reportedly told an orderly: "When one is being seen as mentally ill, one has all sorts of thoughts," suggesting an element of self-doubt. UAT 669/28711 (treatment dates March 17 to May 30, 1917).

119. Schmidt, *Forensisch-Psychiatrishe Erfahrungen im Kriege*, 11.

120. For an example of the particular attention given to the "oral and written propaganda" spread by conscientious objectors, see Max Levy-Suhl, "Psychiatrisches und Neurologisches aus einem Kriegslazarett," *Neurologisches Centralblatt* 23 (1916): 949; Chickering, *Imperial Germany and the Great War*, 45–50; Shand, "Doves among the Eagles," especially 96, 98, 99; Riesenberger, *Geschichte der Friedensbewegung*, 108–11; Stöcker, *Lebenserinnerungen: Die unvollendete Autobiographie einer frauenbewegten Pazifisten, Helene Stöcker*, eds. Reinhold Lüttgemeier-Davin and Kerstin Wolff (Vienna: Bohlau, 2015), 204–6, 230, 317; Erpenbeck, *Wilhelm Pieck*, 48–49, 53; Jörger, "Über Dienstverweigerer," 117–18; Hoppe, "Militärischer Ungehorsam," 401, 411; Hübner, *Über Wahrsager*, 19; BAF, RM 43/1301. For an article about men in Britain refusing to serve, see "Gehorsamsverweigerung britischer Seeleute," *Germania*, February 19, 1917. According to friends of Wilhelm Pieck, who was one of the few soldiers to later publish on his experiences, the authorities did not want family members to know what was going on: "His relatives were not permitted officially to know about that. He was only allowed to correspond, as if he was in the garrison just as before. . . . One apparently wanted to avoid something about the case getting out into the public." BAB-Li, NY 4036/13, letter from Käte to Hermann Duncker on July 17, 1917.

121. Lange, *Hans Paasches*, 164–85; Schwantje, *Hans Paasche*, 13–18.

122. Stöcker, *Lebenserinnerungen*, 207, 230.

123. Lange, *Hans Paasche*, 185, 196–97, 200–201. Unfortunately, I have not been able to track down the actual medical records.

124. Lerner has artfully summarized many of these connections in *Hysterical Men*, especially chapters 1–2. See also Wetzell, *Inventing the Criminal*, especially 40; Wetzell, "Psychiatry and Criminal Justice," 272–73; Lengwiler, "Auf dem Weg," 247; Weindling, "Bourgeois Values, Doctors and the State," 199; Quinkert, Rauh, and Winkler, "Einleitung," 13; Peckl, "Krank," 33–34. As Doris Kaufmann notes, however, doctors did not succeed in their desire to make their opinions binding on the court in such cases. "Psychiatrie und Strafjustiz," 24.

125. Brock concluded: "The COs' fate depended solely on the attitude of the examining psychiatrist. . . . Indeed, throughout, the confined COs remained silent partners in the process to which they were involuntarily submitted." "Confinement of Conscientious Objectors," 258. On the more general underestimation of patient agency, see the discussion in the introduction.

126. Hermes does suggest that soldiers may have been using psychiatric treatment to get out of service, but she appears to be discussing cases of simulation. *Krankheit: Krieg*, 268.

127. BAF, RM 43/1301, report from December 29, 1916. Interestingly, this is also around the time when cases of explicit conscientious objection begin appearing with more frequency, as will be discussed below.

128. BAF, RM 121-I/908, letter from Zetzmann [father of an accused sailor] to the military [naval] court on August 31, 1918. This concerned father also plays the "soldier card" in his request for leniency, mentioning the service of three of his other sons as well.

129. Quoted in Steinitz, Misar, and Stöcker, *Kriegsdienstverweigerung*, 13. See also Grünewald, *Zur Geschichte der Kriegsdienstverweigerer*, 33–36.

130. Steinitz, Misar, and Stöcker, *Kriegsdienstverweigerung*, 14.

131. BAB-Li, NY 4036/13 (italics mine).

132. Artur Zickler, *Im Tollhause* (Berlin: Singer, 1919), 21. Zickler does not provide dates in his account.

133. Ibid., 53–54.

134. Ibid., 54.

135. Lange, *Hans Paasche*, especially 185–194; Wette, *Ernstfall Frieden*, 227–29; Wolfram Wette, "Justiz und pazifistische Offiziere in der Zeit der Weimarer Republik," in Kramer and Wette, *Recht ist*, 131.

136. See especially Wolff, "Medikalisierung von unten?"; and Loetz, "Medikalisierung in Frankreich, Grossbritanien und Deutschland."

137. Scholars have noted these potential benefits (usually just in passing) more generally, though not in connection with conscientious objection specifically. Moreover, they also overlook the space for individual agency created by this medicalization. See Bröckling, *Disziplin*, 230; Hermes, *Krankheit: Krieg*, 268; Lerner, *Hysterical Men*, 7.

138. Zicker, *Im Tollhause*, 35.

139. Steinitz, Misar, and Stöcker, *Kriegsdienstverweigerung*, 14.

140. UAT 669/28711 (treatment dates March 17 to May 30, 1917).

141. Lange, *Hans Paasche*, 197–98.

142. Grünewald, *Zur Geschichte der Kriegsdienstverweigerung*, 9. American objector Briehl noted the harsh treatment he experienced in prison. See, for example, Kroch Library Manuscript Collections, Cornell University, Fred Briehl Papers, Box 1, folder 19, letter from Fred Brieh to his partner Edna on August 28, 1918. With the passage of the Selective Training and Service Act of 1940, the situation for American objectors improved significantly in World War II, when options for civilian work were included. Nonetheless, thousands were still imprisoned. Taylor, *Acts of Conscience*, 15, 22, 386.

143. Ceadel, *Pacifism*, chapter 4; Hecker, *Die Kriegsdientsverweigerung im deutschen und ausländischen Recht*, 16–18; Graham, *Conscription and Conscience*, 213, 313. Ohrtmann, *Die Bewegung der Kriegsdienstgegner*, 19.

144. Michael Noone Jr., "Legal Aspects of Conscientious Objection: A Comparative Analysis," in Moskos and Chambers, *The New Conscientious Objection*, especially 194.

145. Armin T. Wegner, *Die Verbrechen der Stunde—Die Verbrechen der Ewigkeit: Drei Reden wider der Gewalt* (Berlin: Verlag Neues Vaterland, 1922), 51–54; Ohrtmann, *Die Bewegung der Kriegsdienstgegner*, 12–13, 29; Moskos and Chambers, "Introduction," 12.

146. Shepard, *War of Nerves*, 101.

147. Hecker, *Die Kriegsdientsverweigerung im deutschen und ausländischen Recht*, 10; Kraft, *Fahnenflucht und Kriegsneurose*, 24–25; Hahnenfeld, *Kriegsdienstverweigerung*, 27; Schreiber, "Kriegsdienstverweigerung," 82–83; Ulrich Finckh, "Justiz und Kriegsdienstverweigerung in der Bundesrepublik," in Kramer and Wette, *Recht ist*, 255–56.

148. Schmidt, *Forensisch-Psychiatrishe Erfahrungen im Kriege*, 12.

149. Chickering, *World without War*; Stöcker, *Lebenserinnerungen*, 189; Linse, *Organisierter Anarchismus*, especially 313–20; Grünewald, *Nieder die Waffen*, 58–59; Wette,

Ernstfall Frieden, 208; Garbe, *Between Resistance*, 33; Grünewald and Dungen, *Twentieth-Century Peace Movements*, 11; Ziemann, "Verweigerungsformen," 100.

150. Hans Paasche, *Meine Mitschuld am Weltkrieg* (Berlin: Verlag Neues Vaterland, 1919), especially 4–9; Lange, *Hans Paasche*, 58, 135, 153, 164; Schwantje, *Hans Paasche*, 13.

151. BAB-Li, NY 4036/13; Erpenbeck, *Wilhelm Pieck*, 49–52.

152. Friedrich G. (treatment dates January 30 to February 22, 1917), HAPUH, Patientenakten, Box Gauss-Glock.

153. Wilhelm H. (treatment dates March 29 to May 23, 1917), ALVR, Düren Krankenakten, Box for March 28 to April 24, 1917.

154. BAF, PERS 9 13814 (Box 01.01.1891 Mül-N), Sennes N. (treatment dates October 5 to October 31, 1917).

155. UAT 669/28711 (treatment dates March 17 to May 30, 1917); UAT 669/28709 (treatment dates October 9 to October 25, 1917).

156. Garbe, *Between Resistance*, 33.

157. Stertz, "Verschrobene Fanatiker," 588; Robert Gaupp, "Die gerichtsärtzliche Beurteilung der militärischen Dienstverweigerung aus religiösen Gründen," *ZNPRE* 15 (1918): 92.

158. Hoppe, "Militärischer Ungehorsam," 410.

159. Ibid., 411.

160. Gaupp, "Dienstverweigerung aus religiösen (und politischen) Gründen," (1918), 168.

161. It is interesting to consider the less frequently discussed mutiny of 1917 in Wilhelmshaven. While clearly a lapse in military discipline, and diverse accounts add different details, the "several hours milling about the town's taverns" undertaken by four hundred to six hundred sailors, who quickly returned to their posts later that evening, was also quite a different phenomenon than the conscientious objection noted here. For the source of the quote, see Chickering, *Imperial Germany and the Great War*, 181. See also Holger Herwig, *The First World War: Germany and Austria*, 2nd ed. (London: Bloomsbury, 2014), 365; Daniel Horn, *The German Naval Mutinees* (New Brunswick, NJ: Rutgers University Press, 1969), chapter 4.

Epilogue

1. Magnus Schwantje, "Hat der Krieg die Friedensbewegung vernichtet?," in *Friedens-Heldentum: Pazifistische Aufsätze aus der Zeitschrift "Ethische Rundschau," 1914 und 1915*, ed. Magnus Schwantje (Berlin: Verlag Neues Vaterland, 1919), quotes from 9–10.

2. Magnus Schwantje, "Vorwart," in Schwantje, *Friedens-Heldentum*, 5; Chickering, *Imperial Germany and the Great War*, especially 47–50; Shand, "Doves among the Eagles"; Riesenberger, *Geschichte der Friedensbewegung*, 98–123; Ziemann, "German Pacifism," 421; "Zum Weltfrieden durch Kriegsdienstverweigerung," 376. See also chapter 1.

3. Schwantje, "Vorwart," 5.

4. Ernst Friedrich, "Das Anti-Kriegsmuseum" [1932], in Mytze, *Ernst Friedrich zum 10. Todestag*, 33.

5. Rudolf Goldscheid, "Weltreaktion und Pazifismus," *Friedens-Warte* 23 (1923): 65–68, collected in BAB-Li, R 43-I/510 "Pazifistische Bestrebungen und Verbände, Band I"; Hellmut von Gerlach, "Die Krisis im deutschen Pazifismus," *Vossische Zeitung*, January 15, 1930, collected in BAB-Li, R 8019/1 "Abwehr von Pressenangriffen im Zusammenhang mit Auseinandersetzung innerhalb der Friedensbewegung"; Wolfram Wette, "Einleitung: Probleme des Pazifismus in der Zwischenkriegzeit," in *Pazifismus in der Weimarer Republic: Beiträge zur historischen Friedensforschung*, ed. Karl Holl and Wolfram Wette (Paderborn: Schöningh, 1981), 11, 20; Wette, *Ernstfall Frieden*, 88; Grünewald, *Nieder die Waffen*, 72; Ziemann, "German Pacifism," 426; Guido Grünewald, "War Resisters in Weimar Germany," in *Challenge to Mars: Essays on Pacifism from 1918 to 1945*, ed. Peter Brock and Thomas Socknat (Toronto: University of Toronto, 1999), 69, 74; Kramer and Wette, "Pazifisten im Visier," 28; Benjamin Ziemann, *Contested Commemorations: Republican War Veterans and Weimar Political Culture* (Cambridge: University of Cambridge Press, 2013), 38–39; Reinhold Lüttgemeier-Davin and Kerstin Wolff, "Helene Stöcker—Frauenbewegung und Pazifismus im Kaiserreich und in der Weimarer Republik. Eine Einordnung," in Lüttgemeier-Davin and Wolff, *Lebenserinnerungen*, 325, 333.

6. Guido Grünewald, "Friedenssichering durch radikale Kriegsdienstgegnerschaft: Der Bund der Kriegsdienstgegner (BdK) 1919–1933," in Holl and Wette, *Pazifismus in der Weimarer Republik*, 78; Grünewald, "War Resisters," 69–70, 72; "Kurt Hillers 'neuer' Pazifismus: Kriegsdienstverweigerung oder Kriegsvorbeugung," *Friedens-Warte* 22 (1920): 293–96; Ziemann, "German Pacifism," 426; Stöcker, *Lebenserinnerungen*, especially 220–53.

7. H. Runham Brown, *Der Durchbruch* (Middlesex, UK: War Resisters International, 1930).

8. Jason Crouthamel, "Mobilizing Psychopaths into Pacifists: Psychological Victims of the First World War in Weimar and Nazi Germany," *Peace and Change* 30 (2005): especially 205–7, 210, 213–14, 218, 221, 223; Crouthamel, *Great War and German Memory*; Lange, *Hans Paasches*, 200–201; Wette, "Einleitung," 11, 20; Grünewald, "Friedenssichering durch radikale Kriegsdienstgegenerschaft," 88; Moskos and Chambers, "Introduction," 17; Jürgen Kuhlmann and Ekkehard Lippert, "The Federal Republic of Germany: Conscientious Objection as Social Welfare," in Moskos and Chambers, *The New Conscientious Objection*, 98–105.

9. The accounts by both Ziemann and Crouthamel foreground the agency of the soldiers in these struggles over memorialization. Ziemann, *Contested Commemorations*, especially 143–64; Crouthamel, "Mobilizing Psychopaths"; Lerner, *Hysterical Men*, 193–94, 213–14, 221; Neuner, *Politik und Psychiatrie*, especially 165–96; Greg A. Eghigian, "The Politics of Victimization: Social Pensioners and the German Social State in the Inflation of 1914–1924," *Central European History* 26 (1993): 375–403; Deborah Cohen, *The War Come Home: Disabled Veterans in Britain and Germany, 1914–1939* (Berkeley: University of California Press, 2001), 2–3, 9, 89. While this book has examined the wartime events and has not focused on the Weimar era itself and how the psychiatric discourse may or may not have changed, it is important to remember that postwar rationalizations and attempts to construct memory do not necessarily match up with the realities

of the war itself. For an example of this dissonance between postwar constructions and wartime reality, see Jahr, *Genwöhnliche Soldaten*, 300, 388n22.

10. On this issue, see Blackbourn, *Fontana History of Germany*, 383. See also similar ideas in Rosenblum, *Beyond the Prison Gates.*

11. Nazi-era investigations into some veterans' mental health and diagnoses are evident in medical files begun during World War I—and often dormant for decades—that continued to be added to when various officials of the Third Reich inquired further about the individuals. See also Henry Friedlander, *The Nazi Origins of Genocide: From Euthanasia to the Final Solution* (Chapel Hill: University of North Carolina Press, 1995), 81–82, 174.

Bibliography

Archival Sources

Archiv des Landschaftsverbandes Rheinland (ALVR)

Altakten Rheinische Kliniken Düren, Krankenakten (1914–1918)
Heil- und Pflegeanstalt Galkhausen, Krankenakten (Boxes A–E, G)
Heil- und Pflegeanstalt Grafenberg, Krankenakten (1914–1918)
Rheinische Prov. Heil- und Pflegeanstalt Bedburg-Hau (Kr. Cleve), 23113 Abgelehnte Aufnahme=Anträge

Bundesarchiv Berlin-Lichtenberg (BAB-Li)

NY 4036/13 Aufzeichnungen Wilhelm Piecks im Militärgefängnis Kattowitz
R 43-I/510 Pazifistische Bestrebungen und Verbände, Band I
R 8019/1 Abwehr von Pressenangriffen im Zusammenhang mit Auseinandersetzung innerhalb der Friedensbewegung

Bundesarchiv Freiburg (BAF)

PERS 9 Krankenunterlagen von Angehörigen der Preußischen Armee, Preußischen Marine, Kaiserlichen Marine, Schutztruppen, Reichswehr, und Wehrmacht

PH 2/729 Heranziehung von Mennoniten u.a. Sekten zum Kriegsdienst.- Schriftwechsel
PH 8-I/713 Verfahrensakte
PH 22-II/730 Festungs- und Hauptlazarett II Königsberg, Arrestanstalt und Psychiatrische Abteilung
RM 27-XIV/50 Gericht der I. Marine-Inspektion in Kiel.—Untersuchung wegen Fahnenflucht und Raub
RM 27-XV/48 Gericht der 2. Marine-Inspektion.—Fahnenflucht.-Bestimmungen über das Verfahren gegen Abwesende
RM 43/1301 Landesverrat und Fahnenflucht
RM 121-I/906 Gericht der I. Marinedivision.—Verfahren wegen Fahnenflucht
RM 121-I/908 Gericht der I. Marinedivision.—Verfahren wegen Fahnenflucht und Kriegsverrat

Carl A. Kroch Library, Rare and Manuscript Collections, Cornell University

Fred Briehl Papers

Haus 5, LVR-Klinik Düren

Bewahrungshaus Krankenakten

Historisches Archiv der Psychiatrischen Universitätsklinik Heidelberg (HAPUH)

Reserve=Lazarett XVI, Die Psychiatrische Klinik zu Heidelberg, Patientenakten

Universitätsarchiv, Albert-Ludwigs-Universität Freiburg (UAF)

B0253 Psychiatrische Universitätsklinik, Patientenakten

Universitätsarchiv, Eberhard Karls Universität Tübingen (UAT)

308/42 Gaupp
308/89 Kriegsneurose (1914–1918)
308/90 Reservelazarett II
669 Nervenklinik, Krankengeschichten, Reserve-Lazarett II Tübingen

Newspaper Source

Germania (1914–1918)

Published Primary Sources

Birnbaum, Karl. *Die psychopathische Verbrecher: Die Grenzzustände zwischen geistiger Gesundheit und Krankheit in ihren Beziehungen zu Verbrechen und Strafwesen.* Berlin: Langenscheidt, 1914.

———. "Ergebnisse der Neurologie und Psychiatrie: 48. Kriegsneurosen und -psychosen auf Grund der gegenwärtigen Kriegsbeobachtungen." *Zeitschrift für die gesamte Neurologie und Psychiatrie: Referate und Ergebnisse* 11 (1915): 321–69.

———. "Ergebnisse der Neurologie und Psychiatrie: 49. Kriegsneurosen und -psychosen auf Grund der gegenwärtigen Kriegsbeobachtungen." *Zeitschrift für die gesamte Neurologie und Psychiatrie: Referate und Ergebnisse* 12 (1916): 1–89.

———. "Ergebnisse der Neurologie und Psychiatrie: 50. Kriegsneurosen und -psychosen auf Grund der gegenwärtigen Kriegsbeobachtungen." *Zeitschrift für die gesamte Neurologie und Psychiatrie: Referate und Ergebnisse* 12 (1916): 317–83.

———. "Ergebnisse der Neurologie und Psychiatrie: 56. Kriegsneurosen und -psychosen auf Grund der gegenwärtigen Kriegsbeobachtungen." *Zeitschrift für die gesamte Neurologie und Psychiatrie: Referate und Ergebnisse* 13 (1917): 457–533.

———. "Ergebnisse der Neurologie und Psychiatrie: 58. Kriegsneurosen und -psychosen auf Grund der gegenwärtigen Kriegsbeobachtungen." *Zeitschrift für die gesamte Neurologie und Psychiatrie: Referate und Ergebnisse* 14 (1917): 193–351.

———. "Ergebnisse der Neurologie und Psychiatrie: 62. Kriegsneurosen und -psychosen auf Grund der gegenwärtigen Kriegsbeobachtungen." *Zeitschrift für die gesamte Neurologie und Psychiatrie: Referate und Ergebnisse* 16 (1918): 1–78.

———. "Ergebnisse der Neurologie und Psychiatrie: 67. Kriegsneurosen und -psychosen auf Grund der gegenwärtigen Kriegsbeobachtungen." *Zeitschrift für die gesamte Neurologie und Psychiatrie: Referate und Ergebnisse* 18 (1919): 1–76.

———. "Kastan, Die strafbaren Handlungen psychisch kranker Angehöriger des Feldheeres/ Stiefler, Forensisch-psychiatrische Beobachtungen im Felde" (review), *Archiv für Kriminologie* 69 (1918): 300–301.

Bleuler, Eugen. *Lehrbuch der Psychiatrie*. 1916. Reprint, New York: Springer, 1983.

Boas, K. "Fahnenflucht und unerlaubte Entfernung im Kriege, von Max Meier." *Neurologisches Centralblatt* 38 (1919): 40–41.

Böhmig, H. "Bericht der Nervenabteilung des Reservelazaretts I. Dresden." *Deutsche Militärärztliche Zeitschrift* 45 (1916): 158–81.

Brauer, Wilhelm. *Handbuch des Deutschen Militärstrafrechts*. Erlangen: Enke, 1872.

Fauser, August. "Über die Bedeutung der neueren Entwicklung der Psychiatrie für die gerichtliche Medizin." *Juristisch-psychiatrische Grenzfragen* 2 (1904): 69–79.

Friedrich, Ernst. "Das Anti-Kriegsmuseum" [1932]. In *Ernst Friedrich zum 10. Todestag*, edited by Andreas W. Mytze, 32–35. Berlin: Mylet-Druck, 1977.

Gaupp, Robert. "Die gerichtsärtzliche Beurteilung der militärischen Dienstverweigerung aus religiösen Gründen." *Zeitschrift für die gesamte Neurologie und Psychiatrie: Referate und Ergebnisse* 15 (1918): 92–93.

———. *Die Nervenkranken des Krieges: Ihre Beurteilung und Behandlung. Ein Wort zur Aufklarung und Mahnung unseres Volkes*. Stuttgart: Evangelischer Presseverband für Württemberg, 1917.

———. "Dienstverweigerung aus religösen (und politischen) Gründen und ihre gerichtsärztliche Beurteilung." *Medicinisches Correspondenz-Blatt* 88 (1918): 167–69, 175–77.

———. "Dienstverweigerung aus religiösen (und politischen) Gründen und ihre gerichtsärztliche Beurteilung." *Zeitschrift für die gesamte Neurologie und Psychiatrie: Referate und Ergebnisse* 17 (1919): 84–85.

Gregor, Adalbert. *Lehrbuch der Psychiatrischen Diagnostik*. Berlin: Karger, 1914.

"Gründsätze für die Behandlung und Beurteilung der sogennanten Kriegsneurotiker." *Deutsche Militärärztliche Zeitschrift* 47 (1918): 433–46.

Hoppe, Adolf. "Militärischer Ungehorsam aus religiöser Überzeugung," *Zeitschrift für die gesamte Neurologie und Psychiatrie: Originalien* 45 (1919): 393–412.

Horstmann, W. "Religiosität oder Wahn?" *Zeitschrift für die gesamte Neurologie und Psychiatrie: Originalien* 49 (1919): 218–42.

Hösslin, C. von. "Über Fahnenflucht." *Zeitschrift für die gesamte Neurologie und Psychiatrie: Originalien* 47 (1919): 344–55.

Hübner, A. H. *Über Wahrsager, Weltverbesserer, Nerven=und Geisteskrankheiten im Krieg: Vortrag gehalten in der Anthropologischen Gesellschaft zu Bonn*. Bonn: Marcus & Webers Verlag, 1918.

Jannasch, Lilli. "Die angelsächsische Bruderhand." *Die Weltbühne* 16 (1920): 428–30.

Jörger, Johann. "Über Dienstverweigerer und Friedensapostel." *Zeitschrift für die gesamte Neurologie und Psychiatrie: Originalien* 43 (1918): 117–33.

Jünger, Ernst. *Storm of Steel*. Translated by Michael Hofmann. 1920. Reprint, London: Penguin, 2003.

Kastan, Max. "Die strafbare Handlungen psychisch-kranker Angehöriger des Feldheeres." *Archiv für Psychiatrie und Nervenkrankheiten* 56, nos. 2 & 3 (1916): 573–631, 725–97.

Koch, Julius. *Die Psychopathischen Minderwertigkeiten*. Ravensburg: Otto Maier, 1891–1893.

Kraepelin, Emil. *Psychiatrie: Ein kurzes Lehrbuch für Studirende und Aerzte*. 8th ed., vollständig umgearbeitete Auflage, 4 Bände. Leipzig: Barth, 1909–1915.

"Kurt Hillers 'neuer' Pazifismus: Kriegsdienstverweigerung oder Kriegsvorbeugung," *Friedens-Warte* 22 (1920): 293–96.

Laehr, M. "Kriegsärztlicher Abend der Zehlendorfer Lazarette am 24. Juli 1918." *Neurologisches Centralblatt* 37 (1918): 703–4.

Levy-Suhl, Max, "Psychiatrisches und Neurologisches aus einem Kriegslazarett." *Neurologisches Centralblatt* 23 (1916): 946–59.

Liebermeister, Gustav. "Über den jetzigen Stand der Lehre von den Kriegsneurose." *Deutsche Militärärztliche Zeitschrift* 47 (1918): 321–29.

Loeb, S. "Dienstverweigerung aus religiösen Gründen und ihre gerichtsärztliche Beurteilung." *Psychiatrisch-Neurologische Wochenschrift* 20 (1918): 191–204.

Martineck, Otto. "Tagung der in der Kriegsneurotikerbehandliung tätigen Ärzte der Heeresverwaltung am 9. Oktober d.j., Kurzer Bericht." *Deutsche Militärärztliche Zeitschrift* 47 (1918): 404–7.

Meier, Max. "Fahnenflucht und unerlaubte Entfernung im Krieg." Doctoral diss., Universität Bonn, 1917.

Militär-Straftgesetzbuch. Vom 20. Juni 1872. Berlin: Mittler and Son, 1883.

Morel, Bénédict-Augustin. *Traité des Dégénérescences Physiques, Intellectuelles et Morales de L'espèce Humaine et Des Causes qui Produisent des Variétés Maladives*. Paris: J. B. Baillière, 1857.

Oppenheim, Hermann. *Lehrbuch der Nervenkrankheiten für Ärzte und Studierende*. Berlin: Hirschwald, 1894.

Paasche, Hans. *Meine Mitschuld am Weltkrieg*. Berlin: Verlag Neues Vaterland, 1919.

Peretti, Josef. "Erfahrungen über psycho-pathologische Zustände bei Kriegsteilnehmern." *Schmidts Jahrbücher* 84 (1917): 257–66.

Pönitz, Karl. "Psychologie und Psychopathologie der Fahnenflucht im Kriege." *Archiv für Kriminologie* 68 (1917): 260–81.

Richthofen, Manfred von. *Der Rote Kampflieger*. Berlin: Ullstein Verlag, 1917.

Runham Brown, H. *Der Durchbruch*. Middlesex, UK: War Resisters International, 1930.

Sanitätsbericht über das Deutsche Heer (Deutsches Feld- und Besatzungsheer) im Weltkriege 1914/1918, Band III. Berlin: E. S. Mittler und Sohn, 1934.

Schmidt, Wilhelm. *Forensisch-Psychiatrische Erfahrungen im Krieg*. Berlin: Karger, 1918.

Schwantje, Magnus. *Hans Paasche: Sein Leben und Wirken*. Berlin: Verlag Neues Vaterland, 1921.

——. "Hat der Krieg die Friedensbewegung vernichtet?" In *Friedens-Heldentum: Pazifistische Aufsätze aus der Zeitschrift "Ethische Rundschau," 1914 und 1915*, edited by Magnus Schwantje, 9–33. Berlin: Verlag Neues Vaterland, 1919.

——. "Vorwart." In *Friedens-Heldentum: Pazifistische Aufsätze aus der Zeitschrift "Ethische Rundschau," 1914 und 1915*, edited by Magnus Schwantje, 5–6. Berlin: Verlag Neues Vaterland, 1919.

Schwarzwald, B. "Die Kriegsdelikte der Psychopathen." *Zeitschrift für die gesamte Neurologie und Psychiatrie: Originalien* 43 (1918): 215–59.

Steinitz, Martha. *Die englischen Kriegsdienstverweigerer: mit einem Anhang: Klassischer Pazifismus und Kriegsdienstverweigerung*. Berlin: Verlag Neues Vaterland, 1921.

Steinitz, Martha, Olga Misar, and Helene Stöcker. *Kriegsdienstverweigerer in Deutschland und Österreich*. Berlin: Die Neue Generation Verlag, 1923.

Stertz, Georg. "Verschrobene Fanatiker." *Berliner Klinische Wochenscrift* 56 (1919): 586–88.

Stiefler, Georg. "Forensich-Psychiatrish aus dem Felde." *Wiener Medizinische Wochenschrift* 69 (1919): 1416–20, 1472–74.

Stier, Evald. *Fahnenflucht und unerlaubte Entfernung: Eine psychologische, psychiatrische und militärrechtliche Studie*. Halle: Verlag Carl Marhold, 1905.

Stöcker, Helene. "Kriegsdienstverweigerung." In *Die Friedensbewegung; ein Handbuch der Weltfriedensströmungen der Gegenwart*, edited by Walter Fabian and Kurt Lenz, 121. 1922. Reprint, Cologne: Bund, 1985.

——. *Lebenserinnerungen: Die unvollendete Autobiographie einer frauenbewegten Pazifisten, Helene Stöcker*. Edited by Reinhold Lüttgemeier-Davin and Kerstin Wolff. Vienna: Bohlau, 2015.

Stoll, H. *Ergebnisse psychiatrischer Begutachtung beim Kriegsgericht*. Halle: Carl Marhold Verlag, 1918.

Storch, Alfred. "Beiträge zur Psychopathologie der unerlaubten Entferung und Fahnenflucht im Felde." *Zeitschrift für die gesamte Neurologie und Psychiatrie: Originalien* 46 (1919): 348–67.

Strafgesetzbuch für das Deutsche Reich. Nördlingen: C. H. Beck'schen Buchdruckerei, 1871.

Suttner, Bertha von. *Die Waffen nieder! Eine Lebensgeschichte*. Dresden: Pierson, 1899.

Verein für wissenschaftliche Heilkunde, Königsberg. "Offizielles Protokoll." *Deutsche Medizinische Wochenscrift* 44 (1918): 645.

Viszanik, Michael. *Irrenheil- und Pflegeanstalten Deutschlands, Frankreichs, sammt der Cretinen-Anstalt auf dem Abendherberg in der Schweiz, mit eigenen Bemerkungen*. Wien: Verlag von Carl Gerold, 1845.

Voss, G. "Begehrungsvorstellungen und Hysterie." *Deutsche Militärärztliche Zeitschrift* 47 (1918): 35–36.

——. "Der Einfluss der sozialen Lage auf Nerven- und Geisteskrankheiten, Selbstmord und Verbrechen." In *Krankheit und soziale Lage*, edited by Max Mosse and Gustav Tugendreich, 400–472. Munich: J.F. Lehmanns, 1913.

——. "Die Ätiologie der Psychosen." In *Handbuch der Psychiatrie*, part 3, edited by G. Aschaffenburg, 1–115. Leipzig: Deuticke, 1915.

——. "Zur Frage der 'Begehrungsvorstellungen' und ihrer Bedeutung für die Entstehung der Hysterie." *Medizinishe Klinik* 32 (1917): 862–63.

Wegner, Armin T. *Die Verbrechen der Stunde—Die Verbrechen der Ewigkeit: Drei Reden wider die Gewalt*. Berlin: Verlag Neues Vaterland, 1922.

Weiler, Karl. "Ein Jahr Kriegsneurotikerbehandlung." *Münchener Medizinische Wochenschrift* 66 (1919): 401–7.

——. "Kriegsgerichtspsychiatrische Erfahrungen und ihre Verwertung für die Strafrechtspflege im Allgemeinen." *Monatsschrift für Kriminalpsychologie und Strafrechtsreform* 12/13 (1921/1922): 282–31, 165–92.

——. "Versorgung und weitere Behandlung der psychopathischen, hysterischen und neurotischen Kriegsteilnehmer." *Münchener Medizinische Wochenschrift* 67 (1919): 531–36.

Zickler, Artur. *Im Tollhause*. Berlin: Singer, 1919.

"Zum Weltfrieden durch Kreigsdienstverweigerung." *Die Neue Generation* 18 (1922): 376–77.

Published Secondary Sources

Abercrombie, Nicholas, Stephen Hill, and Bryan S. Turner. *The Penguin Dictionary of Sociology*. 3rd ed. London: Penguin, 1994.

Ackerknecht, Erwin. *A Short History of Psychiatry*. 2nd rev. ed. Translated by Sula Wolff. New York: Hafner, 1968.

Adams, Rachel, Benjamin Reiss, and David Serlin, eds. *Keywords for Disability Studies*. New York: New York University Press, 2015.

Andrews, Jonathan. "Case Notes, Case Histories, and the Patients' Experience of Insanity at Gartnavel Royal Asylum, Glasgow, in the Nineteenth Century." *Social History of Medicine* 11, no. 2 (1998): 255–81.

Atack, Iain. "Pacifism and Perpetual Peace." *Critical Studies on Security* 6, no. 2 (2018): 207–20.

Bacopoulous-Viau, Alexandra, and Aude Fauvel. "The Patient's Turn: Roy Porter and Psychiatry's Tales, Thirty Years On." *Medical History* 60, no. 1 (2016): 1–18.

Becker, Joachim. "Die Geschichte des Rheinischen Landeskrankenhauses Düsseldorf-Grafenberg von 1876 bis 1918." Med. diss., Universität Düsseldorf, 1978.

Beddies, Thomas. "'Aktivere Krankenbehandlung' und 'Arbeitstherapie': Anwendungsformen und Begründungszusammenhänge bei Hermann Simon und Carl Schneider." In *"Heroische Therapien": Die deutsche Psychiatrie im internationalen Vergleich 1918–1945*, edited by Hans-Walter Schmuhl and Volker Roelcke, 268–86. Göttingen: Wallstein Verlag, 2013.

Bennette, Rebecca Ayako. *Fighting for the Soul of Germany: The Catholic Struggle for Inclusion after Unification*. Cambridge, MA: Harvard University Press, 2012.

——. "Remapping the German Homeland: Germania and Catholic Efforts to Mobilise Continued Support during the First World War." *Immigrants and Minorities* 35, no. 3 (2017): 237–55.

Bergen, Leo van. *Before My Helpless Sight: Suffering, Dying and Military Medicine on the Western Front, 1914–1918*. Translated by Liz Waters. London: Routledge, 2016.

Bernet, Claus. "Kriegsdienstverweigerung im 19. Jahrhundert: Ein Beitrag zum Klischee des Militärstaats Preußen." *Militär und Gesellschaft in der Frühen Neuzeit* 12, no. 2 (2008): 204–22.

Beveridge, Allan. "Voices of the Mad: Patient Letters from the Royal Edinburgh Asylum 1873–1908." *Psychological Medicine* 27, no. 4 (1997): 899–908.

Blackbourn, David. *The Fontana History of Germany, 1780–1918: The Long Nineteenth Century*. London: Fontana, 1997.

Blasius, Dirk. *"Einfache Seelenstörung": Geschichte der deutsche Psychiatrie 1800–1945*. Frankfurt am Main: Fischer, 1994.

Blom, Ida, Karen Hagemann, and Catherine Hall. *Gendered Nation: Nationalisms and Gender Order in the Long Nineteenth Century*. Oxford: Berg, 2000.

Bourke, Joanna. "The Emotions of War: Fear and the British and American Military, 1914–45." *Historical Research* 74 (2001): 314–30.

——. *An Intimate History of Killing: Face-to-Face Killing in Twentieth-Century Warfare*. New York: Basic, 1999.

——. "Suffering and the Healing Profession: The Experience of Military Medicine in the First and Second World Wars." In *War and Medicine*, edited by Melissa Larner, James Peto, and Nadine Monem, 108–25. London: Black Dog, 2008.

Brand-Claussen, Bettina, and Maike Rotzoll. "Uniform und Eigensinn: Reflexe des Militarismus in psychiatrischen Anstalten des deutschen Kaiserreichs." In *Schlachtschrecken-Konventionen: Das Rote Kreuz und die Erfindung der Menschlichkeit im Kriege*, edited by Wolfgang U. Eckart and Philipp Osten, 229–53. Freiburg: Centaurus, 2011.

Braun, Salina. *Heilung mit Defekt: Psychiatrisches Praxis an den Anstalten Hofheim und Siegburg, 1820–1878*. Göttingen: Vandenhoeck & Ruprecht, 2008.

Brock, Peter. "Confinement of Conscientious Objectors as Psychiatric Patients in World War I Germany." *Peace and Change* 23, no. 3 (1998): 247–64.

——. *Pacifism in Europe to 1914*. Princeton, NJ: Princeton University Press, 1972.

——. "Prison Samizdat of British Conscientious Objectors in the Two World Wars." In *Against the Draft*, edited by Peter Brock, 222–42. Toronto: University of Toronto Press, 2006.

Bröckling, Ulrich. *Disziplin: Soziologie und Geschichte militärischer Gehorsamsproduktion*. Paderborn: Fink, 1997.

——. "Psychopathische Minderwertigkeit? Moralischer Schwachsinn? Krankhafter Wandertrieb? Zur Pathologisierung von Deserteuren im Deutschen Kaiserreich vor

1914." In *Armeen und ihre Deserteure: Vernachlässigte Kapitel einer Militärgeschichte der Neuzeit*, edited by Ulrich Bröckling and Michael Sikora, 161–86. Göttingen: Vandenhoeck & Ruprecht, 1998.

Bröckling, Ulrich, and Michael Sikora. "Einleitung." In *Armeen und ihre Deserteure: Vernachlässigte Kapitel einer Militärgeschichte der Neuzeit*, edited by Ulrich Bröckling and Michael Sikora, 7–15. Göttingen: Vandenhoeck & Ruprecht, 1998.

Burch, Susan. "Disorderly Pasts: Kinship, Diagnoses, and Remembering in American Indian-U.S. Histories." *Journal of Social History* 50 (2016): 362–85.

Burch, Susan, and Kim E. Nielsen. "History." In *Keywords for Disability Studies*, edited by Rachel Adams, Benjamin Reiss, and David Serlin, 95–98. New York: New York University Press, 2015.

Caplan, Eric Michal. "Trains, Brains, and Sprains: Railway Spine and the Origins of Psychoneuroses." *Bulletin of the History of Medicine* 69, no. 3 (1995): 387–419.

Carlson, Licia. "Institutions." In *Keywords for Disability Studies*, edited by Rachel Adams, Benjamin Reiss, and David Serlin, 109–12. New York: New York University Press, 2015.

Carpenter, R. Charli. "'Women and Children First': Gender, Norms, and Humanitarian Evacuation in the Balkans 1991–95." *International Organization* 57, no. 4 (2003): 661–94.

Castan, Joachim. *Der Rote Baron: Die ganze Geschichte des Manfred von Richthofen*. Stuttgart: Klett-Cotta, 2007.

Ceadel, Martin. *Pacifism in Britain 1914–1945: The Defining of a Faith*. New York: Oxford University Press, 1980.

Chase, Ronald. *The Making of Modern Psychiatry*. Berlin: Logos, 2018.

Chickering, Roger. *Imperial Germany and a World without War: The Peace Movement and German Society, 1892–1914*. Princeton, NJ: Princeton University, 1975.

———. *Imperial Germany and the Great War, 1914–18*. 2nd ed. Cambridge: Cambridge University Press, 2004.

Cocks, Geoffrey, and Konrad H. Jarausch. *German Professions, 1800–1950*. New York: Oxford University Press, 1990.

Cohen, Deborah. *The War Come Home: Disabled Veterans in Britain and Germany, 1914–1939*. Berkeley: University of California Press, 2001.

Condrau, Flurin. "The Patient's View Meets the Clinical Gaze." *Social History of Medicine* 20, no. 3 (2007): 525–40.

Conrad, Peter. "Medicalization and Social Control." *Annual Review of Sociology* 18 (1992): 209–32.

Conrad, Peter, and Joseph W. Schneider. *Deviance and Medicalization: From Badness to Sickness*. Columbus, OH: Merrill, 1985.

Conway, Daniel. *Masculinities, Militarisation and the End Conscription Campaign: War Resistance in Apartheid South Africa*. New York: Manchester University Press, 2012.

Cowan, Michael. *Cult of the Will: Nervousness and German Modernity*. University Park, PA: Penn State University Press, 2008.

Crossley, Nick. "R. D. Laing and the British Anti-psychiatry Movement: A Sociohistorical Analysis." *Social Science & Medicine* 47 (1998): 877–89.

Crouthamel, Jason. *The Great War and German Memory: Society, Politics and Psychological Trauma, 1914–45*. Exeter: University of Exeter Press, 2009.

———. *An Intimate History of the Front: Masculinity, Sexuality, and German Soldiers in the First World War*. New York: Palgrave Macmillan, 2014.
———. "Mobilizing Psychopaths into Pacifists: Psychological Victims of the First World War in Weimar and Nazi Germany." *Peace and Change* 30 (2005): 205–30.
Dales, Joanna. "John William Graham and the Evolution of Peace: A Quaker View of Conflict before and during the First World War." *Quaker Studies* 21, no. 2 (2016): 169–92.
DasGupta, Sayantani. "Medicalization." In *Keywords for Disability Studies*, edited by Rachel Adams, Benjamin Reiss, and David Serlin, 120–21. New York: New York University Press, 2015.
Davies, Owen. *A Supernatural War: Magic, Divination, and Faith during the First World War*. New York: Oxford University Press, 2018.
Deist, Wilhelm. *Militär, Staat und Gesellschaft: Studien zur prussische-deutschen Militärgeschichte*. Munich: Oldenbourg, 1991.
———. "The Military Collapse of the German Empire." *War in History* 3, no. 2 (1996): 186–207.
Deutscher Kulturbund. *Wilhelm Pieck. 1870–1960*. [East] Berlin: Deutscher Kulturbund, 1960,
Dross, Fritz. "'. . . die Gemüse könnten füglich irgendwo anders gereinigt werden'—Beobachtungen zur Geschichte der Anstalt als Irren- und als Krankenhaus." In *"Moderne" Anstaltspsychiatrie im 19. und 20. Jahrhundert—Legitimation und Kritik*, edited by Heiner Fangerau and Karen Nolte, 43–66. Stuttgart: Franz Steiner Verlag, 2006.
Dungen, Peter van den. "Achievements of Peace Movements." In *Twentieth-Century Peace Movements: Successes and Failures*, edited by Guido Grünewald and Peter van den Dungen, 15–31. Lewiston, NY: Edwin Mellen Press, 1995.
Eckart, Wolfgang. "Kriegsgewalt und Psychotrauma im Ersten Weltkrieg." In *Verletzte Seelen: Möglichkeiten und Perspecktiven einer historischen Traumaforschung*, edited by Günter Seidler and Wolfgang Eckart, 85–105. Giessen: Psychosozial-Verlag, 2005.
———. *Medizin und Krieg: Deutschland 1914–1924*. Paderborn: Schöningh, 2014.
____. *Die Wunden heilen sehr schön: Feldpostkarten aus dem Lazarett 1914–1918*. Stuttgart: Franz Steiner Verlag, 2013.
Eckart, Wolfgang, and Robert Jütte. *Medizingeschichte: Eine Einführung, 2. Auflage*. Köln: Böhlau Verlag GmbH und Cie, 2014.
Eghigian, Greg A. "A Drifting Concept for an Unruly Menace: A History of Psychopathy in Germany." *Isis* 106, no. 2 (2015): 283–309.
———. "The German Welfare State as a Discourse of Trauma." In *Traumatic Pasts*, edited by Mark S. Micale and Paul Lerner, 92–112. Cambridge: Cambridge University Press, 2001.
———. "The Politics of Victimization: Social Pensioners and the German Social State in the Inflation of 1914–1924." *Central European History* 26 (1993): 375–403.
Emirbayer, Mustafa, and Ann Mische. "What Is Agency?" *American Journal of Sociology* 103 (1998): 962–1023.
Engstrom, Eric. "Assembling Professional Selves: On Psychiatric Instruction in Imperial Germany." In *Psychiatrie im 19. Jahrhundert. Forschungen zur Geschichte von psychiatrischen Institutionen, Debatten und Praktiken im deutschen Sprachraum*, edited by Eric J. Engstrom and Volker Roelcke, 116–52. Basel: Schwabe Verlag, 2003.

——. *Clinical Psychiatry in Imperial Germany: A History of Psychiatric Practice*. Ithaca, NY: Cornell University Press, 2003.

——. "Topographies of Forensic Practice in Imperial Germany." *International Journal of Law and Psychiatry* 37, no. 1 (2014): 63–70.

Engstrom, Eric, and Volker Roelcke. "Die 'alte Psychiatrie'? Zur Geschichte und Aktualität der Psychiatrie im 19. Jahrhundert." In *Psychiatrie im 19. Jahrhundert. Forschungen zur Geschichte von psychiatrischen Institutionen, Debatten und Praktiken im deutschen Sprachraum*, edited by Eric J. Engstrom and Volker Roelcke, 9–25. Basel: Schwabe Verlag, 2003.

Erpenbeck, Fritz. *Wilhelm Pieck: Ein Lebensbild*. Berlin: Dietz, 1951.

Finckh, Ulrich. "Justiz und Kriegsdienstverweigerung in der Bundesrepublik." In *Recht ist, was den Waffen nützt. Justiz und Pazifismus im 20. Jh.*, edited by Wolfram Wette and Helmut Kramer, 255–74. Berlin: Aufbau Verlag, 2004.

Fischer-Homberger, Ester. "Der Begriff 'Krankheit' als Funktion aussermedizinischer Gegebenheiten: Zur Geschichte der traumatischen Neurose." *Sudhoff's Archiv* 54 (1970): 225–41.

Fredette, Raymond H. *The Sky on Fire: The First Battle of Britain, 1917–1918*. Tuscaloosa: University of Alabama Press, 2007.

Frevert, Ute. *A Nation in Barracks: Modern Germany, Military Conscription and Civil Society*. Oxford: Berg, 2004.

——. "Wartime Emotions: Honour, Shame, and the Ecstasy of Sacrifice." In *1914-1918-online. International Encyclopedia of the First World War*, edited by Ute Daniel, Peter Gatrell, Oliver Janz, Heather Jones, Jennifer Keene, Alan Kramer, and Bill Nasson, issued by Freie Universität Berlin, Berlin (updated October 8, 2014), doi: 10.15463/ie1418.10409.

Friedlander, Henry. *The Nazi Origins of Genocide: From Euthanasia to the Final Solution*. Chapel Hill: University of North Carolina Press, 1995.

Friedman, Matthew J., Patricia A. Resick, Richard A. Bryant, and Chris R. Brewin. "Considering PTSD for DSM-5." *Depression and Anxiety* 28 (2011): 750–69.

Frith, John. "Syphilis—Its Early History and Treatment until Penicillin and the Debate on Its Origins." *Journal of Military and Veterans' Health* 20 (2012): 49–58.

Gahlen, Gundula. "'Always Had a Pronouncedly Psychopathic Predisposition': The Significance of Class and Rank in First World War German Psychiatric Discourse." In *Psychological Trauma and the Legacies of the First World War*, edited by Jason Crouthamel and Peter Leese, 81–113. Basingstoke, UK: Palgrave Macmillan, 2017.

Garbe, Detlef. *Between Resistance and Martyrdom: Jehovah's Witnesses in the Third Reich*. Translated by Dagmar G. Grimm. Madison: University of Wisconsin Press, 2008.

——. "Radikale Verweigerung aus Prinzipientreue und Gewissensgehorsam: Kriegsdienstverweigerung im 'Dritten Reich.'" In *Ausübung, Erfahrung und Verweigerung von Gewalt in Kriegen des 20: Jahrhunderts*, edited by Andreas Gestrich, 132–58. Münster: Lit, 1996.

Geary, Patrick J. *The Myth of Nations: The Medieval Origins of Europe*. Princeton, NJ: Princeton University Press, 2002.

Germann, Urs. "'Entmündung der Fachjustiz' oder 'Reserveengel der Jurisprudenz'? Psychiatrische Deutungsmacht im Kontext justizieller Entscheidungsprozesse. Das Beispiel der gerichtspsychiatrischen Begutungspraxis im Kanton Bern 1885–1920." In *Psychiatrie im 19: Jahrhundert*, edited by Eric Engstrom and Volker Roelcke, 219–44. Basel: Schwabe, 2003.

Geroulanos, Stefanos, and Todd Meyers. *The Human Body in the Age of Catastrophe: Brittleness, Integration, Science, and the Great War.* Chicago: University of Chicago Press, 2018.

Gilman, Sander L. "Madness." In *Keywords for Disability Studies*, edited by Rachel Adams, Benjamin Reiss, and David Serlin, 114–19. New York: New York University Press, 2015.

Goldberg, Ann. *Honor, Politics, and the Law in Imperial Germany, 1871–1914.* Cambridge: Cambridge University Press, 2010.

——. "The Limits of Medicalization: Jewish Lunatics and Nineteenth-Century Germany." *History of Psychiatry* 7 (1996): 265–85.

——. "The Mellage Trial and the Politics of Insane Asylums in Wilhelmine Germany." *Journal of Modern History* 74, no. 1 (2002): 1–32.

——. "A Reinvented Public: 'Lunatic Rights' and Bourgeois Populism in the Kaiserreich." *German History* 21, no. 2 (2003): 159–82.

——. *Sex, Religion, and the Making of Modern Madness: The Eberbach Asylum and German Society 1815–1849.* New York: Oxford University Press, 1999.

Goldmann, Renate, Erhard Knauer, and Eusebius Wirdeier. *Moderne, Weltkrieg, Irrenhaus: Bruche in der Psychiatrie, 1900–1930.* Essen: Klartext Verlag, 2014.

Goossen, Benjamin W. *Chosen Nation: Mennonites and Germany in a Global Era.* Princeton, NJ: Princeton University Press, 2017.

Graham, J. W. *Conscription and Conscience: A History, 1916–1919.* London: Allen & Unwin, 1922.

Grossman, Dave. *On Killing: The Psychological Cost of Learning to Kill in War and Society.* Boston: Little Brown, 1995.

Grünewald, Guido. "Friedenssichering durch radikale Kriegsdienstgegnerschaft: Der Bund der Kriegsdienstgegner (BdK) 1919–1933." In *Pazifismus in der Weimarer Republic: Beiträge zur historischen Friedensforschung*, edited by Karl Holl and Wolfram Wette, 77–90. Paderborn: Schöningh, 1981.

——. *Nieder die Waffen! Hundert Jahre Deutsche Friedensgesellschaft 1892–1992.* Bremen: Donat, 1992.

——. "War Resisters in Weimar Germany." In *Challenge to Mars: Essays on Pacifism from 1918 to 1945*, edited by Peter Brock and Thomas Socknat, 67–88. Toronto: University of Toronto, 1999.

——. *Zur Geschichte der Kriegsdienstverweigerung.* Essen: Deutsche Friedensgesellschaft, 1982.

Haase, Norbert. *Deutsche Deserteure.* Berlin: Rotbuch Verlag, 1987.

Haenel, Thomas. *Zur Geschichte der Psychiatrie: Gedanken zur allgemeinen und Baseler Psychiatriegeschichte.* Basel: Springer Basel, 1982.

Hahnenfeld, Günter. *Kriegsdienstverweigerung.* Hamburg: Decker's Verlag, 1966.

Harrison, Mark. "The Medicalization of War—the Militarization of Medicine." *Social History of Medicine* 9, no. 2 (1996): 267–76.

———. "War and Medicine in the Modern Era." In *War and Medicine*, edited by Melissa Larner, James Peto, and Nadine Monem, 10–27. London: Black Dog, 2008.

Hausen, Karin. "Die Polarisierung der 'Geschlechtscharacktere'—Eine Spiegelung der Dissoziation von Erwerbs- und Familienleben." In *Sozialgeschichte der Familie in der Neuzeit Europas: Neue Forschungen*, edited by Werner Conze, 363–93. Stuttgart: Klett, 1976.

Hecker, Hellmuth. *Die Kriegsdienstverweigerung im deutschen und ausländischen Recht mit Übersetzung der ausländischen Texte*. Frankfurt am Main: Alfred Metzner Verlag, 1954.

Hermes, Maria. *Krankheit: Krieg: Psychiatrische Deutungen des Ersten Weltkriegs*. Essen: Klartext, 2012.

Herwig, Holger. *The First World War: Germany and Austria*. 2nd ed. London: Bloomsbury, 2014.

Hirschmüller, Albrecht. "The Development of Psychiatry and Neurology in the Nineteenth Century." Translated by Madga Whitrow. *History of Psychiatry* 10 (1999): 395–423.

Hofer, Hans-Georg. "Beyond Freud and Wagner-Jauregg: War Psychiatry and the Hapsburg Army." In *War, Trauma and Medicine in Germany and Central Europe (1914–1939)*, edited by Hans-Georg Hofer, Cay-Rüdiger Prüll, and Wolfgang U. Eckart, 49–71. Freiburg: Centaurus, 2011.

———. *Nervenschwäche und Krieg: Modernitätskritik und Krisenbewältigung in der österreichischen Psychiatrie (1880–1920)*. Vienna: Böhlau, 2004.

Holl, Karl. "Pazifismus." In *Geschichtliche Grundbegriffe: Historisches Lexikon zur politisch- sozialen Sprache in Deutschland, Bd. 4*, edited by Otto Brunner, Werner Conze, and Reinhart Koselleck, 767–87. Stuttgart: Klett-Cotta, 1978.

———. "Why Do Peace Movements Fail?" In *Twentieth-Century Peace Movements: Successes and Failures*, edited by Guido Grünewald and Peter van den Dungen, 3–14. Lewiston, NY: Edwin Mellen Press, 1995.

Horn, Daniel. *The German Naval Mutinees*. New Brunswick, NJ: Rutgers University Press, 1969.

Huerkamp, Claudia. "The Making of the Modern Medical Profession, 1800–1914: Prussian Doctors in the Nineteenth Century." In *German Professions 1800–1914*, edited by G. Cocks and K. H. Jarausch, 66–84. New York: Oxford University Press, 1990.

Hull, Isabel V. *Absolute Destruction: Military Culture and the Practices of War in Imperial Germany*. Ithaca, NY: Cornell University Press, 2005.

Hurn, Juliet D. "The History of General Paralysis of the Insane in Britain, 1830 to 1950." PhD diss., University of London, 1998.

Jahr, Christoph. "'Der Krieg zwingt die Justiz, ihr Innerstes zu revidieren.' Desertion und Militärgerichtsbarkeit im Ersten Weltkrieg." In *Armeen und ihre Deserteure: Vernachlässigte Kapitel einer Militärgeschichte der Neuzeit*, edited by Ulrich Bröckling and Michael Sikora, 187–221. Göttingen: Vandenhoeck & Ruprecht, 1998.

———. *Gewöhnliche Soldaten: Desertion und Deserteure im deutschen und britischen Heer 1914–1918*. Göttingen: Vandenhoeck & Ruprecht, 1996.

Jansen, Christian. "Pazifismus in Deutschland: Entwicklung und innere Widersprüche (1800–1940)." In *Recht ist, was den Waffen nützt: Justiz und Pazifismus im 20. Jh.*, edited by Wolfram Wette and Helmut Kramer, 59–78. Berlin: Aufbau Verlag, 2004.

Jeismann, Michael. *Das Vaterland der Feinde: Studien zum nationalen Feindbegriff und Selbstverständnis in Deutschland und Frankreich, 1792–1918.* Stuttgart: Klett-Cotta, 1992.

Jones, Edgar, and Simon Wessely. "War Syndromes: The Impact of Culture on Medically Unexplained Symptoms." *Medical History* 49, no. 1 (2005): 55–78.

Kaczmarek, Emilia. "How to Distinguish Medicalization from Over-Medicalization." *Medicine, Health Care and Philosophy* 22 (2019): 119–28. doi: 10.1007/s11019-018-9850-1.

Kaufmann, Doris. "Psychiatrie und Strafjustiz im 19. Jahrhundert: die gerichtsmedizinischen Gutachten der Medizinischen Fakultät der Universität Tübingen 1770–1860." *Medizin, Gesellschaft und Geschichte* 10 (1991): 23–39.

——. "Science as Cultural Practice: Psychiatry in the First World War and Weimar Germany." *Journal of Contemporary History* 34, no. 1 (1999): 125–44.

Keegan, John. *The Face of Battle.* New York: Viking, 1976.

Kendler, Kenneth S. "The Clinical Features of Paranoia in the 20th Century and Their Representation in Diagnostic Criteria from DSM-III through DSM-5." *Schizophrenia Bulletin* 43, no. 2 (2017): 332–42.

Kliche, Christian. "Die Stellung der deutschen Militärärzte im Ersten Weltkrieg." PhD diss., FU-Berlin, 1968.

Kloocke, Ruth, Heinz-Peter Schmiedebach, and Stefan Priebe. "Psychological Injury in the Two World Wars: Changing Concepts and Terms in German Psychiatry." *History of Psychiatry* 16 (2005): 43–60.

Knauer, Erhard, Friedel Schulz, and Heinz Lepper. *125 Jahre Rheinische Kliniken Düren: gestern, heute, morgen: Von der Provinzialanstalt zur Fachklinik.* Cologne: Rheinland Verlag, 2003.

Knippenschild, Dieter. "Deserteure im Zweiten Weltkrieg: Der Stand der Debatte." In *Armeen und ihre Deserteure: Vernachlässigte Kapitel einer Militärgeschichte der Neuzeit*, edited by Ulrich Bröckling and Michael Sikora, 222–51. Göttingen: Vandenhoeck & Ruprecht, 1998.

Kocka, Jürgen. "Looking Back on the Sonderweg." *Central European History* 51 (2018): 137–42.

Köhne, Julia Barbara. *Kriegshysteriker: Strategische Bilder und mediale Techniken militärpsychiatrischen Wissens (1914–20).* Husum: Matthiesen, 2009.

——. "Screening Silent Resistance: Male Hysteria in First World War Medical Cinematography." In *Psychological Trauma and the Legacies of the First World War*, edited by Jason Crouthamel and Peter Leese, 49–79. Basingstoke, UK: Palgrave Macmillan, 2017.

Komo, Günter. *"Für Volk und Vaterland": Die Militärpsychiatrie in den Weltkriegen.* Münster: Lit Verlag, 1992.

Kraft, Thomas. *Fahnenflucht und Kriegsneurose: Gegenbilder zur Ideologie des Kampfes in der deutschsprachigen Literatur nach dem Zweiten Weltkrieg.* Würzburg: Königshausen & Neumann, 1994.

Kramer, Helmut, and Wolfram Wette. "Pazifisten im Visier der Justiz. Ein bedrückendes Kapitel der deutschen Geschichte des 20. Jahrhunderts." In *Recht ist, was den Waffen nützt: Justiz und Pazifismus im 20. Jahrhundert*, edited by Helmut Kramer and Wolfram Wette, 11–58. Berlin: Aufbau-Verlag, 2004.

Krumeich, Gerd. "Vorwort zur Wiederveröffentlichung." In *Krieg dem Kriege*, edited by Ernst Friedrich, 1–16. 1924. Reprint, Munich: Deutsche Verlags-Anstalt, 2004.

Kuhlmann, Jürgen, and Ekkehard Lippert. "The Federal Republic of Germany: Conscientious Objection as Social Welfare." In *The New Conscience Objection: From Sacred to Secular Resistance*, edited by Charles C. Moskos and John Whiteclay Chambers II, 98–105. New York: Oxford University Press, 1993.

Lange, Werner. *Hans Paasches Forschungsreise ins innerste Deutschland: Eine Biographie*. Bremen: Donat, 1995.

Leed, Eric J. *No Man's Land: Combat & Identity in World War I*. Cambridge: Cambridge University Press, 1979.

Leins, Claudia. "Robert Eugen Gaupp: Leben und Werk." Doctoral diss., Universität Tübingen, 1991.

Lemmers, Franz. "Zur Entwickelung der Militärpsychiatrie in Deutschland zwischen 1870 und 1918." *Abhandlungen zur Geschichte der Medizin und der Naturwissenschaften* 69 (1994): 35–44.

Lengwiler, Martin. "Auf dem Weg zur Sozialtechnologie: Die Bedeutung der frühen Militärpsychiatrie für die Professionalisierung der Psychiatrie in Deutschland." In *Psychiatrie im 19 Jahrhundert: Forschungen zur Geschichte von psychiatrischen Institutionen, Debatten und Praktiken im deutschen Sprachraum*, edited by Eric J. Engstrom and Volker Roelcke, 245–62. Basel: Schwabe Verlag, 2003.

———. "Psychiatry beyond the Asylum: The Origins of German Military Psychiatry before World War I." *History of Psychiatry* 14, no. 1 (2003): 41–62.

Lerner, Paul. "From Traumatic Neurosis to Male Hysteria: The Decline and Fall of Hermann Oppenheim, 1889–1919." In *Traumatic Pasts: History, Psychiatry, and Trauma in the Modern Age, 1870–1930*, edited by Mark S. Micale and Paul Lerner, 140–71. Cambridge: Cambridge University Press, 2001.

———. *Hysterical Men: War, Psychiatry, and the Politics of Trauma in Germany, 1890–1930*. Ithaca, NY: Cornell University Press, 2003.

Levsen, Sonja. "Masculinities." In *1914-1918-online. International Encyclopedia of the First World War*, edited by Ute Daniel, Peter Gatrell, Oliver Janz, Heather Jones, Jennifer Keene, Alan Kramer, and Bill Nasson, issued by Freie Universität Berlin, Berlin (updated January 7, 2015), doi: 10.15463/ie1418.10531.

Linden, Stefanie Caroline, and Edgar Jones. "German Battle Casualties: The Treatment of Functional Somatic Disorders during World War I." *Journal of the History of Medicine and Allied Sciences* 68, no. 4 (2013): 627–58.

Linse, Ulrich. "Biographische Daten." In *Ernst Friedrich zum 10: Todestag*, edited by Andreas W. Mytze, 64–71. Berlin: Mylet-Druck, 1977.

———. *Organisierter Anarchismus im Deutschen Kaiserreich von 1871*. Berlin: Duncker & Humblot, 1969.

Lipp, Karlheinz. *Pazifismus in der Pfalz vor und während des Ersten Weltkrieges: Ein Lesebuch*. Nordhausen: Verlag Traugott Bautz, 2015.

Loetz, Francisca. "Medikalisierung in Frankreich, Grossbritanien und Deutschland, 1750–1850: Ansätze, Ergebnisse und Perspektiven der Forschung." In *Das europäische Gesundheitssystem: Gemeinsamkeiten und Unterschiede in historischer Perspektive*, edited by Wolfgang U. Eckart and Robert Jütte, 123–61. Stuttgart: Steiner, 1994.

Lorimer, John G. "Why Would Modern Military Commanders Study the Franco-Prussian War?" *Defense Studies* 5 (2005): 108–23.

Loth, Wilfried. *Katholiken im Kaiserreich*. Düsseldorf: Droste, 1984.

Lüttgemeier-Davin, Reinhold, and Kerstin Wolff. "Einleitung: Helene Stöckers unvollendete Lebenserinnerungen." In *Lebenserinnerungen: Die unvollendete Autobiographie einer frauenbewegten Pazifisten, Helene Stöcker*, edited by Reinhold Lüttgemeier-Davin and Kerstin Wolff, 11–30. Vienna: Bohlau, 2015.

———. "Helene Stöcker—Frauenbewegung und Pazifismus im Kaiserreich und in der Weimarer Republik. Eine Einordnung." In *Lebenserinnerungen: Die unvollendete Autobiographie einer frauenbewegten Pazifisten, Helene Stöcker*, edited by Reinhold Lüttgemeier-Davin and Kerstin Wolff, 281–339. Vienna: Bohlau, 2015.

Mamali, Ioanna. "'Das "naturwissenschafliche" Ideal': Von der Zwangsbehandlung zur NS- Erbgesundheitspolitik. Ferdinand Kehrer, 1915–1945." In *"Heroische Therapien": Die deutsche Psychiatrie im internationalen Vergleich 1918–1945*, edited by Hans-Walter Schmuhl and Volker Roelcke, 251–67. Göttingen: Wallstein Verlag, 2013.

McClelland, Charles E. *The German Experience of Professionalization: Modern Learned Professions and Their Organizations from the Early Nineteenth Century to the Hitler Era*. Cambridge: Cambridge University Press, 1991.

Meagher, Sharon M., and Patrice DiQuinzio. "Introduction: Women and Children First." In *Women and Children First: Feminism, Rhetoric, and Public Policy*, edited by Sharon M. Meager and Patrice DiQuinzio, 1–13. Albany: SUNY Press, 2005.

Michl, Susanne. *Im Dienste des 'Volkskörpers': Deutsche und französiche Ärzte im Ersten Weltkrieg*. Göttingen: Vandenhoeck & Ruprecht, 2007.

Million, Theodore, Erik Simonsen, and Morton Birket-Smith. "Historical Conceptions of Psychopathy in the United States and Europe." In *Psychopathy: Antisocial, Criminal, and Violent Behaviors*, edited by Theodore Million, Erik Simonsen, Morton Birket-Smith, and R. D. Davis, 3–31. New York: Guilford Press, 1998.

Mintz, Susannah B. "Invisibility." In *Keywords for Disability Studies*, edited by Rachel Adams, Benjamin Reiss, and David Serlin, 113–14. New York: New York University Press, 2015.

Moskos, Charles C., and John Whiteclay Chambers II. "Introduction: The Secularization of Conscience." In *The New Conscientious Objection: From Sacred to Secular Resistance*, edited by Charles C. Moskos and John Whiteclay Chambers II, 3–20. New York: Oxford University Press, 1993.

Mosse, George. *The Image of Man: The Creation of Modern Masculinity*. New York: Oxford University Press, 1996.

Neuner, Stephanie. *Politik und Psychiatrie: Die staatliche Versorgung psychisch Kriegsbeschädigter in Deutschland, 1920–39*. Göttingen: Vandenhoeck & Ruprecht, 2011.

Noll, Richard. *American Madness: The Rise and Fall of Dementia Praecox*. Cambridge, MA: Harvard University Press, 2011.

———. "The Blood of the Insane." *History of Psychiatry* 17 (2006): 406–9.

——. *The Encyclopedia of Schizophrenia and Other Psychotic Disorders*. 3rd ed. New York: Facts on File, 2007.

Noone, Michael, Jr. "Legal Aspects of Conscientious Objection: A Comparative Analysis." In *The New Conscientious Objection: From Sacred to Secular Resistance*, edited by Charles C. Moskos and John Whiteclay Chambers II, 177–95. New York: Oxford University Press, 1993.

Norkowska, Katarzyna. "Der Dichter in der Uniform: Gottfried Benns Verhältnis zum Militär." In *Benn Forum: Beiträge zur literarischen Moderne*, edited by Joachim Dyck, Hermann Korte, and Nadine Jessica Schmidt, 113–33. Berlin: De Gruyter, 2001.

Ohrtmann, Johann. *Die Bewegung der Kriegsdienstgegner: Ein schlichter Bericht von schlichtem Heldentum*. Heide: Riechert, 1932.

Oram, Gerard. *Military Executions during World War I*. Basingstoke, UK: Palgrave Macmillan, 2003.

Orend, Brian. "Kant's Just War Theory." *Journal of the History of Philosophy* 37, no. 2 (1999): 323–53.

Overy, Richard. *The Bombing War: Europe 1939–1945*. London: Penguin, 2014.

Parsons, Talcot. *The Social System*. 1951. Reprint, Abingdon, UK: Routledge, 1991.

Peckl, Petra. "Krank durch die 'seelischen Einwirkungen des Feldzuges'? Psychische Erkrankungen der Soldaten im Ersten Welkrieg und ihre Behandlung." In *Krieg und medikale Kultur: Patientenschicksale und ärztliches Handeln in der Zeit der Weltkriege, 1914–1945*, edited by Livia Prüll and Philipp Rauh, 30–89. Göttingen: Wallstein, 2014.

——. "What the Patient Records Reveal: Reassessing the Treatment of 'War Neurotics' in Germany (1914–1918)." In *War, Trauma and Medicine in Germany and Central Europe (1914–1939)*, edited by Georg Hofer, Livia Prüll, and Wolfgang Eckart, 139–59. Freiburg: Centarus, 2011.

Pilling, Merrick D., Andrea Daley, Margaret F. Bigson, Lori E. Ross, and Juveria Zaheer, "Assessing 'Insight', Determining Agency, and Autonomy: Implicating Social Identities." In *Containing Madness: Gender and 'Psy' in Institutional Contexts*, edited by Jennifer Kilty and Erin Dej, 191–213. Cham: Palgrave Macmillan, 2018.

Pleitner, Berit. *Die 'vernünftige' Nation: Zur Funktion von Stereotypen über Polen und Franzosen im deutschen nationalen Diskurs 1850 bis 1871*. Frankfurt am Main: Peter Lang, 2001.

Porter, Dorothy, and Roy Porter. *Patient's Progress: Doctors and Doctoring in Eighteenth-Century England*. Stanford, CA: Stanford University Press, 1989.

Porter, Roy. *Madness: A Brief History*. Oxford: Oxford University Press, 2002.

——. "The Patient's View: Doing Medical History from Below." *Theory and Society* 14, no. 2 (1985): 175–98.

Prüll, Cay-Rüdiger. "Die Bedeutung des Ersten Weltkrieges für die Medizin im Nationalsozialismus." In *Nationalsozialismus und Erster Weltkrieg*, edited by Gerd Krumeich, 363–78. Essen: Klartext, 2010.

——. "The Exhausted Nation—Psychiatry and Medicine on the Home Front (1914–1918). The Case of Robert Sommer and the City of Giessen." *Neuere Medizin- und Wissenschaftsgeschichte Quellen und Studien* 26 (2011): 30–48.

——. "Rationale Therapie oder Unmenschlichkeit? Die deutsche Psychiatrie und die Behandlung der Soldaten im Ersten Weltkrieg." *Praxis: Schweizerische Rundschau für Medizin* 89 (2000): 1073–82.

Prüll, Livia, and Phillip Rauh. "Militär und medikale Kultur in Deutschland 1914–1945: Eine Einleitung." In *Krieg und medikale Kultur: Patientenschicksale und ärztliches Handeln in der Zeit der Weltkriege, 1914–1945*, edited by Livia Prüll and Philipp Rauh, 7–29. Göttingen: Wallstein, 2014.

Quinkert, Babette, Philipp Rauh, and Ulrike Winkler. "Einleitung." In *Krieg und Psychiatrie 1914–1950*, edited by Babette Quinkert, Philipp Rauh, and Ulrike Winkler, 9–28. Göttingen: Wallstein, 2010.

Radkau, Joachim. *Das Zeitalter der Nervosität: Deutschland Zwischen Bismarck und Hitler.* Munich: Carl Hanser Verlag, 1998.

Ralser, Michaela. "Tagungsbericht: Psychiatrische Krankenakten als Material der Wissenschaftsgeschichte. Methodisches Vorgehen am Einzelfall, 17.05.2007—19.05.2007 Berlin." *H-Soz-Kult*, June 10, 2007. https://www.hsozkult.de/conferencereport/id/tagungsberichte-1602.

Rauh, Philipp. "Die militärpsychiatrischen Therapiemethoden im Ersten Weltkrieg—Diskurs und Praxis." In *"Heroische Therapien": Die deutsche Psychiatrie im internationalen Vergleich, 1918–1945*, edited by Hans-Walter Schmuhl und Volker Roelcke, 31–49. Göttingen: Wallstein, 2013.

Rauh, Philipp, and Livia Prüll. "Krank durch den Krieg? Der Umgang mit psychisch kranken Veteranen in Deutschland in der Zeit der Weltkriege." In *Psychische Versehrungen im Zeitalter der Weltkriege*, edited by Gundula Gahlen, Wencke Meteling, and Christoph Nübel. Chemnitz: Portal Militärgeschichte, 2015. https://doi.org/10.15500/akm.24.06.2015.

Regulski, Christoph. *Die Reichskanzlerschaft von Georg Michaelis 1917: Deutschlands Entwickelung zur parlementarisch-demokratischen Monarchie im Ersten Weltkrieg.* Marburg: Tectum, 2003.

Riedesser, Peter, and Axel Verderber. *Aufrüstung der Seelen: Militärpsychiatrie und Militärpsychologie in Deutschland und Amerika.* Freiburg: Dreisam-Verlag, 1985.

——. *"Maschinengewehre hinter der Front": Zur Geschichte der deutschen Militärpsychiatrie.* Frankfurt am Main: Fischer, 1996.

Riesenberger, Dieter. *Geschichte der Friendensbewegung in Deutschland: Von den Anfängen bis 1933.* Göttingen: Vandenhoeck & Ruprecht, 1985.

Roelcke, Volker. "Continuities or Ruptures? Concepts, Institutions and Contexts of Twentieth- Century German Psychiatry and Mental Health Care." In *Psychiatric Cultures Compared: Psychiatry and Mental Health Care in the Twentieth Century*, edited by Marijke Gijswijt-Hofstra, Harry Oosterhuis, Joost Vijselaar, and Hugh Freeman, 162–82. Amsterdam: Amsterdam University Press, 2005.

Roper, Michael. "Nostalgia as an Emotional Experience in the Great War." *Historical Journal* 54 (2011): 421–51.

Rosenblum, Warren. *Beyond the Prison Gates: Punishment and Welfare in Germany, 1850–1933.* Chapel Hill: University of North Carolina Press, 2008.

Sadler, John Z. *Values and Psychiatric Diagnoses.* New York: Oxford University Press, 2004.

Scharfe, Martin. "Briefe aus dem Irrenhaus: Selbstzeugnisse von Patientinnen aus der Frühzeit der Marburger Anstalt." In *Heilbar und nützlich: Ziele und Wege der Psychiatrie in Marburg an der Lahn*, edited by Peter Sander, Gerhard Aumüller, and Christina Vanja, 163–83. Marburg: Jonas, 2001.

Schmiedebach, Heinz-Peter. "Eine 'antipsychiatrische Bewegung,' um die Jahrhundertwende." In *Medizinkritische Bewegungen im Deutschen Reich (ca. 1870-ca. 1933)*, edited by Martin Dinges, 127–59. Stuttgart: Franz Steiner Verlag, 1996.

——. "Sozialdarwinismus, Biologismus, Pazifismus—Ärztestimmen zum Erstenweltkrieg." In *Medizin und Krieg: Vom Dilemma der Heilberufe 1865–1985*, edited by Johanna Blecker and Heinz-Peter Schmiedebach, 93–121. Frankfurt am Main: Fischer, 1987.

——. "Zum Verständniswandel der 'psychopathische' Störungen am Anfang der naturwissenschaftlischen Psychiatrie in Deutschland." *Nervenarzt* 56 (1985): 140–45.

Schott, Heinz, and Rainer Tölle. *Geschichte der Psychiatrie: Krankheitslehren, Irrwege, Behandlungsformen*. Munich: Beck, 2006.

Schreiber, Jürgen. "Kriegsdienstverweigerung: Eine historische und rechtsvergleichende Untersuchung." Doctoral diss., Universität Bonn, 1952.

Shand, James D. "Doves among the Eagles: German Pacifists and Their Government during World War I." *Journal of Contemporary History* 10 (1975): 95–108.

Sharp, Ingrid. "Life Was Even Tougher for the German Conscientious Objectors of World War 1." The Conversation, May 15, 2014. https://theconversation.com/life-was-even-tougher-for-the-german-conscientious-objectors-of-world-war-i-26715.

Shepard, Ben. *A War of Nerves: Soldiers and Psychiatrists in the Twentieth Century*. Cambridge, MA: Harvard University Press, 2003.

Showalter, Elaine. *The Female Malady: Women, Madness, and English Culture 1830–1980*. New York: Pantheon, 1985.

Siemen, Hans Ludwig. *Menschen bleiben auf der Strecke . . . Psychiatrie zwischen Reform und Nationalsozialismus*. Gütersloh: Verlag Jakob-van-Hoddis, 1987.

Simmonds, Alan G. *Britain and World War I*. New York: Routledge, 2012.

Sisti, Dominic, Michael Young, and Arthur Caplan. "Defining Mental Illnesses: Can Values and Objectivity Get Along?" *BMC Psychiatry* 13 (2013): 346.

Stahnke, Karl-Heinz. "Die Kriegsdienstverweigerung in der Literatur." *Jahresbibliographie der Bibliothek für Zeitgeschichte* 35 (1963): 510–49.

Stevenson, David. *With Our Backs to the Wall: Victory and Defeat in 1918*. Cambridge, MA: Belknap: 2011.

Stibbe, Matthew. *Germany, 1914–1933: Politics, Society and Culture*. New York: Routledge, 2013.

Stompe, Thomas. "Psychopathie—Geschichte und Dimensionen." *Neuropsychiatrie* 23 (2009): 3–9.

Swain, Kelley. "'Extraordinarily Arduous and Fraught with Danger': Syphilis, Salvarsan, and General Paresis of the Insane." *The Lancet: Psychiatry* 5 (2018): 687–768.

Taylor, Stephen J. *Acts of Conscience: World War II, Mental Institutions, and Religious Objectors*. Syracuse, NY: Syracuse University Press, 2009.

Treitel, Corinna. *Eating Nature in Modern Germany: Food, Agriculture, and Environment, c. 1870–2000*. Cambridge: Cambridge University Press, 2017.

Ulrich, Bernd. "Krieg als Nervensache." *Die Zeit*, November 22, 1991.

Voren, Robert van. "Political Abuse of Psychiatry—an Historical Overview." *Schizophrenia Bulletin* 36, no. 1 (2010): 33–35.

Wagenblast, Jörg. *Die Tübinger Militärpsychiatrie im Zweiten Weltkrieg*. Stuttgart: Franz Steiner Verlag, 2016.

Watson, Alexander. *Enduring the Great War: Combat, Morale and Collapse in the German and British Armies, 1914–1918*. Cambridge: Cambridge University Press, 2014.

Weindling, Paul. "Bourgeois Values, Doctors and the State: The Professionalization of Medicine in Germany 1848–1933." In *The German Bourgeoisie: Essays on the Social History of the German Middle Class from the Late Eighteenth to the Early Twentieth Century*, edited by David Blackbourn and Richard J. Evans, 198–223. New York: Routledge, 1991.

Weißer, Ulfried. *Die Bundesrepublik Deutschland-ein Erfolgsprojekt*. Berlin: Frank & Timm, 2015.

Welch, David. *Germany, Propaganda and the Total War 1914–1918: The Sins of Omission*. New Brunswick, NJ: Rutgers, 2000.

Welch, Steven R. "Military Justice." In *1914-1918-online. International Encyclopedia of the First World War*, edited by Ute Daniel, Peter Gatrell, Oliver Janz, Heather Jones, Jennifer Keene, Alan Kramer, and Bill Nasson. Berlin: Freie Universität Berlin, 2014. https://doi.org/10.15463/ie1418.10393.

Wette, Wolfram. "Einleitung: Probleme des Pazifismus in der Zwischenkriegzeit." In *Pazifismus in der Weimarer Republic: Beiträge zur historischen Friedensforschung*, edited by Karl Holl and Wolfram Wette, 9–26. Paderborn: Schöningh, 1981.

——. *Ernstfall Frieden: Lehren aus der deutschen Geschichte seit 1914*. Bremen: Donat, 2017.

——. "Justiz und pazifistische Offiziere in der Zeit der Weimarer Republik." In *Recht ist, was den Waffen nützt: Justiz und Pazifismus im 20. Jahrhundert*, edited by Helmut Kramer and Wolfram Wette, 127–42. Berlin: Aufbau Verlag, 2004.

——. "Militärgeschichte von unten." In *Krieg des kleinen Mannes: Eine Militärgeschichte von unten*, edited by Wolfram Wette, 9–47. Munich: Piper, 1992.

Wetzell, Richard F. *Inventing the Criminal: A History of German Criminology, 1880–1945*. Chapel Hill: University of North Carolina Press, 2000.

——. "Psychiatry and Criminal Justice in Modern Germany, 1880–1933." *Journal of European Studies* 39, no. 3 (2009): 270–89.

Wolff, Eberhard. "Medikalisierung von unten? Das Beispiel der jüdischen Krankenbesuchgesellschaften." In *Zwischen Aufklärung, Policey und Verwaltung: Zur Genese des Medizinalwesens 1750–1850*, edited by Bettina Wahrig and Werner Sohn, 179–90. Wiesbaden: Harrassowitz Verlag, 2003.

Wulf, Stefan. "Nonne, Max." In *Neue Deutsche Biographie*, vol. 19, edited by the Historische Komission bei der Bayerischen Akademie der Wissenschaften, 333–35. Berlin: Dunker and Humblot, 1999.

Ziemann, Benjamin. *Contested Commemorations: Republican War Veterans and Weimar Political Culture*. Cambridge: University of Cambridge Press, 2013.

——. "'Der Hauptmann von Köpenick'—Symbol für den Sozialmilitarismus im wilhelmischen Deutschland?" In *Grenzüberschreitungen oder der Vermittler Bedrich*

Loewenstein. Festschrift zum 70. Geburtstag eines europäischen Historikers, edited by Vilém Prečan, Milena Janišová, and Matthias Roeser, 252–64. Prague: Institute for Contemporary History of the Academy of Sciences of the Czech Republic, 1999.

——. "German Pacifism in the Nineteenth and Twentieth Centuries." *Neue Politische Literatur* 60, no. 3 (2015): 415–37.

——. "Militarism." In *The Ashgate Research Companion to Imperial Germany*, edited by Mathew Jeffries, 367–82. Farnham: Ashgate, 2015.

——. "Verweigerungsformen von Frontsoldaten in der deutschen Armee 1914-1918." In *Gewalt im Krieg: Ausübung, Erfahrung und Verweigerung von Gewalt in Kriegen des 20: Jahrhunderts*, edited by Andreas Gestrich, 99–122. Münster: Lit, 1996.

——. *Violence and the German Soldier in the Great War: Killing, Dying, Surviving.* Translated by Andrew Evans. London: Bloomsbury, 2017.

Zürcher, Erik-Jan. "Refusing to Serve by Other Means: Desertion in the Late Ottoman Empire." In *Conscientious Objection: Resisting Militarized Society*, edited by Özgur Heval Çinar and Coşkun Üsterci, 45–52. London: Zed, 2009.

Index

An 'm' or 'n' following a page number indicates a map or endnote, respectively.

CPSIA information can be obtained
at www.ICGtesting.com
Printed in the USA
LVHW091941041120
670713LV00015B/186/J

9 781501 751202